LINGUISTIC CATEGORIES:
AUXILIARIES AND RELATED PUZZLES
VOLUME ONE

SYNTHESE LANGUAGE LIBRARY

TEXTS AND STUDIES IN
LINGUISTICS AND PHILOSOPHY

VOLUME 19

LINGUISTIC CATEGORIES: v.1.
AUXILIARIES
AND RELATED PUZZLES

Volume One: Categories

Edited by

FRANK HENY

Dept. of Linguistics, Groningen University

and

BARRY RICHARDS

School of Epistemics, University of Edinburgh

D. REIDEL PUBLISHING COMPANY

A MEMBER OF THE KLUWER ACADEMIC PUBLISHERS GROUP

DORDRECHT / BOSTON / LANCASTER

Library of Congress Cataloging in Publication Data
Main entry under title:

Linguistic categories.

(Synthese language library; v. 19–20)
Based on papers presented at the Fourth Groningen Round Table, held in July
1980 and organized by the Institute for General Linguistics of Groningen University.
Includes indexes.
Contents: v. 1. Categories – v. 2. The scope, order, and distribution of English
auxiliary verbs.
   1. Grammar, Comparative and general – Grammatical categories – Congresses.
2. Grammar, Comparative and general – Auxiliaries – Congresses. 3. English language
– Auxiliary verbs – Congresses. I. Heny, Frank. II. Richards, Barry, 1942–
III. Groningen Round Table (4th: 1980) IV. Rijksuniversiteit te Groningen. Instituut
voor Algemene Taalwetenschap. V. Series.
P240.5.L56 1983   415   83–11050
ISBN 90–277–1478–9 (v. 1)
ISBN 90–277–1479–7 (v. 2)

Published by D. Reidel Publishing Company,
P.O. Box 17, 3300 AA Dordrecht, Holland.

Sold and distributed in the U.S.A. and Canada
by Kluwer Academic Publishers
190 Old Derby Street, Hingham, MA 02043, U.S.A.

In all other countries, sold and distributed
by Kluwer Academic Publishers Group,
P.O. Box 322, 3300 AH Dordrecht, Holland.

TABLE OF CONTENTS
VOLUME ONE

TABLE OF CONTENTS
VOLUME TWO

PREFACE

Virtually all the papers in these volumes originated in presentations at the Fourth Groningen Round Table, held in July 1980. That conference, organized by the Institute for General Linguistics of Groningen University was the fourth in an irregular series of meetings devoted to issues of topical interest to linguists. Its predecessor, the Third Round Table, was held in June 1976, and dealt with the semantics of natural language. A selection of the papers was published as *Syntax and Semantics 10, Selections from the Third Groningen Round Table*, ed. by F. Heny and H. Schnelle, Academic Press, 1979. This fourth meeting was more narrowly focussed. The original intention was to examine the hypothesis of Akmajian, Steele and Wasow in their paper 'The Category AUX in Universal Grammar', *Linguistic Inquiry* 10, 1—64. Ultimately the topic was broadened considerably to encompass not only the syntax, semantics and morphology of auxiliaries and related elements, but to tackle the problem (implicit in the original work of Akmajian, Steele and Wasow) of justifying the selection of categories for the analysis of natural language.

In the summer of 1979, a workshop and short, informal conference were held at the University of Salzburg, in preparation for the Round Table. These were organized in conjunction with the Summer Institute of the Linguistic Society of America. The cooperation of the LSA and of the University of Salzburg, and in particular of the Director of that Institute, Professor Gaberell Drachman, is hereby gratefully acknowledged. The debate in Salzburg contributed greatly to the success of the ensuing Round Table, and hence to the quality of these volumes. Among the issues which began to dominate the discussions there was the problem of determining what linguists might mean by a category — in particular by the category AUX, or auxiliary. The contribution of Timothy Potts of the University of Leeds may be worth singling out, particularly as he was unable to attend the Round Table itself. However, all the participants contributed very significantly to the definition of the problems that occupied the speakers at the Round Table and are addressed in these pages.

This is in no sense simply a proceedings of the conference itself. A number of papers were not available for inclusion, and those that appear here have

vii

been refereed and in most cases quite extensively revised. We should like to take this opportunity to thank the almost fifty scholars who generously helped in this process of selection and review. Whatever merit the volume has it would have had less without their anonymous contributions. At the meeting itself it was agreed that other related papers of high quality might be included in a volume issuing from the Round Table; the paper by Schmerling, which came to our attention late in 1980, seemed an ideal candidate, and after the usual review has been included. On the other hand, a number of papers on semantics, which originated at the Round Table but are less closely related in theme to those included here, have been published separately as *Linguistics and Philosophy* 5, No. 1, under the title *The Semantics of Temporal Elements*.

The papers that we do include in these two volumes are remarkably closely related, though they clearly fall into three distinct categories. The first deals rather directly with the original AUX hypothesis. The second, a larger group of papers, tackles the general problem of defining and justifying categories for the analysis of natural language. These first two groups of papers make up Volume One. The third group of papers, which constitute the second volume, deal with the scope, order and distribution of the English auxiliary verbs (one paper deals with an English creole, Sranan).

Thanks are due to the Faculty of Letters, University of Groningen, for their very generous support and to the *Ministerie voor Onderwijs en Wetenschappen* of the Netherlands, which contributed not only directly to the expenses of the conference but also to the costs of an exchange program between the School of Epistemics of the University of Edinburgh and the Institute for General Linguistics in Groningen. The British Council also helped finance that exchange program, and it was through the support we received from these two sources that we were able to co-operate before, during and after the Round Table.

Finally, Jet van Everdingen and Hennie Zondervan-Kimsma have spent hours typing, photocopying and doing the other chores that come with running a meeting and editing a book. They have done a splendid job. The many others who have contributed we will have to thank collectively.

April 1982   FRANK HENY
                                                      BARRY RICHARDS

INTRODUCTION .

A few years ago, all but a handful of generative linguists were native speakers of English and would have been very content with a theory that provided an elegant analysis for their own language. Today we are likely to look askance even at a framework that yields a fair description of English, Bulgarian, Arabic and Dutch unless it also gives us a systematic basis for insightful comparison between and within these languages.

To meet this demand, linguistic theory must incorporate the means to identify certain elements as invariant. Among these invariant items may be word classes, grammatical features, rules − or yet more abstract elements. They may be complex or they may be analytical primitives. There is no reason to suppose a priori that any one class of constructs is necessarily invariant. The question is empirical: which choices yield the best results? Which permit the most insightful account of observed variance?

And like every other such empirical question, this one is theory dependent. If as we pass from language to language, we hold one element or another constant, unvarying, then this has significance only within the context of a theory within which other constituents may be permitted to vary − or also held constant. The question is therefore always relative: to account for the observed variance, what must be held constant, and what permitted to vary?

Anyone who has had contact with more than one language has been confronted with the problem on at least a pretheoretical level, and is likely to be more or less aware of how hard it is to decide of two items whether they should be regarded as like or unlike. Without a highly articulated framework, it is virtually impossible, for example, to even make sense of the question whether two words, W_1 from one language L_1, and W_2 from another, L_2, are 'the same' or not. Quine's celebrated thesis of indeterminacy in his *Word and Object* can be seen as little more than a very sophisticated expression of his awareness of that fact. Quine was of course concerned with the semantics, but he could have made his point by reference to any other grammatical sub-system − and could have looked at the passive construction instead of the word for rabbit. Without a theory in which to embed a systematic analysis the answer would have been the same: the question makes no sense.

ix

Akmajian, Steele and Wasow (1979) (ASW) were concerned with 'categories' of words rather than words themselves, but in essence their question was the same as Quine's, and if they came up with a different answer, this was because they were taking for granted a theoretical framework relative to which the answer could apparently be given. Is there a language independent category AUX? Within a given approach to grammatical description, that amounts to the question whether the most insightful account of observed variance within the chosen domain can be given when some item AUX defined by the theory remains constant while others vary. In the framework originally assumed by ASW, invariant constructs could be drawn from just three sources: the phrase structure trees, the (PS) rules defining those trees, and the grammatical transformations. Lexical categories were represented by nodes in the phrase structure trees and hence if AUX was to be an invariant word category it would be represented by a phrase structure node in all grammars. The observed inter-language variance — which is obviously considerable in this area — would have to be accounted for by some other variance, in this instance by the differing properties of the words inserted under the AUX node.

Since what was permitted to vary were the properties of the items belonging to AUX, the question arose whether lexical items differing in the necessary ways could properly be inserted under a single node in the theory within which ASW were working. At the same time, it was natural to question whether within that theoretical framework the postulating of an invariant AUX node was really the best way of accounting for the relevant data. The first two papers of this volume address themselves to such questions.

In Steele *et al.* (1981) the essential idea is that an analysis in which crucial use is made of a node with the criterial properties ascribed to AUX will automatically result in a significant number of a set of non-definitional properties being assigned to that node. It is the clustering of these further properties (the addition of further, non-necessary partial invariance) which constitutes the main explanatory power of such analyses. The papers by Rudin on Bulgarian and Jelinek on Arabic pursue these ideas further; they argue that a node with the minimum of properties required by the hypothesis will also exhibit a significant set of the other non-definitional properties. Because of the way in which the basic definition of AUX is set up, this permits a great deal of superficial variation in the material appearing under that category while, it is claimed, also predicting a non-trivial set of consequences resulting from the invariant properties of AUX in each language.

By hypothesis, the AUX is a node (in a transformational grammar) with, minimally, syntactic properties distinct from those of all other nodes in the language. Moreover, it at least dominates Tense. These then are the invariant, defining properties of (or associated with) AUX. To put it another way, the AUX hypothesis of ASW, which is taken further in these two papers, attributes a degree of invariance to all languages which is fixed by the node AUX and the invariant properties associated universally with this node. The observed variance is attributed to the fact that in each language other properties will be associated with elements inserted under AUX.

Further development of the original concerns of ASW may proceed in a number of directions; the AUX hypothesis itself need not represent the immediate focus of research which nevertheless remains closely related in spirit to their work. Recall that one of the criterial properties of AUX was that it dominate Tense. Tense in turn is intimately related to sentencehood; to be more precise, finiteness appears to be a property which only (but not all) sentences possess, and a language is defined in terms of its sentences. Against that background, it seems obvious that insight into the criterial properties of natural language itself may well be expected to emerge from a study of finiteness and the properties which are commonly associated with it, . . . and hence perhaps also with sentencehood. Accepting only the observational aspects of the work by Steele and her collaborators, one could therefore hope to approach the category 'Sentence' (and hence in turn 'Language') by investigating the nature of the relationships which hold between Tense, finiteness, modality, negation, and so on, that is, between all the notional and other properties which according to the work of Steele *et al.* are associated with the AUX node.

Edmondson, in the first paper of the second section of this volume does just that. He explores the properties of negative polarity items occurring in AUX-like positions, using data from a number of languages, and emphasizes how the behavior of these items must be analysed partly in pragmatic terms. Richards and Heny, and Hintikka, in the issue of *Linguistics and Philosophy* which is a companion to this volume, have given analyses of Tense in which essentially pragmatic factors play a central role. Those papers may thus be relevant to any attempt to pursue this line of research further.

Carlson's paper, the second in Part Two, also relates the problem of defining the putative category AUX to that of defining sentencehood, but generalizes the AUX hypothesis in other ways: he distinguishes, as have many before him, between function and content morphemes and suggests that the observations of Steele *et al.* regarding positional properties of AUX, together with certain observations of his own (for example that tense tends to be realized as a bound morpheme) can be subsumed under general principles for the interpretation of function morphemes – in particular morphemes which like Tense map members of a category (such as 'sentence') onto members of the same category. Such items, which he introduces into the syntax as operators will also be *interpreted* as operators. Often they will show up as bound morphemes within the constituent on which they operate, following principles which he programmatically discusses. It is from these principles, he suggests, that the observations of Steele *et al.* regarding AUX and the notional elements associated with it can be derived. More generally, his analysis may also provide some explicit motivation for thinking that the syntax of natural language is closely related (in an unexpected way) to the semantics.

Reuland's paper generalizes the AUX hypothesis in another direction. He relates it to the problem of defining sentencehood in yet other ways – and in the process argues that it must be modified. He points out that while Tense may seem relevant to the definition of finiteness, it is Agreement rather than Tense which is crucial in that conception of finiteness which is relevant to the definition of opacity in the Government Binding theory of Chomsky's *Lectures on Government and Binding*. He argues that what the AUX-hypothesis should have singled out was the INFL node, which in the Government Binding framework dominates both Tense and Agreement features and which is the head of the basic sentence. The AUX of Steele *et al.* is, he suggests, merely a special case of INFL and is certainly not present in all sentences. In fact, he argues, AUX is simply the INFL of root (i.e. main) clauses. If correct, this might go some way to accounting for the observed relation between AUX and various pragmatic (speech act) phenomena. Reuland's argument is based largely on English and Dutch un-tensed clauses.

Cremers' paper, which follows, also deals with untensed forms, and also with the category 'sentence', though his main concern is to argue that certain constructions, which have generally been assumed to be sentential or at least semantically propositional must, even in the semantics, be analysed as lacking a subject, and hence be identified with properties rather than propositions. It happens that Cremers' discussion is quite closely related even in detail to that of Reuland; for the latter, in arguing for a distinct INFL node in S, used data indicating that several Dutch verbs not normally thought of as good candidates for auxiliary status, like **willen** 'want', must indeed be sometimes generated under the INFL node and take 'VP complements'. Cremers' totally independent, semantic argument would seem to extend this class to **proberen** 'try' and others – though it must be explicitly pointed out that Cremers' claim is only that they take VP complements; not that they appear in INFL or AUX. The relationships thus become yet more complex — and interesting — between the loose class of 'auxiliaries', the category 'setnence' and the node INFL or AUX, which, whether or not it is head of the basic sentence (i.e. the sentence internal to the complementizer, if any) is clearly intimately bound up with the nature of sentencehood.

There is another direction in which the AUX hypothesis can be extended, this time not to the sentence at all, but to the general problem of defining categories in natural language. If AUX or INFL is head of S, then it is probably so in the sense suggested by Carlson, namely as an operator, a function from sentences to sentences. There are other kinds of phrasal head. It has long been a pre-theoretical assumption of linguists (and their precursors) that the heads of certain phrases — heads like verbs, nouns, etc. — somehow determine what can occur in those phrases. If heads, whether those like INFL or those like nouns and verbs determine what can occur in their phrases then of course they determine the nature (i.e. *category*) of those phrases. From this it follows that if the syntax of natural language is to be directly associated with a standard semantics — one that is more or less compositional, if not Fregean — then the type of the interpretation of the phrase as a whole will depend only on the type of the interpretation of its head. Viewed this way, Case assignment, sub-categorization and the properties lexically associated with heads, might be expected to interact to define a highly complex categorial grammar. In such a grammar (roughly the syntax of Chomsky's *Lectures* — mentioned above), the central role is assigned to the heads of phrases, and insight into the categorial structure of natural language should result primarily from examination of the lexical properties of these heads.

Van Riemsdijk deals in effect only with the Case assignment properties of German adjectives, but his discussion has wider implications. He argues that abstract Case assignment is in turn dependent upon the composition of the head in question, whether that is analysed in terms of the feature $[\pm V]$, $[\pm N]$ of the $\overline{X}$ system. (Cf., for example, Jackendoff's $\overline{X}$-*Syntax*.) Given the immediately preceding discussion this would strongly suggest that these features would constitute the analytical bases of a grammar built along the lines suggested by van Riemsdijk's work, and that the categories of that grammar would be defined over these features rather than being based on constituents of a more traditional sort like *noun* and *adjective*. Support for this position is indeed provided in van Riemsdijk's paper. He shows how several superficial differences between German and English adjectives follow naturally from his hypothesis that the feature make-up of German adjectives is neutralized in the phrase structure (which he takes to define the categories), while that of the English ones is not. This would appear to imply that whatever is the case with INFL or AUX, the adjective is not a universal category, though the features which define it are. Given the line of reasoning we have been pursuing, this would seem to imply that there should be some identifiable difference between the type, i.e. semantics of German and English adjectives based on their feature make up. That question certainly seems worth asking in future research.

At first it might seem that the class of items found among the English auxiliaries, or those associated with AUX is so irregular that any attempt to relate the problem of defining natural language categories in general to the problem of characterizing AUX will be misguided. However Maling, in the final paper of this volume, argues that there are members of the categories Preposition and Adjective in English which display highly idiosyncratic properties — but can nevertheless be unambiguously assigned to one or the other of these categories. Perhaps we should call them word-classes. For Maling also argues that at least the sub-categorial properties of many items do not depend on the structural class of the selected phrase. So a lexical head may require a locative argument rather than, say, a prepositional phrase, noun phrase or adverb. If so, the relationship between features of the X system, subcategorization in the widest sense and 'categories' in the sense intended in categorial grammar may well be much more complex than would be suggested by our earlier discussion of van Riemsdijk's paper.

One thing is perfectly clear, not only from the paper by Maling and that of Carlson, but also from several of the contributions in the second volume: there is considerable distance between syntactic operations and semantically relevant syntactic categories.

This collection does not pretend to offer an integrated, unified view of AUX, auxiliaries or the problem of isolating in a motivated way the categories of natural language. What it does seem to offer is a very rich source of ideas for further research in an extremely important area of universal grammar — whether spelled with small letters or large.

PART ONE

THE *AUX* HYPOTHESIS

CATHERINE RUDIN

DA AND THE CATEGORY *A UX* IN BULGARIAN

The particle **da** in Bulgarian has traditionally been classified as some sort of conjunction, and in the few existing generative treatments of Bulgarian (e.g. Dolapchieva, 1976) it has generally been described as a complementizer. In this paper I will show that **da** is not a complementizer and that it can in fact be analyzed as belonging to the AUX, given the definition of AUX proposed by Akmajian, Steele, and Wasow (1979) (henceforth 'ASW'). The paper will include a brief sketch of some other elements of the AUX in Bulgarian and a discussion of the status of AUX as a constituent.

1. WHY DA IS NOT A COMPLEMENTIZER

At first glance, **da** does seem very much like a complementizer. It often seems to introduce embedded sentences in the same way as the complementizers **če** 'that' and **dali** 'whether', and the choice of **da**, **če**, or **dali** in the complement sentence is determined by the verb of the higher clause.[1]

(1) a. Kazvat če pejat decata.
        say-3p that sing-3p children-the

   They say the children are singing.

   b. Pitajte dali pejat decata.
        ask-2p-imp whether sing-3p children-the

   Ask whether the children are singing.

   c. Iskam da pejat decata.
        want-1s to sing-3p children-the

   I want the children to sing.

However, upon further investigation it becomes obvious that **da** differs from **če** and **dali** in several ways. One of these is its position relative to the FOCUS position. In the examples in (1) there is no focused element in the embedded clause so this difference is not visible. When focused material is present, it

3

F. Heny and B. Richards (eds.), Linguistic Categories: Auxiliaries and Related Puzzles, Vol. One, 3–20.

always precedes **da** but normally follows **če** and **dali** ((2a–c) differ from (1a–c) only in emphasis). Example (2d) shows that the focused NP **decata** cannot follow **da**.

(2) a. Kazvat če *decata* pejat.

    b. Pitajte dali *decata* pejat.

    c. Iskam *decata* da pejat.

    d. * Iskam da *decata* pejat.

The focused NP in (2c) is a nominative subject, as is demonstrated by the case-marked pronouns in (3); its position is not due to raising to object of the higher clause.

(3) a. Iskam   te   da   pejat.
         want-1s   they-nom   to   sing-3p.
         I want them to sing.

    b. * Iskam   gi   da   pejat.
         want-1s   them-acc   to   sing-3p.

The difference in surface position does not in itself prove that **če** and **dali** are complementizers and **da** is not; **da** could, for example, originate in COMP and be moved into immediately preverbal position after Focusing had applied. This analysis is not satisfactory, however, for at least two reasons, both having to do with a restriction against a doubly filled COMP position in Bulgarian.

First, **da** can occur in the same simple sentence as either of the complementizers, **če** or **dali**, but they cannot cooccur with each other:

(4) a. *Dali*   *da*   ja   popitam?
         whether   to   her-acc   ask-1s
         (*I wonder*) *should I ask her?*

    b. Toj se   dvoumi   *dali*   *da* se   vŭrne   obratno.
         he refl   debated-3s   whether   to refl   turn-3s   back
         He debated whether to turn back.

    c. Ženata   sedna   taka   če   da   me   vižda.
         woman-the   sat-3s   thus   that   to   me   see-3s
         The woman sat so that she could see me.

d. Tolkova blesteše če očite *da* te zaboljat.
so shone-3s that eyes-the to you-acc begin-to-hurt-3p.

It shone so (brightly) that your eyes would begin to hurt.

but never:

e. * ... če dali ...
f. * ... dali če ...

This can be accounted for by a restriction against COMP containing more than one element, provided that da is not in COMP at any stage in the derivation. If da were generated in COMP and later moved out, all the sentences in (4) would have doubly filled COMP nodes in underlying structure; [$_{COMP}$ dali da] and [$_{COMP}$ če da], in which case the non-occurrence of [$_{COMP}$ če dali] or [$_{COMP}$ dali če] would be an unexplained and isolated exception.

Če and dali also do not cooccur with the clitic question particle li, which presumably originates in COMP and cliticizes onto the verb or other questioned word from there.[2] Da however does cooccur with li (compare (4ab) above):

(5) a. *Da* ja popitam *li*?
to her ask-1s Q

Should I ask her?

b. Toj se dvoumi *da* ne se *li* vŭrne obratno.
he refl debated-3s to neg refl Q turn-3s back

He debated whether to turn back.

Secondly, a similar argument can be made on the basis of WH-words, which cooccur freely with da but not with če or dali:

(6) a. *Kakvo da* pravim?
what to do-1p

What should we do?

b. Toj ne znae *kogo da* pita.
he neg know-3s whom to ask

He doesn't know who to ask.

c. Tŭrsi   kniga   *kojato*   *da*   mu   haresa.
   seek-3s   book   which   to   him-dat   please-3s

He is looking for a book that he'll like.

but never:

d. * dali kakvo, * kakvo dali, * če kogo, * kojato če, etc.

Again, this is easily accounted for if **da** is not in COMP at the point in the
derivation when WH-Movement occurs.

I conclude that **da** is not in COMP position and is therefore not a complementizer.

2. WHY **DA** IS IN AUX

According to ASW, "AUX is a category — i.e. distinct in its syntactic behavior
from the behavior of other syntactic categories — labelling a constituent
that includes elements expressing the notional categories of Tense and/or
Modality". This definition consists of two basic criteria for AUX-hood: one
syntactic ("a constituent", "distinct in its syntactic behavior") and one
semantic ("expressing . . . Tense and/or Modality"). The particle **da** fits both
criteria, and certain verbal elements in Bulgarian also seem to fit the criteria
to varying degrees; these will be discussed below.

Syntactically, **da** is unlike anything else in Bulgarian. The surface position
of **da** is always immediately before the verb complex, which consists of the
verb with its clitics (dative and accusative personal and reflexive pronouns,
the clitic forms of the verb **sŭm** (to be), and the negative particle **ne**). These
clitics always attach to the left of the verb unless this would make them
utterance initial, in which case they ·attach to the right of the verb. Example
(7a) illustrates the normal preverbal position and (7b) shows the postverbal
positioning of clitics to avoid their being initial, as in the ungrammatical (7c).

(7) a. Včera   toj   *mi*   *ja*   dade.
       yesterday   he   me-dat   it-f   gave-3s

   Yesterday he gave it to me.

   b. Dade   *mi*   *ja*.
      gave-3s   me-dat   it-f

   (He) gave it to me.

c. * *Mi*   *ja*   dade.
     me-dat   it-f   gave-3s.

When **da** and one or more clitics occur together, the order is *da – clitic(s) – V*; no other order is possible:

(8) a.   Iskam   da   mi   ja   dade.
         want-1s   to   me-dat   it-f   give-3s
         I want him to give it to me.

     b. * Iskam   mi   ja   da   dade.
         want-1s   me-dat   it-f   to   give-3s

However, other than the clitics, no material can ever intervene between **da** and the verb. Even adverbials, which can occur nearly anywhere else in the sentence, cannot separate them; the following would be good if the adverb were in some other position.

(9) a. * Kakvo   da   sega   pravim?
         what   to   now   do-1s
         (*What should we do now?*)

     b. * Iskat   da   napŭlno   svŭršim   rabotata   do   utre.
         want-3p   to   fully   finish-1p   work-the   by   tomorrow
         (*They want us to completely finish the work by tomorrow.*)

Assuming the clitics and V to be dominated by a single node – call it V′ for convenience – **da** is always immediately pre-V′. The restriction of **da** to this position is constant in both root and embedded S's, direct and indirect questions, relative clauses, in short, everywhere; and this restriction is not shared by any major category. Bulgarian NPs and AdjPs occur in various positions both before and after the verb. Verbs obviously do not have to be preverbal, and adverbials, conjunctions, articles, complementizers, prepositions, and other categories also do not follow this particular restriction. The only other elements that are always preverbal are several verb-like modals, which will be discussed below and shown to be in AUX as well. It would, of course, be possible to account for the placement of **da** by a rule moving it there from some other deep structure position, but there is no evidence as to what that source position would be. It has already been shown that COMP is not a viable candidate.

I conclude, therefore, that **da** is generated in its surface position before the VP; (10) is a preliminary approximation of the base structure of a sentence containing **da**.

(10)

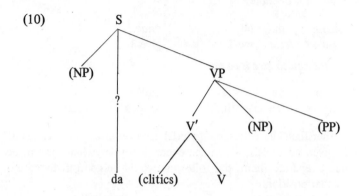

The node marked "?" can in fact be analyzed as AUX, given the ASW definition, as we shall see below.

I turn now to the semantic criteria for AUX-hood, namely, that the AUX node should dominate elements expressing tense and/or modality. **Da** does not express tense (although it does correlate with certain tenses),[3] but it does express modality, and the other elements I propose to include in AUX all express either tense or modality as well. The exact semantics of **da** is a question which has given rise to considerable controversy among Bulgarian scholars. I will not attempt an in-depth treatment of this problem here, but will simply give a brief overview of the subject.

Da has at least four more or less distinct usages (or 'meanings'), all of which are, however, probably relatable to a common semantic core of counterfactuality combined with possibility and/or desirability. The major usages of **da** are:

(I) Conditional ('if, even if, if only'): see (11).

(II) (quasi-)Imperative ('lets, let him') [**da** in this sense is used most often with first and third persons, which have no other imperative; but it can occur with second person subjects as well] : see (12).

(III) Purpose ('in order to'): see (13).

(IV) Introduces complement to verbs, nouns, and adjectives of desire, expectation, and the like ('prospective' complements): see (14).

Examples:

(11) a. No   i   da bjaha   zabeljazali tija   nešta . . .
       but and to were-3p noticed-pl these things
       But even if they had noticed these things . . .

    b. Daže da umra,   pak njama   da gi   pija.
       even to die-1s still won't to them drink
       Even if I die I won't drink them.

(12) a. Sekretarite   da zapisvat.
       secretaries-the to take-notes-3p
       Let the secretaries take notes.

    b. Da svŭršim s   tozi razgovor!
       to end-1p with this conversation
       Let's put an end to this conversation.

(13) a. Legnete   da vidim   kak ste.
       lie-down-2p to see-1p how are-2p
       Lie down so we can see how you are.

    b. Dojdoha hora   da slušat   lekciite   ti.
       came-3p people to hear-3p lectures-the your
       People came to hear your lectures.

(14) a. Vie iskate   da mŭlčim.
       you want-2p to be-quiet-1p
       You want us to ge quiet.

    b. Predpočitam da igraja   tenis.
       prefer-1s to play-1s tennis
       I prefer to play tennis.

In all of these cases the **da** clause is counterfactual in that it either did not occur (11a) or has not yet occurred either at the time of the utterance or at the time indicated by the higher clause. The elements of possibility/potentiality and of an intention or wish for that potential to be realized are also recurring themes, although they do not hold for all cases. A number of scholars have studied the modal properties of **da** (see for example Mutafchieva (1970), Penchev (1973), Schick (1977)) and have come to various conclusions,[4] but all of them that I am aware of agree in including some sort of modality in their analyses of the meaning of **da**. I concur with the majority of Bulgarian linguists in believing that **da** does express modality, although that modality has yet to be precisely defined. **Da** thus fits ASW's semantic criterion for being an AUX, as well as at least part of the syntactic criterion; that is, it is distinct in its syntactic behavior from other categories. Consideration of the constituent status of the AUX in Bulgarian must be deferred until after taking a brief look at some other possible components of the AUX.

3. THE AUXILIARY VERBS

All of the likely candidates for inclusion in the Bulgarian AUX other than **da** are verbs or at least verblike elements, which occur both as fully inflected main verbs and in an invariant ('uninflected') form as auxiliaries. The verbs in question are the following:

	Meaning when uninflected	Meaning when inflected
šte	*will*	*want*
njama	*will not*	*be nonexistent*
trjabva	*must/should*	*be necessary*
biva	*ought*	*happen, be*

When these occur in constructions like those in (15), that is, when they are in the position between (FOCUS) and (**da**)-V, they appear in the invariant form, identical to the third person singular inflected form, regardless of the person and number of the subject. In other types of constructions (cf. the examples in (16)), they agree in person and number with the subject, like ordinary verbs.

(15) a. Ti *šte* izpusneš vlaka.
      you will miss-2s train-the
      You'll miss the train.

b. Nie *njama* da zabravim.
we won't to forget-1p
We won't forget.

c. Ti *trjabva* da otideš.
you must to go-2s
You should go.

d. Ti ne *biva* da izpuskaš urocite.
you neg ought to miss-2s lessons-the
You shouldn't skip classes.

(16) a. Da praviš kakvoto si šteš.
to do-2s what refl want-2s.
Do whatever you want.

b. Nie *njamame* vreme.
we don't-have-1p time
We don't have time.

c. Ti mi *trjabvaš*.
you me-dat are-necessary-2s
I need you.

d. Sŭbranijata *bivat* vednŭž v sedmicata.
meetings-the are-3p once in week-the
Meetings take place once a week.

The opposite distribution of inflections is never possible. The fully inflected form of these four verbs cannot occur before (da)-V, nor can the invariant form occur as a main verb. Compare (17) to (15b, 16b).

(17) a.* Nie *njamame* da zabravim.
we don't-have-1p to forget-1p

b.* Nie *njama* vreme.
we won't-1p time.

The uninflected verbs in (15) fit ASW's criteria for AUX-hood quite well: they express the notional categories of Tense (**šte, njama**) or Modality (trjabva, biva), and they differ syntactically from ordinary verbs, including those in (16), in not taking person/number agreement. Other verbs do agree with the subject in V-da-V constructions, even if they require identical subjects for the two verbs. See (18a–c) and examples throughout this paper.

(18) a. Az prodŭlžavam da peja.
    I   continue-1s to sing-1s

    I keep singing.

  b. Ti   prodŭlžavaš da peeš.
    you continue-2s to sing-2s

    You keep singing.

  c. Te   prodŭlžavat da pejat.
    they continue-3p to sing-3p

    They keep singing.

These facts warrant giving serious consideration to the possibility that **njama, trjabva**, etc. are not true verbs, but rather auxiliaries, in the non-inflecting type of construction. **Šte** behaves like a 'real' verb in terms of person/number agreement in the past tense, but **njama, trjabva**, and **biva** remain uninflected; here again the invariant form is morphologically third person singular.

(19) a. Az štjah   da četa.
    I would-1s to read 1-s

    I was going to read.

  b. Ti   šteše   da četeš.
    you would-2s to read-2s

    You were going to read.

  c. Nie štjahme da četem.
    we would-1p to read-1p

    We were going to read.

d. Az $\begin{Bmatrix} \text{njamaše} \\ \text{trjabvaše} \\ \text{ne bivaše} \end{Bmatrix}$ da četa.

$I \begin{Bmatrix} \textit{wasn't going to} \\ \textit{had to (should have)} \\ \textit{ought not to have} \end{Bmatrix} \textit{read.}$

e. Ti $\begin{Bmatrix} \text{njamaše} \\ \text{trjabvaše} \\ \text{ne bivaše} \end{Bmatrix}$ da četeš.

$You \begin{Bmatrix} \textit{weren't going to} \\ \textit{had to (should have)} \\ \textit{ought not to have} \end{Bmatrix} \textit{read.}$

f. Nie $\begin{Bmatrix} \text{njamaše} \\ \text{trjabvaše} \\ \text{ne bivaše} \end{Bmatrix}$ da četem.

$We \begin{Bmatrix} \textit{weren't going to} \\ \textit{had to (should have)} \\ \textit{ought not to have} \end{Bmatrix} \textit{read.}$

When not followed by (**da**)-V, **njama** etc. do inflect for person and number in the past tense, just as they do in the present; compare (16b) and (20).

(20) Nie njamahme   vreme.
      we   didn't-have-1p time

We didn't have time.

There are a few other so-called 'impersonal' verbs in Bulgarian, that is, verbs which exhibit a lack of person/number agreement in certain constructions, where they occur in a morphologically third person singular form regardless of the subject of the sentence. These verbs differ from the auxiliaries, however, in that they precede rather than follow the FOCUS. The following are some examples containing one such verb, **može** 'can, is possible'.[5]

(21) a. Ne   može   nie da dojdem   dnes.
       neg is-possible we to come-1p   today.

       We can't come today.

   b. Može   li   az da peja?
       is-possible Q   I   to sing-1s

       May I sing?

It is clear that **može** and similar verbs are properly analyzed as being in a higher S; they are outside of the clause which contains the NP translated into English as the subject of the whole sentence, and therefore have no reason to agree with it. This is not true of the verbal auxiliaries, which are, on the contrary, clearly in the same clause as the subject, at least in surface structure, and should be expected to agree with the subject if they were true verbs.

Another element which might be considered an auxiliary verb is **sŭm** 'to be', which is used in the formation of several of the past tenses or aspects:

(22) a. Az četoh.

      I read.

   b. Az sŭm čel.

      I (m.) have read.

   c. Az bjah čel.

      I (m.) had read.   (**bjah** = past tense of **sŭm**)

However, **sŭm** differs from the other proposed auxiliary verbs in several rather crucial ways: (1) **Šte, njama, trjabva**, and **biva**, as well as **da**, are followed by a tensed verb with regular verbal morphology, while **sŭm** is followed by a participle, that is, basically an adjective with regular adjective morphology, gender agreement, etc. (2) **Sŭm** itself is fully inflected as a verb in all its uses, while a characteristic feature of the other proposed auxiliaries is their lack of person/number agreement, their only inflection being for past vs present tense. (3) **Sŭm** is a clitic on the participle[6] and forms a constituent with the other clitics (*Az [sŭm go] čel / Čel [sŭm go]* 'I have read it'), while none of the other proposed auxiliaries are part of the clitic group. Because of these syntactic and morphological traits I consider **sŭm** to be a verb (albeit a slightly odd one, considering its clitic status) and not an auxiliary.[7]

The elements which I propose including under the node AUX, then, are **da, šte, njama, trjabva,** and **biva.** It should be noted that two or even three of these can occur together: **njama, trjabva, biva,** and in certain non-standard dialects also **šte,** require a following **da** (cf. examples (15)), and the sequence **šte trjabva da** also occurs:

(23) Šte   trjabva   da   mi   pišeš.
      will must   to   me-dat write-2s

You'll have to write to me.

One crucial question remains for our analysis of these elements as an AUX, namely that of constituent status. In order to claim that, for example, the sequence **šte trjabva da** (or any other existing sequence of the proposed auxiliaries) constitutes an AUX in the sense of ASW, it is necessary to show that it is a constituent. This is unfortunately not easy to do. There are, to the best of my knowledge, no rules which move the auxiliary sequence or any part of it, nor can it be replaced by any sort of pro-form, nor deleted, so the usual tests for constituency do not work. There is, however, some evidence suggesting that the auxiliary sequence is a constituent, based on the constituents which surround it.

The position of the auxiliaries is between the FOCUS and the Verb-clitic group (V'). The FOCUS consists of some material, usually an NP or PP, which is moved into the underlying subject position by a Focusing rule. If movement rules can only move constituents, then the FOCUS is a constituent by definition. The clitic group which immediately follows AUX is a constituent by the same reasoning, since it permutes around the following verb (see examples (7)). The verb and clitics together are also presumably a constituent, since if V deletes (e.g. by Gapping) or moves, the clitics must go with it; they cannot attach to anything other than V. The auxiliaries lie between the FOCUS constituent and the V' and belong to neither of them; this at least suggests that they form another constituent, i.e. AUX. The phrase structure rules under this analysis will include something like (24); (25) shows the structure of a sentence containing a focused NP, AUX, and clitics.

(24) a. S $\longrightarrow$ NP   AUX   VP

  b. AUX $\longrightarrow$ (šte) $\left(\left\{ \begin{array}{l} \text{trjabva} \\ \text{njama} \\ \text{biva} \end{array} \right\} \right)$ (da)

(25)

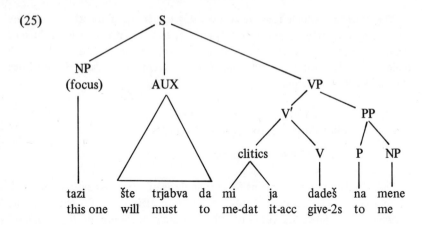

You'll have to give this one to me.

Another type of evidence often used to show that two or more elements are a single constituent is whether any material can be inserted between them. If a sequence is uninterruptable, it is likely that it forms a constituent, on the assumption that material can be inserted at constituent margins. However, if some material can be inserted, the sequence is not *necessarily* proved not to be a constituent; constituents can sometimes be interrupted. For example, in certain (rather archaic) styles in Bulgarian, clitics can interrupt an NP:

(26)   Hubava   si   e   moma   mila.
       pretty   refl   is   girl   washed-f.

A pretty girl washed herself.

In (26), **hubava moma** is clearly an NP. In this style, clitic placement ignores constituent structure altogether and puts the clitics after the first *word* of the utterance regardless of whether that word is a complete major constituent or not (and not necessarily adjacent to V, as in modern standard Bulgarian).

Returning to AUX, the string FOCUS – šte – $\begin{Bmatrix} \text{njama} \\ \text{trjabva} \\ \text{biva} \end{Bmatrix}$ – da – V can be interrupted after FOCUS (i.e. before the start of the postulated AUX constituent) and before **da**, but not anywhere else. The following example uses the adverb **nepremenno** (definitely) to illustrate the possibilities for insertion.

(27)   A   na nego (nepremenno)   šte   (*nepremenno)   trjabva
        but to him   will   must

(nepremenno)   da (*nepremenno)   ja   dadeš.
               to   it-f-acc   give-2s

But you'll definitely have to give it to him.

The impossibility of inserting adverbs after **šte** and **da** may have to do with the fact that, unlike **trjabva, njama, biva,** they are stressless and form a single phonological word with whatever follows them. If adverb transportation is a very late rule, applying after **šte** and **da** have become attached (by some cliticization process, presumably) to the following word, the lack of insertion after them would be accounted for. Note the similar restriction on such sequences as *have to* (*hafta*) and *got to* (*gotta*) in English, where nothing can be inserted in between the two elements which form a surface phonological word:

(28) a.* I have absolutely to get out of here.

   b.* I have got absolutely to get out of here.

but:

   c. I have absolutely got to get out of here.

The insertion facts fail to give any firm evidence for AUX as a constituent in Bulgarian — the cases where insertion is impossible can be independently accounted for by the cliticization of **da** and **šte** onto the following word — but, as pointed out above, they cannot prove it is *not* a constituent at any stage of the derivation either. We are thus left with no definitive evidence for the constituent status of AUX but also no definitive evidence against it.

The fact that **da** and V' cannot be separated suggests at first glance that **da** might in fact be part of V' rather than being in AUX, or perhaps even that the entire AUX is dominated by VP rather than being its sister under S. The analysis of **da** as cliticizing onto the following V' makes it unnecessary to account for their inseparability by placing **da** in the same (deep structure) constituent as V', although it of course does not rule out such an analysis. Note however that whatever evidence there is for **da** being in VP holds for **šte** as well, since no adverb can be inserted between **šte** and V' either, when **šte** is the last auxiliary:

(29)   Az šte (*nepremenno)   vi   dam   knigata.
         I will   definitely   you-dat   give-1s   book-the
         (*I will definitely give you the book.*)

Thus if **da** is in VP, the rest of the proposed AUX must also be there.

Although its constituent status remains somewhat uncertain, I tentatively conclude that Bulgarian does have an AUX (assuming, of course, the correctness of the ASW definition), and that it contains the particle **da** as well as the four non-agreement-marking verbs **šte, njama, trjabva,** and **biva. Da** appears historically to have been a complementizer; it is a complementizer in closely related languages (e.g. Serbocroatian) and retains many complementizer-like functions even in Bulgarian. The other auxiliaries are all clearly verbal in origin. The boundary between auxiliaries and complementizers, on the one hand, and auxiliaries and verbs, on the other, remains quite fuzzy; the problems of precisely how and where to draw the line between these categories, and the question of what kinds of historical and synchronic relations there are between them are clearly areas which deserve much more research.

Indiana University

NOTES

[1] Some verbs, of course, can take more than one complement type, and nouns and adjectives also subcategorize for a complement with **da, če,** or **dali:**

i.   Vidjah *če* horata igrajat.

       I saw that the people were dancing.

ii.   Vidjah horata *da* igrajat.

       I saw the people dancing.

iii.   Vidja li *dali* igrajat horata?

       Did you see if the people were dancing?

iv.   čuvstvoto *če*   (vs)   želanie *da*   (vs)   vǔprosǔt *dali*
       feeling that   desire to   question whether

v.   dobre *če*   (vs)   gotov *da*   (vs)   ne sigurno *dali*
       good that   ready to   not certain whether

[2] **Li** may in fact be identical to **dali** in underlying representation: a single question element may be 'spelled out' as **dali** if it remains in COMP and as **li** if it moves to some

other position. There are, however, some problems with this analysis which need not concern us here. In any case, the identity or non-identity of **li** and **dali** is not crucial to the present argument.

[3] The verb following **da** is virtually always present tense except in the conditional usage, where it is usually past.

[4] Mutafchieva states that **da** in at least some constructions expresses modality in that the action is desired to various degrees, ranging from a wish to a command. Penchev considers the modal properties of **da** to be desirability and obligation, and hypothesizes that these properties are due to an abstract underlying verb 'to demand', which has the features [+ desire, + obligation] in those cases where **da** is not governed by a verb in a higher clause. Schick gives a rather long list of features compatible with the modality of **da**: possibility, necessity, ability, readiness, etc., and symbolizes the features of **da** itself with the abstract synbol [± H].

[5] **Može** also occurs after the FOCUS, but there it does inflect for person/number agreement and attributes ability to the subject rather than possibility to the situation:

i.   Az   moga   da   peja.
        I   can-1s   to   sing-1s

        I can sing.

[6] It should be noted that **sům** also occurs in copular constructions where it is followed by an AP, NP, or AdvP rather than a participal form. Although **sům** is clearly the main (and only) verb in such sentences, it is still a clitic and cannot occur S-initially (cf. example (7)):

i.   Az   sům   lekar   (štastliv, v gradinata)
        I   am   doctor   (happy, in garden-the)

        I am a doctor (happy, in the garden).

ii.   Lekar (štastliv, v gradinata) sům.

but:

iii.   * Sům lekar (štastliv, v gradinata).

Evidently, cliticness is not incompatible with verb status, any more than it is with other categories, such as pronoun or AUX.

[7] Kaisse (1981) argues against a Bulgarian AUX consisting of the clitic forms of **sům** and the pronominal clitics. This has absolutely no relation to the AUX I am proposing, which contains **da** and the uninflected modals, but neither **sům** nor any pronouns. Kaisse's hypothetical AUX is the clitic group which I consider to be attached to V under V'.

BIBLIOGRAPHY

Akmajian, Adrian, Susan Steele, and Thomas Wasow: 1979, 'The Category AUX in Universal Grammar', *Linguistic Inquiry* **10**, 1–64.
Kaisse, Ellen M.: 1981, 'Luiseño Particles and the Universal Behavior of Clitics', *Linguistic Inquiry* **12**, 424–434.

Moneva-Dolapchieva, Raina S.: 1976, *Transformational Treatment of Some Problems in Bulgarian Syntax*, Unpublished Ph.D. dissertation, SUNY buffalo.

Mutafchieva, Zara Genadieva: 1970, *Podchinitelnijat sŭjuz da v sŭvremennija bŭlgarski ezik*, BAN, Sofia.

Penchev, Jordan: 1973, 'Upotreba na sŭjuz da v njakoi konstrukcii', *Bŭlgarski Ezik* 23, 546–551.

Schick, Ivanka Petkova: 1977, 'Die bulgarischen da-Konstruktionen als Träger spezifischer Modalitäten', *Linguistische Studien* 43, 117–185.

ELOISE JELINEK

PERSON-SUBJECT MARKING IN *A UX* IN
EGYPTIAN ARABIC

0. INTRODUCTION

Arguments will be presented here in support of an analysis of indicative sentences in Egyptian Arabic that recognizes a sentential constituent that we may label 'AUX'.[1] Steele has provided a language independent definition of AUX as follows:

> Given a set of language internal analyses, in terms of constituents, those constituents which may contain only a specified (i.e., fixed and small) set of elements, crucially containing elements marking tense and/or modality, will be identified as non-distinct (Steele *et al.*, 1981, Chap. 2.).

Steele's definition of AUX is to be validated by demonstrating its instantiation in the grammars of particular languages. I will show that there is a constituent of indicative sentences in Egyptian Arabic where tense is marked, that tense is never marked elsewhere, and that this constituent has a small, closed inventory. Accordingly, I propose that this constituent may be identified as an instantiation of Steele's language independent definition of AUX, and that the constituent labeled 'AUX' in Egyptian Arabic is equivalent to the AUX constituent Akmajian, Steele and Wasow (1979) have proposed for English and Luiseño.

Akmajian, Steele, and Wasow (ASW) draw attention to the interesting parallels between a constituent of English sentences and a constituent of Luiseño sentences that in each language is the locus for the marking of tense and modality. ASW argue that these cross-language parallels suggest that AUX is at least an available category for the description of other languages, and that AUX may in fact be a universal grammatical feature.

Pullum and Wilson (1977), as summarized by Pullum (1981, p. 435) argued that

(A) The node label 'AUX' should be abolished.

(B) The 'auxiliaries' are just a special subset of the verbs.

(C) 'Auxiliaries' are main verbs.

Pullum and Wilson's position on the analysis of English is that "all modals are well as other auxiliaries should be generated in the same way as verbs".

21

F. Heny and B. Richards (eds.), Linguistic Categories: Auxiliaries and Related Puzzles, Vol. One, 21–46.
Copyright © 1983 by D. Reidel Publishing Company.

(1977, p. 741). Pullum (1981) argues against an AUX constituent in both English and Luiseño, and furthermore denies that there are significant parallels between these two languages with respect to a constituent where tense and modality are marked:

It is worth noting here, however, that even if my arguments . . . failed, that is, if there were an 'AUX' constituent in both Luiseño and English, ASW's hope for a universal theory of 'AUX' would not be realized, or its prospects significantly bettered. As we shall see in detail below, the claimed 'AUX' node of Luiseño contains a cluster of particles indicating tense, the person and number of the subject NP, and the assorted 'modal' notions mentioned above. The English 'AUX' postulated by ASW contains (at surface structure) a finite auxiliary verb. The properties of the two alleged constituents are markedly different, in ways made fairly clear by ASW or by Steele in earlier work. (1981, p. 438)

According to Pullum, then, aside from questions of constituency, the elements ASW assign to an AUX constituent in English are best seen as a subset of main verbs, while the elements assigned to AUX in Luiseño are simply particles. He sees no significant parallels, semantic or otherwise, that would lead him to recognize a cross-language equivalence between AUX in Luiseño and AUX in English.

Egyptian Arabic presents an interesting case with regard to the properties of AUX identified by ASW, since, as I will show, the AUX in Egyptian Arabic shares features of both the Luiseño AUX and the English AUX. That is, in some sentence types, to be specified below, AUX in Egyptian Arabic is represented by an inflection of a finite verb, the copula. In other sentence types, the AUX constituent will be shown to consist of particles that are without question non-verbal, that mark tense and person-subject, as the Luiseño particles do. Therefore, the items that I will specify as belonging to the small, closed inventory of AUX in Egyptian Arabic cannot all be assimilated to the lexical category *verb* on the one hand, or identified simply as particles on the other. Since the Egyptian Arabic AUX resembles both the English AUX and the Luiseño AUX, it strengthens ASW's claim as to the significant parallels between AUX in these two languages, and provides an additional independent case of the cross-language parallels that suggest the availability of a syntactic category AUX as a feature that the grammars of particular languages may select.

My first task will be to argue for the constituency of AUX in Egyptian Arabic; that is, to argue that there is a constituent of indicative sentences in the language, syntactically independent of the predicate, where tense is marked. I will argue that finite (indicative) sentences contain this constituent, whereas non-finite (imperative and subjunctive) sentences do not, and that there are both finite and non-finite embedded clause types in the language, where the former have an AUX constituent and the latter do not. It is this distribution of the constituent across sentences types, as well as the best available translation, that will substantiate my claim for tense marking in this constituent. This will be the goal of Section 1 of this paper. In Section 2, I will show how a rule of Egyptian Arabic grammar, NEG-attachment, crucially makes reference to the AUX constituent of indicative sentences in the language. In Section 3, I will show how the conditions on the appearance of independent subjects must be stated with reference to AUX. In Section 4, I will present some conclusions.

1. AUX AS A CONSTITUENT OF INDICATIVE SENTENCES IN EGYPTIAN ARABIC

1.1. *The Indicative Mood and the Copula*

The copula is a feature of indicative sentences in Egyptian Arabic. By 'indicative' is meant here declarative and interrogative sentences. Both declarative and interrogative sentences in the language are finite, that is, carry tense marking. Declarative and yes/no interrogative sentences differ only in intonation; therefore, all the examples in this section that are translated as declaratives could be rendered interrogative by an appropriate change in intonation contour.[2]

Across languages, copular verbs often differ syntactically in significant respects from other verbs in a language; copular sentence types may be defined which are distinct from other sentence types. Copular verbs together with a subject often do not constitute a complete sentence, as may be the case with other verb-subject concatenations. Copular verbs may co-occur with predicate nouns, predicate adjectives, participles, etc. (*John is angry, John is running*), to form what have sometimes been termed 'compound predicates', as distinct from 'simple' verbal predicates, where no copula is required (*John ran*). Egyptian Arabic does not distinguish among sentence types in this way; we can, if we like, classify all indicative sentences in the language as copular sentences. This is not to say that there are no other verbal predicates in the language. The point is that all verbal as well as all non-verbal predicates in the language occur with some inflection of the copula to mark tense contrasts in indicative sentences, as the following examples will show.[3]

(1) Predicate noun

    a. ʕali ʕaskari
       Ali is a policeman.

    b. ʕali kaan ʕaskari
       Ali was a policeman.

    c. ʕali ḥaykuun ʕaskari
       Ali will be a policeman.

(2) Predicative adjective

    a. ʕali zaʕlaan
       Ali is angry.

    b. ʕali kaan zaʕlaan
       Ali was angry.

    c. ʕali ḥaykuun zaʕlaan
       Ali will be angry.

Note that there is no present tense copula, as is not unusual across languages. The inflection of the copula **kaan** marks past tense and third person masculine singular. The inflection **ḥaykuun** marks future tense and third person masculine singular. Other predicate types include:

(3) Locative prepositional phrase

    a. ʕali   fil-beet   dil-wa't
       Ali   in-the house now
       Ali is at home now.

    b. ʕali kaan fil-beet
       Ali was at home

    c. ʕali ḥaykuun fil-beet
       Ali will be at home.

In addition to these predicate types, there are two forms traditionally known as the Active and Passive Participles. These forms do not mark person, but are inflected for number and gender, as nouns and adjectives are. They mark aspect, and they also mark voice:

(4) Active Participle

    a.   ʕali   raayiḥ   maṣr
        ACT PART Egypt
        masc. sg.

        Ali is going to Egypt.

    b.   ʕali kaan raayiḥ maṣr

        Ali was going to Egypt.

    c.   ʕali ḥaykuun raayiḥ maṣr

        Ali will be going to Egypt.

The active participle marks imperfective or continuative aspect and active voice in these sentences.

(5) Passive Participle

    a.   ʕali   masguun
        PASS PART
        masc. sg.

        Ali is imprisoned.

    b.   ʕali kaan masguun

        Ali was imprisoned.

    c.   ʕali ḥaykuun masguun

        Ali will be imprisoned.

The passive participle marks perfective aspect and passive voice. The following examples show the verbal paradigms of the indicative mood:

(6) 'Perfect' (perfective aspect)

    a.   ʕali   katab
        PERF 3ms.

        Ali wrote, has written.

  b. ʕali kaan katab

    Ali had written

  c. ʕali ḥaykuun katab

    Ali will have written.

The form **katab** is an inflection of the root KTB 'write' and marks perfective aspect and third person masculine singular.

  (7) '**bi**-Imperfect' (imperfective aspect)

    a. ʕali biyiktib

      bi-IMPF 3ms.

     Ali is writing.

    b. ʕali kaan biyiktib

     Ali was writing.

    c. ʕali ḥaykuun biyiktib

     Ali will be writing.

  (8) '**ḥa**-Imperfect' (prospective aspect)

    a. ʕali ḥayiktib

      ḥa-IMPF 3ms.

     Ali is going to write.

    b. ʕali kaan ḥayiktib

     Ali was going to write.

The form **biyiktib** marks imperfective or continuative aspect and third person masculine singular, while **ḥayiktib** marks prospective aspect and third person masculine singular.[4] These verbal paradigms mark aspect, as the participles do. But they do not mark voice contrasts. They are inflected for person, while participles are not, and thus are clearly semantically and morphologically distinct from participles. They resemble participles in that they occur with the copula to mark tense contrasts, as is the case with all predicate types in the language.

  The copula is a regular member of the morphological class *verb*, and is inflected for person, number, and gender (in the singular) as all other verbs are. But the copula is semantically distinct in that it alone marks tense contrasts; all other verbs and participles mark aspect. The following are the tense-marking paradigms of the copula:

(9)   A. PAST   B. FUTURE
                  'Perfect'   'ḥa-Imperfect'

	Sing.	Plu.	Sing.	Plu.
1	kunt	kunna	ḥakuun	ḥankuun
2m.	kunt	kuntu	ḥatkuun	ḥatkuunu
f.	kunti		ḥatkuuni	
3m.	kaan	kaanu	ḥaykuun	ḥaykuunu
f.	kaanit		ḥatkuun	

No inflection of the copula is ever used to mark present tense.[5]

All of the example sentences given above correspond to one of the following schemata:

(10) a. Subject Predicate (present tense)

   b. Subject Copula Predicate (non-present tense)

But there is another word order that is equally acceptable for the non-present tense sentences, not illustrated above. The copula may precede the subject, in both declarative and interrogative sentence types.

(11) a. ʕali ʕaskari

   Ali is a policeman.

   b. kaan ʕali ʕaskari

   Ali was a policeman.

   c. ḥaykuun ʕali ʕaskari

   Ali will be a policeman.

This word order is an acceptable alternate with each of the predicate types illustrated above. Therefore, we may revise our sentence schemata for indicative sentences as follows:

(12) a. Subject Predicate (present tense)

      b. $\left\{\begin{array}{l}\text{Subject Copula} \\ \text{Copula Subject}\end{array}\right\}$ Predicate (non-present tense)

In addition to the subject of the sentence, an adverbial phrase may optionally
intervene between the copula and the predicate:

(13) ḥaykuun ʕali   fil-wa't da   biyiktibu
      be 3ms   at-that-time   writing-it
      FUTURE   ADV P   V 3ms-PRO

Ali will be writing it at that time.

In answer to a question, such as

(14) kaan   il-walad   biyibiiʕ burtu'aan   fi-s-suu'?
      be 3ms   the-boy   selling   oranges   in the market
      PAST   V 3ms

Was the boy selling oranges in the market?

A suitable reply might be:

(15)   la', makanš
      no, NEG be 3ms
               PAST

No, he wasn't.

I take the fact that the subject and optional adverbial phrases may intervene
between the copula and the predicate, and the fact that the copula may
appear without the predicate in responsives, as evidence for the syntactic
independence of the copula from the predicate.

1.2. *Non-finite Sentence Types*

Many languages that mark tense have some sentence types where tense is not
marked. Across languages, imperative and subjunctive sentences often do not
carry tense-marking. Accordingly, we might expect that such sentence types
in Egyptian Arabic might not be tensed. If so, they should not exhibit any of
the finite inflections of the copula seen above; and this is the case.

1.2.1. *The imperative mood*. There is an imperative inflection of the verb in Egyptian Arabic, as follows:

(16) a. ruuḥ   b. ruuḥi   c. ruuḥu
     go! masc. sg.   go! fem. sg.   go! pl.

This inflection is distinct from the indicative paradigms seen above. There is also an imperative inflection of the copula itself:

(17)   kuun   mu' addab
        be   ms. polite

        Be polite!

This non-finite inflection of the copula does not mark tense.

1.2.2. *The subjunctive mood*. There is a subjunctive/jussive verbal paradigm in Egyptian Arabic, traditionally known as the 'Imperfect'. This paradigm has replaced an older subjunctive paradigm still in use in Standard Arabic.[6] These subjunctive/jussive forms occur in independent clause types with a non-finite reading.

(18)   yiruuḥ   maṣr
        go   Egypt
        SBJT 3ms.

        Let him (may he) go to Egypt!

Finite inflections of the copula do not occur in these sentences. There is, however, a subjunctive inflection of the copula itself:

(19)   yikuun   ʕali   ʕaskari
        be   Ali   policeman
        SBJT 3ms

        Ali a policeman?!

        (Is it possible, could it be - - -?!)

Compare example (1) above, a finite sentence used to make an assertion. Note that these non-finite imperative and subjunctive sentences differ from present tense indicative sentences, which also lack a finite inflection of the copula, in that the non-finite sentences contain a non-indicative verbal predicate.[7]

1.2.3. *Embedded clause types*. Many languages that mark tense have both finite and non-finite embedded clauses. Finite embedded clauses are frequently the complement of epistemic 'dicto-cognitive' predicates, referring to some act of speech or cognition.

(20)   ana kunt   ʕaarif   innu   kaan   raayiḥ
        I   be 1s. knowing   that-he   be 3ms.   going
             PAST ACT PART ms. COMP-PRO PAST   ACT PART ms.

        I knew that he was going.

Non-finite embedded clauses are frequently the complement of some deontic dicto-cognitive predicate, referring to some state or act of desire or coercion.[8]

(21)   ana kunt   ʕaawiz   innu   yiruuḥ
        I   be 1s   wanting   that-he   go 3ms.
             PAST ACT PART ms. COMP-PRO SBJT

        I wanted him to go.

The matrix clause in (20) and (21) is finite. In (20), the embedded clause is also finite, and has a finite inflection of the copula. In (21), the embedded clause is non-finite, and no finite inflection of the copula may occur.

(22)   * ana kunt   ʕaawiz   innu   kaan   yiruuḥ
        I   be 1s. wanting   that-he   be 3ms.   go 3ms.
             PAST ACT PART ms. COMP-PRO PAST   SBJT

There is also a kind of adverbial clause in Egyptian Arabic where the verbal paradigms that appear in indicative clauses may appear with no accompanying finite inflection of the copula. These appositive predicates are traditionally known in Arabic grammar as **ḥaal** or 'condition' clauses.

(23)   ʕali rigiʕ   biʕ ayyaṭ
             returned   weeping
             PERF 3ms.   *bi*-IMPF 3ms.

        Ali (has) returned weeping.

These **ḥaal** constructions are further evidence that the indicative verbal paradigms (as in **biʕ ayyaṭ**) mark aspect alone, while the copula marks tense. Thus, there are some sentence types in Egyptian Arabic that mark tense but do not mark aspect; these are sentences with an inflection of the copula and a non-verbal or non-participial predicate, as in (1–3). There are sentences that mark both tense and aspect; these are sentences with the copula and a verbal or participial predicate, as in (4–8). There are clauses that mark aspect alone, as in the ḥaal example (23). And there are sentences that mark neither tense nor aspect; these are imperatives and subjunctives, as in (16–19). I conclude that tense and aspect are marked separately in Egyptian Arabic, and that the copula marks tense contrasts.

My purpose is to show that finite clauses have an AUX constituent, while non-finite clauses do not. We have seen that the copula has distributional properties that no other verb has; it alone appears with all predicate types in indicative sentences to mark tense contrasts. There are other verb-verb sequences in the language; in some of these sequences, a clause boundary is present, as can be shown by the optional presence of a complementizer or a conjunction. No complementizer or conjunction ever intervenes between the copula and a succeeding predicate. Other verb-verb sequences involve certain aspectual verbs as the first element. In such verb-verb sequences, non-initial verbs must always be in the Imperfect (subjunctive) inflection, whereas the copula precedes verbs in any of the verbal paradigms. Furthermore, these aspectual verb-verb sequences are in turn preceded by the copula to mark tense contrasts. See Jelinek (1981) for a complete inventory and analysis of verb-verb sequence types in Egyptian Arabic.

In sum, the copula, while quite clearly a member of the morphological class *verb*, differs semantically (by marking tense) from other members of that morphological class. The copula also differs syntactically from other verbs in the distributional features described in the preceding sections. Some of the syntactic peculiarities of the copula outlined here would be consistent with an interpretation of the copula as the initial member of a 'compound' predicate. The fact that finite inflections of the copula are excluded from certain non-finite sentence types, including imperatives and ḥaal or 'condition' clauses, and the fact that the subject and/or an adverbial phrase may intervene between the copula and the predicate, are evidence in support of the position that some rules of the grammar refer to a sentential constituent where tense is marked, that is syntactically independent of the predicate. In the next section, evidence will be presented that demonstrates that items other than the finite inflections of the copula may appear in this sentential constituent. In specifying these items, we will complete the small, closed inventory of elements that may appear in the AUX constituent of indicative sentences in Egyptian Arabic.

2. NEG-ATTACHMENT IN EGYPTIAN ARABIC

In this section, I will describe the phenomena of NEG-attachment in Egyptian Arabic, and show how any generalization that captures these phenomena crucially makes reference to the AUX constituent. The assumption here is that the syntactic rules of a language define the sentential constituents. An adequate statement of NEG-attachment in Egyptian Arabic provides support for the AUX constituent proposed here. A first approximation of this generalization is as follows:

    (24)   NEG attaches to any item appearing in the AUX constituent.

Examples:

(25) a. ʕali miš ʕaskari
             NEG

      Ali isn't a policeman.

    b. ʕali makanš ʕaskari
             NEG-be 3ms.
             PAST

      Ali wasn't a policeman.

    c. ʕali maḥaykunš ʕaskari
             NEG-be 3ms.
             FUTURE

    or

    c'. ʕali miš ḥaykuun ʕaskari
             NEG-be 3ms.
             FUTURE

      Ali won't be a policeman.

Example (25a) shows that in a present tense sentence, where there is no inflection of the copula, the unattached NEG particle (**miš** or **muš**) appears alone; in non-present tense sentences (25b) and (25c, 25c'), where there is an inflection of the copula, the discontinuous elements **ma - - - - š** appear attached to that inflection. (Some Egyptians say **maḥaykunš**, as in (25c); most educated Cairenes prefer **miš ḥaykuun**, as in (25c'). The point here is that NEG may attach to the copula.)

In other present tense sentences, where there is a verbal predicate, NEG may attach to the predicate.

(26) a. ʕali   makatabš
          NEG- wrote
          PERF 3ms.

  Ali didn't write (hasn't written).

   b. ʕali   makanš   katab
          NEG-be 3ms.   wrote 3ms.
          PAST   PERF

  Ali hadn't written.

   c. ʕali   maḥaykunš   katab
          NEG-be 3ms.   wrote 3ms.
          FUTURE   PERF

   or

   c'. ʕali   miš   ḥaykuun   katab
          NEG   be 3ms.   wrote 3ms.
                    FUTURE   PERF

  Ali won't have written.

Examples (25) and (26) suggest that one of the following generalizations on NEG-attachment might be sufficient, and that reference to AUX might be avoided:

(27)   NEG attaches to the first verb in the sentence.

(28)   NEG attaches to the first predicate in the sentence.

It is the failure of generalizations such as (27) and (28) that will require us to refer to AUX in an adequate statement of NEG attachment. In order to show that (27, 28) are inadequate, we will need to look at predicate types in Egyptian Arabic somewhat more closely than we have done so far.

2.1. *Predicate*₁ *and Predicate*₂

We have seen that all members of the paradigms of the morphological class *verb* in Egyptian Arabic mark person-subject. The copula, as a regular member

of this morphological class, marks person-subject. But morphological classes
and sentential constituents need not coincide; for example, members of the
morphological class *noun* may appear in both the subject constituent and the
predicate constituent (as a predicate noun) in an Egyptian Arabic sentence,
and one member of the morphological class *verb* (the copula) appears in the
AUX constituent, while all others appear in the predicate constituent.

Some predicate types in Egyptian Arabic do not mark person subject,
while others do. I will call those predicates that do not mark person-subject
(predicate nouns, adjectives, participles, etc.) *Predicate*$_1$; and those predicates
that do mark person-subject *Predicate*$_2$. The latter class includes non-copular
verbs, but verbs do not exhaust the inventory of *Predicate*$_2$.[9]

In many languages, possessive and existential sentences are *sui generis*
in syntactic structure, and this is the case in Egyptian Arabic. Possessive
sentences employ one of a set of locative prepositions, with pronominal
suffixes that mark possession elsewhere, as transitive predicates. The paradigm
is as follows:

(29)   ʕand-i   ʕand-ina
        with-me   with us

        I have.   *We have.*

        ʕand-ak   ʕand-ukum
        with-you ms.   with you pl.

        You have.   *You have.*

        ʕand-ik   ʕand-uhum
        with-you fs.   with them

        You have.   *They have.*

        ʕand-u (h)
        with-him

        He has.

        ʕand-aha
        with-her

        She has.

In present tense sentences, NEG attaches to these transitive predicates:

(30) a. ʕandu   kitaab   b. ʕandaha   kitaab
        with-him   book   with-her   book
        PREP-PRO   N   PREP-PRO   N
        He has a book.   *She has a book.*

    c. ma ʕanduuš   kitaab   d. ma ʕandahaaš   kitaab
        NEG-with-him book   NEG-with-her   book
        PREP-PRO   N   PREP-PRO   N
        He doesn't have a book.   *She doesn't have a book.*

The copula marks tense in these sentences just as it does elsewhere, and NEG attaches to the copula in non-present tense sentences.

(31) a. kunt   ʕandi   kitaab   b. makuntiiš   ʕandi   kitaab
        be 1s. at-me   book   NEG-be 1s. at-me   book
        PAST   PAST
        I had a book.   *I didn't have a book.*

In existential sentences, the locative preposition **fi**, 'in, at' with a pronominal suffix marking third person masculine singular, as an abstract subject, is employed. (Compare **il y a**, or **es gibt**.)

(32)   (kaan   \   fiih   ʕaskari   ʕal-baab
       (be 3ms.)   in-it   policeman   at the door
       (PAST   /   PREP-PRO

       There $\dfrac{is}{(was)}$ a policeman at the door.

(33)   mafiiš   ḥadd   yiʕmil   kida
       NEG-in-it   anyone   do   so
       There's no one who would do such a thing.

(34)   makanš   fiih   ḥadd   fil-beet
       NEG-be 3ms.   in-it   anyone   in-the-house
           PAST
       There was nobody at home.

Example (32) shows the copula marking tense in an existential sentence. In (33), NEG attaches to the predicate in a present tense sentence; in (34), NEG attaches to the copula.

NEG also attaches to certain 'nouns of volition' that occur with these same possessive suffixes and serve as transitive predicates. There are perhaps a dozen such volitional predicates, a lexically defined class.[10]

(35) a. biddi   tiffaaḥa   b. mabiddiiš   tiffaaḥa
      wish-my apple   NEG-wish-my apple

      I want an apple.   *I don't want an apple.*

(36) a. kunt   biddi   tiffaaḥa   b. makuntiiš biddi   tiffaaḥa
      be 1s wish-my apple   NEG-be 1s wish-my apple
      PAST   PAST

      I wanted an apple.   *I didn't want an apple.*

Compare:

(37) a. giddi   ḥakiim   b. giddi   miš   ḥakiim
      my-grandfather doctor   my-grandfather NEG doctor

      My grandfather is a doctor   *My grandfather isn't a doctor.*

(38) a. giddi   kaan   ḥakiim
      my grandfather be 3ms. doctor
                    PAST

      My grandfather was a doctor.

    b. giddi   makanš   ḥakiim
        my-grandfather NEG-be 3ms. doctor
                     PAST

      My grandfather wasn't a doctor.

The example sentences in (35, 36) show that NEG attaches to these volitional predicates in present tense sentences; that the copula marks tense contrasts in these sentence types as elsewhere, and that NEG attaches to the copula in non-present tense volitional sentences. Examples (37–38) show a non-volitional noun with a possessive suffix. Such a noun may not function as a predicate, but is the subject of the sentence. The subject never undergoes NEG-attachment.

(39)   *magiddiiš   ḥakiim
      NEG-my-grandfather doctor
      (Compare (37b above.)

Examples (29–36) demonstrate that the generalization stated in (27) on NEG attachment will not suffice, since these predicates are not verbs. We turn to the generalization stated in (28); this fails also, since there are predicates to which NEG never attaches:

(40)   * giddi   maḥakimš
       my-grandfather   NEG-doctor
       (Compare (37b) above.)

Inspection of the preceding examples will reveal that in all the present tense sentences when NEG attaches to the predicate, that predicate is a *Predicate*$_2$, marking person-subject, just as the copula does. This suggests that the following generalization on NEG attachment may suffice:

(41)   NEG attaches to the first word in the sentence that marks person-subject.

If (41) applies, then reference to AUX is not required in an adequate statement of NEG attachment. The following examples will show that (41) does not apply.

2.2. *The 'Pronoun of Separation' and the 'Negative Pronouns'*

We have seen that no inflection of the copula is ever used to mark present tense. Howver, there are pronominal elements that appear in the AUX constituent in certain present tense sentences. If the predicate of the sentence is a definite noun, a pronoun that agrees in number and gender with the NP subject (traditionally called a 'pronoun of separation') must intervene between the subject and the predicate.[11] The following paradigm results:

(42) a. ʕali   huwwa   il- ʕaskari
         he   the-policeman

     Ali is the policeman.

   b. ʕali   kaan   il- ʕaskari
             be 3ms.
             PAST

     Ali was the policeman.

   c. ʕali ḥaykuun il- ʕaskari
      be 3ms.
      FUTURE

Ali will be the policeman.

(43) a. Nagwa hiyya il-mudarrisa
       she   the teacher

Nagwa is the teacher.

   b. Nagwa kaanit il-mudarrisa
      be 3fs.
      PAST

Nagwa was the teacher.

   c. Nagwa ḥatkuun il-mudarrisa
      be 3fs.
      FUTURE

Nagwa will be the teacher.

Li and Thompson (1977) argue that the historical development of 'copular morphemes' from earlier pronominal forms can be demonstrated in Mandarin Chinese, Palestinian Arabic, Hebrew, and Wappo. Hale (1973) suggests that person-subject marking pronouns in AUX in Walbiri and Warramunga resemble in shape and are historically related to independent pronouns in those languages. What I would like to point out here is the parallel between these pronominal forms that mark person-subject and present tense in Egyptian Arabic with the particles that appear in AUX in Luiseño. In the NEG analogues of these sentences, what has been termed a 'negative pronoun' appears:

(44) a. ʕali mahuwwaaš il- ʕaskari
      NEG-he   the-policeman

Ali isn't the policeman.

   b. ʕali makanš il- ʕaskari
      NEG-be 3ms.
      PAST

Ali wasn't the policeman.

   c. ʕali maḥaykunš il- ʕaskari
      NEG-be 3ms.
      FUTURE

      Ali won't be the policeman.

(45) a. Nagwa mahiyyaaš il-mudarrisa
       NEG-she

       Nagwa isn't the teacher.

   b. Nagwa makanitš il-mudarrisa
      NEG-be 3fs.
      PAST

      Nagwa wasn't the teacher.

   c. Nagwa maḥatkunš il-mudarrisa
      NEG-be 3fs.
      FUTURE

      Nagwa won't be the teacher.

The complete set of 'negative pronouns' is as follows:

(46) A. *Pronouns*   B. *'NEG pronouns'*

	Sing.	*Plu.*	*Sing.*	*Plu.*
1	ana	iḥna	maniiš	maḥnaaš
2m.	inta	intu	mantaaš	mantuuš
f.	inti		mantiiš	
3m.	huwwa	humma	mahuwwaaš	mahummaaš
f.	hiyya		mahiyyaaš	

These 'negative pronouns' are optional in, and restricted to, any present tense sentence with a Predicate$_1$ — that is, any sentence where person-subject is not marked elsewhere. Evidence that these 'negative pronouns' are not constructions where NEG attaches to the subject is as follows:

(47)   huwwa mahuwwaaš il- ʕaskari
       he   NEG-he   the-policeman

       He's not the policeman.

The 'pronoun of separation' and the 'negative pronouns' are clearly not verbs, predicates, or subjects, but pronominal elements appearing in AUX. They demonstrate that the generalization stated in (41) does not apply, and that reference to the AUX constituent of Egyptian Arabic sentences is necessary for an adequate statement of NEG-attachment, as follows:

(48)   NEG attaches to any AUX element; if there is no AUX element, then NEG may attach to Predicate$_2$.

Since the 'negative pronouns' are AUX elements, and mark present tense, the analysis given here predicts that they would be excluded from non-finite clause types, and this is the case.

(49)   ir-ra'iis   ʕaawiz   innak   matkunš   kaslaan
         the-boss   wanting   that-you   NEG-be   lazy
                     ACT PART ms.   COMP-PRO   SBJT 3ms.   ADJ ms.

The boss wants you not to be lazy.

Example sentence (49) shows a non-finite embedded clause with the copula inflected in the subjunctive. 'Negative pronouns' may not occur in such sentences. Since there is no AUX element, and since the subjunctive verbal form marks person subject, NEG-attachment to the predicate occurs, and the generalization on NEG attachment given in (48) applies. The 'negative pronouns' are also excluded from any sentence with an imperative verbal inflection. The 'negative pronouns' are comparable to a present tense negative copula. See Comrie (1976) for a discussion of negative verbs in other languages.[12]

3. REQUIRED VS OPTIONAL SUBJECTS

A statement of the conditions on the appearance of subjects in Egyptian Arabic sentences also requires reference to the AUX constituent.

(50)   Where person-subject is marked in AUX or Predicate, no NP subject is required.

In all non-present tense sentences, no NP subject is required to form a complete sentence, since person-subject is marked in (at least) some inflection of the copula, and in some cases, in the predicate as well.

(51) a. ʕaskari
      policeman

    b. kaan ʕaskari
       He was a policeman.

    c. ḥaykuun ʕaskari
       He will be a policeman.

Example (51a) is not a sentence, but an NP. (51b, c) are complete sentences, since person-subject is marked in AUX.

(52) a. katab
      He wrote, has written.

    b. kaan katab
       He had written.

    c. ḥaykuun katab
       He will have written.

Example (52a) is a complete sentence, since person-subject is marked in the predicate. No sentence with a Predicate$_2$ requires an independent subject, regardless of tense. Recall that both AUX and Predicate$_2$ include items other than verbs, so that generalizations such as the following do not cover all the cases:

(53)   Where person-subject is marked in the verbal morphology, no NP subject is required.

(54)   Where person-subject is marked in the predicate, no NP subject is required.

(55)   Where person-subject is marked in some bound pronominal affix, no NP subject is required.

Evidence against (53–55) is as follows: Sentences with a 'negative pronoun' do not require an independent subject.

(56) a. mahuwwaaš naayim
      NEG-he   sleeping
                 ACT PART ms.

      He's not sleeping.

b. makanš   naayim
    NEG-be 3ms. sleeping
    PAST   ACT PART ms.

He wasn't sleeping.

c. maḥaykunš   naayim
    NEG-be 3ms. sleeping
    FUTURE ACT PART ms.

He won't be sleeping.

Since the 'negative pronouns' are neither verbs, predicates, nor bound pronominal affixes, but pronominal elements appearing in AUX where NEG attachment occurs, none of the generalizations in (53, 54, 55) is adequate, and reference to the AUX constituent, as in (50), is required for an adequate statement of the conditions on the appearance of independent subjects.

4. CONCLUSIONS

In the foregoing, I have identified the three primary constituents of Egyptian Arabic sentences — Subject, AUX, and Predicate, and I have described the appearance of these sentential constituents across sentence type. A description of the syntactic structure of Egyptian Arabic sentences in terms of these primary constituents permits a clear and concise statement of the differences that mark sentence mood, and permits us to generalize over a variety of sentence types previously treated as 'irregular' — possessive and volitional sentences, those sentences with a 'pronoun of separation' or a 'negative pronoun', etc. A set of sentence schemata for the language is as follows:

(57)

$$S_{\text{Indicative}} \longrightarrow \left\{ \begin{array}{l} \text{SUBJ} \quad \text{AUX}_1 \quad \text{PRED}_1 \\ \text{(SUBJ)} \left| \begin{array}{l} \text{AUX}_1 \quad \text{PRED}_2 \\ \text{AUX}_2 \left\{ \begin{array}{l} \text{PRED}_1 \\ \text{PRED}_2 \end{array} \right. \end{array} \right. \end{array} \right\}$$

Optional SUBJECT may precede or
follow AUX.

$S_{\text{Imperative}} \longrightarrow$ (SUBJ) PRED_{IMP}

$S_{\text{Subjunctive}} \longrightarrow$ (SUBJ) $\text{PRED}_{\text{SBJT}}$

AUX₁ here refers to those constructions where there is no AUX element, or where the unattached NEG particle appears alone in the AUX constituent; in these sentences, person-subject is not marked in AUX. AUX_2 refers to those constructions where some inflection of the copula or a pronominal element appears in AUX, so that person-subject is marked in AUX. Person-subject is marked in $Pred_2$, and in all imperative and subjunctive predicates.

No movement rules or other transformational rules have been proposed here. As to restrictions on the position of AUX in Egyptian Arabic sentences, a non-definitional property of AUX across languages, the following may be noted: where an NP subject is optional, AUX may be in first or second position, perhaps with slight differences in focus. Where an NP subject is required, AUX is in second position:

(58)   ʕali miš zaʕlaan
       NEG angry

Ali isn't angry.

The position of AUX in an Egyptian Arabic sentence thus varies with the subject requirement, but there is an association of AUX with second position, as is frequently the case across languages.

I have identified a constituent of indicative sentences in Egyptian Arabic where tense is marked, and I have shown that this constituent has a small closed inventory — the finite inflections of the copula and certain pronominal elements. This constituent therefore qualifies as an instantiation of the language independent definition of AUX provided by Steele *et al.* (1981). In the presence of a copular verb in AUX, Egyptian Arabic resembles English; in the presence of pronominal elements, it resembles Luiseño, Walbiri, and Lummi (see Steele *et al.*, 1981). The presence of an auxiliary verb together with items that are unequivocally pronominal and non-verbal in the inventory of AUX in one and the same language provides evidence in support of the parallels that ASW have drawn between languages that have an AUX with an inventory of one kind or the other. Pullum (1981) argues that aside from questions of constituency, there is no semantically natural class in the alleged AUX constituents of English and Luiseño, where tense and modality are marked; and that the two cases are dissimilar since the alleged AUX elements in English are verbs and the Luiseño particles are particles. Since Egyptian Arabic has both verbal inflections and pronominal particles in the inventory of AUX, it provides evidence in support of the parallels between English and Luiseño pointed out by ASW and provides information useful in the development of a typology of AUX across languages.

One of Pullum's principal objections to recognizing a syntactic category AUX is the apparent difficulty in assimilating such a category in $\bar{X}$ theory; recognizing AUX as an available syntactic category would be 'theory-weakening'. Pullum (1981) correctly observes that it would be impossible to identify AUX as Spec V, since AUX need not be syntactically associated with V. The question arises as to whether AUX may be identified, along with COMP, as Spec S. This would be consistent with the role of AUX across languages in marking sentence mood, and in delimiting the speech-act potential of the sentence. The indicative/imperative contrast in English, Luiseño, and Egyptian Arabic crucially rests on AUX. Hale (1973) posits an AUX constituent of imperative sentences in Walbiri that is distinct from AUX in declarative sentences. If this interpretation of AUX can be justified, AUX as a [-Major] category could be assimilated into $\bar{X}$ theory with no 'theory-weakening' consequences.

University of Arizona

NOTES

[1] I thank Adrian Akmajian and Susan Steele for very helpful criticisms of earlier versions of this paper. The analysis of Egyptian Arabic given here stems from their work on the category AUX across languages. I am grateful to the Wenner-Gren Foundation, to the American Council of Learned Societies, and to the National Science Foundation for support at various times during my research on Egyptian Arabic. I benefited from consultations with Prof. Adel S. Gamal on Egyptian Arabic, and from comments by Nagwa Younes and Trandil El Rakhawy on the Arabic analysis. Finally, I want to thank Frank Heny for his skeptical and stimulating criticism of this paper.
[2] See Abdel-Massih *et al.* (1979, p. 222) for a discussion of intonation contours in interrogative sentences in Egyptian Arabic.
[3] The transcription of Egyptian Arabic employed here is standard. ḥ is the voiceless pharyngeal fricative; ʕ, is the voiced pharyngeal fricative. The glottal stop is recorded with '; ṣ and ṭ are pharyngealized consonants. Lexical items are listed in Arabic dictionaries under their radical consonants, typically three in number. Thus the copula may be identified as KWN. The citation form for Arabic verbs is the Perfect, third person masculine singular; for the copula, this form is **kaan**.
[4] The **bi-**Imperfect is said to derive from the Imperfect paradigm with the preposition **bi** (in, by) prefixed. The ḥa-Imperfect is said to derive from the Imperfect plus a particle related to the verb raaḥ (go).
[5] The **bi-**Imperfect of **kaan** is sometimes used to mark future tense. It is in free variation with the ḥa-Imperfect for some speakers before a verb in the **bi-**Imperfect. But **biykuun** is never used to mark present tense.

6 See Abdel-Massih *et al.* (1979, p. 289) for a discussion of the Imperfect as a subjunctive in Egyptian Arabic.

7 Steele (1975) has pointed out another interesting kind of cross-language parallel: the use of past tense to mark *irrealis*. In English, we find past *irrealis* in conditional sentences:

(i)   If you loved me . . . .

(ii)   Were you to tell me . . . .

(iii)   Had I but known . . . .

In Egyptian Arabic, past tense is used in a comparable way in conditional clauses:

(iv)   šuff iza kaan fil-beet
        see   if was   in-the-house

        See if he's at home.

Of the finite inflections of the copula in Egyptian Arabic, past tense alone may occur with both the non-indicative verbal paradigms, the imperative and the subjunctive, to mark *irrealis*.

(v) a.   kunt   ruuh   šuufu
           be 2ms.   go 2ms.   see 2ms. – PRO
           PAST   IMP   IMP
                                                        You could have (should have) gone
     b.   kunt   tiruuh   tišuufu   *to see him.*
           be 2ms.   go 2ms.   see 2ms. – PRO
           PAST   SBJT   SBJT

Future tense is excluded before these non-indicative verbal paradigms. See Jelinek (1981) for an analysis of conditional sentences in Egyptian Arabic.

8 The modal contrasts marked in various types of sentences with embedded clauses is discussed in Jelinek (1981, Chap. 5).

9 The terms Predicate$_1$ and Predicate$_2$ are employed here for expository purposes only. They could be considered lexical features.

10 Nouns of volition that may function as predicates in Egyptian Arabic include the following: **nifs** 'inclination'; **'aṣd** 'intention; **ġarad** 'purpose'; **niyya** 'disposition, appetite'; **xaatir** 'mind, idea'; **ha"** 'right, privilege'.

11 These 'pronouns of separation' differ from the pronominal elements in AUX in Luiseño in that they are not clitics; they receive normal word stress. Steele (1977) suggests that the Luiseño person-marking clitics are historically related to independent (stress-carrying) pronouns, as Hale proposed the derivation of Walbiri and Warramunga AUX elements from independent pronouns. There appear to be two sources for tense and person-subject marking in AUX across languages: verbal morphology (auxiliary verbs) and particles. English provides an example of the former (*am, are, is,* etc.) while Luiseño, Walbiri, Warramunga, etc. provide examples of the latter. Egyptian Arabic exhibits tense and person-subject marking in AUX from both sources.

In sentences with a 'pronoun of separation' there is no pause after the NP subject or any break in the intonation contour that would suggest a topic-comment construction. There are such topic-comment constructions in the language:

(i)   axuuya,   huwwa kaan il- ʕaskari
           my-brother, he   was   the-policeman

In (i) there is a topic, **axuuya**, followed by a comment S with a subject pronoun and an AUX element **kaan**.
[12] I am grateful to an anonymous reviewer for pointing out that my analysis predicts the exclusion of the 'negative pronouns' from these sentence types.

BIBLIOGRAPHY

Abdel-Massih, Ernest T., Zaki N. Abdel-Malik, El-Said M. Badawi, and Ernest N. McCarus: 1979, *A Comprehensive Study of Egyptian Arabic*, Vol. III, Center for Near Eastern and North African Studies, University of Michigan, Ann Arbor.

Akmajian, Adrian, Susan Steele, and Thomas Wasow: 1979, 'The Category AUX in Universal Grammar', *Linguistic Inquiry* 10, 1–64.

Comrie, Bernard: 1976, 'The Negative Auxiliary', mimeographed, King's College Research Center, Cambridge.

Hale, Ken: 1973, 'Person Marking in Walbiri,' in S. R. Anderson and P. Kiparsky (eds.), *A Festschrift for Morris Halle*, Holt, Rhinehart and Winston, New York.

Jackendoff, Ray: 1977, *X̄ Syntax: A Study of Phrase Structure*, Linguistic Inquiry Monograph 2, MIT Press, Cambridge, Mass.

Jelinek, Eloise: 1981, *On Defining Categories: AUX and PREDICATE in Colloquial Egyptian Arabic*, Unpublished Ph.D. dissertation, University of Arizona.

Li, Charles N. and Sandra A Thompson: 1977, 'A Mechanism for the Development of Copula Morphemes,' in Charles Li (ed.), *Mechanisms of Syntactic Change*, University of Texas Press, Austin.

Pullum, G. K.: 1981, 'Evidence against the "AUX" Node in Luiseño and English', *Linguistic Inquiry* 12, 435–463.

Pullum, G. K. and D. Wilson: 1977, 'Autonomous Syntax and the Analysis of Auxiliaries, *Language* 53, 741–788.

Steele, Susan: 1975, 'Past and Irrealis: Just What Does It All Mean?', *International Journal of American Linguistics* 41, 200–217.

Steele, Susan: 1977, 'Clisis and Diachrony,' in Charles Li (ed.), *Mechanisms of Syntactic Change*, University of Texas Press, Austin.

Steele, Susan, Adrian Akmajian, Richard Demers, Eloise Jelinek, Chisato Kitagawa, Richard Oehrle, and Thomas Wasow: 1981, *An Encyclopedia of AUX: A Study in Cross-Linguistic Equivalence, Linguistic Inquiry* Monograph 5, MIT Press, Cambridge, Mass.

PART TWO

SOME ELUSIVE CATEGORIES

J. A. EDMONDSON *

POLARIZED AUXILIARIES

Among the linguistic problems attracting attention in the last decade is the problem of *natural language polarity*. Basically, some lexical items show to varying degrees a characteristic asymmetry in distribution; these items fail to be found in all sentence types. As Bolinger (1977, p. 26) describes it, "A kind of polarizing force attaches itself more or less permanently to certain expressions, pairing them off with others in a negative-affirmative contrast". Klima (1964) is usually credited with bringing the importance of polarity to a wider linguistic public, though Jespersen (1917) had already noticed many aspects of polarity in his famous work on negation. Subsequently, a number of studies have been carried out on various aspects of this phenomenon: Baker (1970), Bolinger (1960, 1977), Borkin (1971), Carlson (1980, 1981), Fauconnier (1975, 1976, 1979), Horn (1970, 1972, 1978), Ladusaw (1980a, 1980b, 1980c, 1980d), LeGrand (1973, 1974, 1975) and Linebarger (1981), though this list doesn't exhaust the contributors.

It has generally been claimed that there exists a distinction between *negative polarity items* (NPI's) and *positive polarity items* (PPI's). The former are sometimes said to occur in environments with the feature [+ affective] and the latter in environments with the feature [− affective]. To cite a familiar example, (1) in the negative, an affective context, is beyond reproach. In the positive, however, it would require strangely counterintuitive states of affairs to hold if it were to be meaningful.

(1) a. Mao didn't die until 1976.

b. *Mao died until 1976.

Until belongs to the set of English NPI's. On the other hand, *excellent* counts as an adjective with positive polarity, being restricted largely to positive statements or those with contrastive stress.[1]

(2) a. This ice cream is excellent.

b. * This ice cream isn't excellent.

49

F. Heny and B. Richards (eds.), Linguistic Categories: Auxiliaries and Related Puzzles,
Vol. One, 49–68.
Copyright © 1983 *by D. Reidel Publishing Company.*

Polarity phenomena have proven so controversial because: (a) they are difficult to *confine* to one component of grammar, (b) the *structural configuration* between an NPI and sanctioning affective trigger can be quite complex, (c) NPI's such as *any* have been *equated with* universal as well as with existential *quantifiers*, (d) there is *variation in the acceptability* of sentences containing polarity items and (e) there have been opposing accounts of the *unity of affectivity*.

These problems may be further elaborated as follows. Firstly the sheer number of polarized items has grown with each new study until today it appears that they form a significant subset of the grammatical system. Furthermore, a polarized item in English doesn't always possess a counterpart of the opposite polarity. Worse still, some items, such as the notoriously difficult item *any*, seem to come in both polarized and unpolarized forms, called respectively *polarized* and *free choice any* by Ladusaw (1980a), Carlson (1980, 1981) and Linebarger (1981). Also, NPI's, in the general case, involve conversational and speaker's real world knowledge in their gross interpretation and thus straddle semantics and pragmatics, as Fauconnier and Linebarger particularly emphasize. These properties vitiate any account relying solely on marking a few items in the lexicon. NPI's must be in the scope of an affective operator, but defining what this scope is has proven difficult. Multiple NPI's and the fact that verbs have different logical properties have further clouded the issue. Scope differs in factive or opaque environments, and is affected by the position of *not* in negative questions.[2]

Thirdly, Quine, Hintikka, LeGrand and other linguists and philosophers have given polarized *any* the value of an *all*-quantifier. The prevailing opinion in recent studies, however, favors an existential translation target for *any* and some other NPI's, cf. Ladusaw, Horn, Linebarger and Carlson. Further, Horn (1970) points out the variation in the behavior of NPI's in different affective environments. Ross and Lawler also have discussed polarity 'squishes' in unpublished work. Linebarger (1981, p. 67f) mentions this feature explicitly, saying that it is presumably "... caused by the varying 'strength' or 'liberality' of different NPI's and by the varying availability of the appropriate implicature" (p. 68). The non-discrete nature of polarity also seems to play a role in Fauconnier's notion of pragmatic scales. Finally, not all the new studies agree about the nature of affectivity. Ladusaw and Fauconnier view affectivity as a unified phenomenon, which they equate respectively with *downward entailment*, essentially a semantic property of negations, questions, conditionals, comparatives, etc. that changes a set-subset entailment into a set-superset entailment, and reversal of a *scalar implicature*,

again an entailment scheme incorporating a pragmatically established scale
and an end point on that scale. Linebarger, following Baker, opts for a non-
unified account, choosing negation as the paradigmatic form of affectivity
and having the literal meaning of the remaining affective environments 'allude'
to an implicature containing a negative.

In this restricted study I have chosen to investigate only two of these
features: the nature of affectivity and the variation of NPI's (in particular
the auxiliaries) across affective contexts in various languages. The data I have
assembled speak for a particular kind of variation of NPI's and affectivity. To
be more precise, there seems to exist a graded, implicational hierarchy of a
type widely known from Keenan and Comrie's (1977) work on accessibility.
This hierarchy can be portrayed as follows:

(3)   comparative ⊃ conditional ⊃ interrogatives ⊃ negatives.

If an NPI can occur in some affective context, it will also appear in all
contexts to the right of this context. Furthermore, this gradience must be a
grammatical characteristic subject to analysis as a type. It seems independent
of the speaker's knowledge of the world and conversational intent, since I
have found the hierarchy to hold when the containing sentence is held constant and only the affective operator varied. This stepped gradience further
supports the name *negative polarity* for the phenomena, as the negative seems
strongest of the four. The findings are, however, too preliminary to take a
stand on the unity of affectivity. They do support Linebarger to the degree
that negation occupies a special place among these operators.

It has not gone unnoticed in previous work that polarity favors auxiliaries.
Grammarians, traditional and modern, point out the linkage between polarization and auxiliarihood, cf. Poutsma (1926, p. 408f), Quirk *et al.* (1972,
p. 83) and Akmajian *et al.* (1979). Exemplifying this tie in English are the
items *need* and *dare*, which show their auxiliary face in affective environments
through the missing *s* of the third person singular, the lack of supportive *do*
in negations and questions and the lack of the complementizer *to* before a
following verb. I illustrate the polarized feature of these forms in the four
affective environments of concern in this paper.

(4)   *positive statements*, requiring non-polarized, non-auxiliary *dare/*
        need:

    a.   John $\left\{ \begin{array}{l} * \text{dare/need} \\ \text{dares/needs to} \end{array} \right\}$ eat a fig.

negations:

b. John $\left\{ \begin{array}{l} \text{dare/need not} \\ \text{doesn't dare/need to} \end{array} \right\}$ eat a fig.

questions:

c. $\left\{ \begin{array}{l} \text{Dare/Need John} \\ \text{Does John dare/need to} \end{array} \right\}$ eat a fig?

conditionals:

d. If John $\left\{ \begin{array}{l} \text{dare/need} \\ \text{dares/needs to} \end{array} \right\}$ eat a fig, . . .

comparatives:

e. The situation is more serious than he $\left\{ \begin{array}{l} \text{dare/need} \\ \text{dares/needs to} \end{array} \right\}$ imagine.

In the following I wish to present evidence that English *dare/need* do not represent isolated cases, but that other languages show a similar distributional pattern and correlation of auxiliarihood and polarization.

As already indicated, not all affective environments are equal in their reaction with NPI's, whether polarized auxiliaries or NPI's in general. Notice, for example, that *until* co-occurs only in combination with overt or covert negation, but not with questions, conditions, etc. Cf. (1) and (5) and also Horn (1970).

(5) a. *Did Mao die until 1976?

b. *If Mao died until 1976, . . .

Thus, *until* and polarized *dare/need* do not behave identically. Indeed, the pattern instantiated in these English NPI's is extremely widespread in natural languages. To be more precise, there will exist NPI's that must be accompanied by negation; others that demand negation or interrogation; others still that require negation, interrogation or conditionals. Finally, some NPI's may co-occur with negation, interrogation, conditionals and comparatives equally well.

As an example of a polarized auxiliary of the first or *until*-type consider Mandarin **yŏu** (there is) or (have). In a fashion strongly reminiscent of

English *dare/need*, **yǒu**, according to Chao (1968) and De Francis (1963), comes in two varieties, one with main verb properties and one with auxiliary properties. And, in complete parallelism with the English case, only the auxiliary shows the polarization. Main verb **yǒu** can be found in main verb and auxiliary contexts alike.

(6) a. tā yǒu xiōngdì jiěmèi.
     he have brothers sisters

     He has siblings.

   b. tā méi(yǒu) xiōngdì jiěmèi.
     he NEG have brothers sisters

     He has no siblings.

   c. tā yǒu xiōngdì jiěmèi ma?
     he have brothers sisters Q

     Does he have siblings?

   d. tā rúguǒ yǒu xiōngdì jiěmèi, . . .
     he if   have brothers sisters

     If he has siblings, . . .

Auxiliary **yǒu**, on the other hand, behaves quite differently. It appears as the NPI-counterpart of the aspect markers **le** 'perfective', **zhe** 'progressive' and **guò** 'indefinite past'. (The names of these aspects are taken from Chao (1968, pp. 120, 248, 251), who also documents a number of syntactic tests distinguishing auxiliary **yǒu** from main verbs). Usually, **yǒu** and its special negator **méi** as well as the aspect markers **zhe** and **guò** surface in denials of sentences in the progressive or indefinite past. Since these cases seem more complicated, I concentrate here on the negative form of the perfective marker **le**, cf. also Li and Thompson (1981).

In positive sentences **le** often will indicate that the speaker has just realized the significance of what's going on, even if it hasn't just started.

(7)   xià yǔ le.
       falls rain ASP

      (I've just noticed) it's raining.

When (7) is negated, however, the negation covers the present moment and extends back into the past.

(8) méi (yǒu) xìa yǔ.
    NEG   falls rain

   It hasn't been/isn't raining.

Pairs such as (7) and (8) led Wang (1965) to propose deriving one form from the other syntactically. Syntax alone cannot give adequate solutions to this suppletion, however, since for verbs expressing actions that start and stop rapidly, two negations are possible, point negation with **bu** and blanket negation with **méiyǒu**.[3]

(9) a. mǎ bu pǎo le.
       horse NEG run ASP

       The horse has stopped running.

   b. mǎ méi (yǒu) pǎo.
      horse NEG   run

      The horse doesn't run, e.g. it's lazy.

Scope offers us a neat solution for these two realizations. The PPI **le** in (9a) lies outside the scope of **bū**, but in (9b) the negation takes wide scope and thus forces the appearance of the NPI, **méi (yǒu)**.

Finally, **yǒu** represents a NPI resembling English *until*, the weakest element on a graded hierarchy. **Yǒu** may not occur with questions, conditionals or comparatives.

(10) a. (*yǒu) xìa yǔ ma.

       Is it raining?

    b. jiǎrú (*yǒu) xìa yǔ, . . .

       If it rains, . . .

    c. nǐ (*yǒu) bǐ wǒ (*yǒu) gāo.
       you compared me   tall

       You are taller than me.

A second example of a polarized auxiliary compatible only with negation, but not with questions, conditionals and comparatives is German *brauchen* 'need'. This item also evidences the now familiar pattern of divided categorial loyalties, having in some cases auxiliary properties and in other main verb traits. Predictably, only the former uses are polarized.

(11)   **No polarization, main verb.**

    a. Ich brauche Zeit.

       I need time.

    b. Ich brauche keine Zeit.

       I need no time.

    c. Brauchen Sie etwas Zeit?

       Do you need some time?

    d. Wenn Sie etwas Zeit brauchen, . . .

       If you need some time, . . .

    e. Sie haben mehr Zeit als Sie brauchen.

       You have more time than you need.

(12)   **Polarized, auxiliary traits**

    positive statements

a. * Ich brauche (zu) kommen.

    I need to come.

    negatives

    b. Ich brauche nicht (zu) kommen.

    I need not come.

    questions

c. * Brauche ich (zu) kommen.

    Need I come?

conditionals

d. *Wenn ich (zu) kommen brauche, . . .

If I need come, . . .

comparatives

e. * Er kommt öfter als ich (zu) kommen brauche.

He comes more often than I need come.

Moving on to a possible example of a polarized tense/aspect (auxiliary) element co-occurring with negatives or questions, consider the following descriptions of the Quechua suffix -ču, cf. Bills *et al.* (1969):

In negative declarative sentences the negative particle **mana** precedes the negated element(s) and the suffix -ču is attached to the end of the negated element(s). (p. 22)

and:

A declarative sentence is transformed into a yes-no interrogative simply by adding the suffix -ču . . . . Since the interrogative marker -ču is identical in form to the negative marker -ču, we shall here treat both cases as a single suffix that we shall call the *nonfactual independent suffix*. (p. 37)

Thus, we can recognize the effect of -ču in questions and answers.

(13) a. tuku-nki-ču kaldo-ta.
finish you soup acc

Have you finished the soup?

b. ari, tuku-ni
yes finish I

Yes, I've finished.

c. mana, mana tuku-ni-ču.
no NEG finish I

No, I've not finished.

The conditional or hypothetical does not contain this -ču suffix, however.

(14) si-čus diya-y kan-mán, curaku-y-man.
if day I be cond. put I cond.

If it were my birthday, I would put it on.

To the Spanish borrowing for *day* is added -y instead of the usual personal
suffix -ni for the 1st singular and the conditional suffix -man is added to the
verbs of both antecedent and consequence clause. Don Burns of SIL has
assured me that despite some similarity between -ču and -čus the Quechua
speaker today does not associate the two, whatever the historical situation
might be.

The description and examples of -ču do not clarify one important point,
though. It might be that Quechua -ču resembles English *do*; that is, it might
function as a necessary constituent in the construction of negatives interrogatives without being in fact a true NPI. It would be quite circular to take
co-occurrence across affective contexts as the defining trait of an NPI. Clearly,
independent evidence of the polarity is demanded to warrant counting this
marker as a polarity item. At this stage of my knowledge about Quechua I
have doubts that -ču is an NPI. Whatever status one might assign to -ču, we
surely do not want to recognize every 'constructional' auxiliary as a polarized
auxiliary. Finding counterexamples to our claim about the affective hierarchy
would be effortless. Even English *would* appears with conditionals but not
with questions and negations.

The third element in the hierarchy I am proposing is seen in Taiwanese
Mandarin and in its substrate language Fujian (Southern Min). One of the
clear syntactic differences between the Northern forms of the Chinese
National Language and the kind of Chinese spoken by people of Taiwan
extraction involves the auxiliary **yǒu** mentioned above. As already pointed
out, **yǒu** is the NPI of the polarized pair **le-yǒu**. Speakers on Taiwan, however,
can and do construct sentences with **yǒu** that Northerners find strange. Cf.
Chao (1967, p. 748).

(15) a. yǒu xìa yǔ   ma
        falls rain Q

    Is it raining?

   b. jǐarú yǒu xìa yǔ, . . .
      if   falls rain

    If it rains, . . .

It is tantalizing to suppose that this oddity stems perhaps from a parallel
construction in the indigenous form of Chinese, which is called Fujian,
Fukian, Hokkian or Taiwanese. Negative and question forms in Taiwanese
have been the subject of several recent studies, cf. Li (1971) and Cheng

(1977, 1978, 1980, 1981). The situation here is in a sense more regular than in Mandarin, as **u**, the Taiwanese equivalent of Mandarin **yǒu**, also surfaces in positive sentences. When it does, however, it imparts to it a special 'modality'. Consider these data from Cheng (1977, 1978). (Tone marks have been omitted.)

(16) a. I　khi.
　　　　he go

　　　　He goes/went.

　　b. I　u　khi.
　　　　he　 go

　　　　He does/did go.

　　c. *I　neg khi.　　(This is Cheng's way of indicating (16a) has no
　　　　he　　go　　counterpart without a 'modality').

　　d. I　bo　khi.
　　　　he NEG go

　　　　He does/did not go.

　　e. *I　khi neg khi?
　　　　he go　　 go

　　　　He goes or not, i.e. does he go?

　　f. I　u　khi bo
　　　　he　 go

　　　　Does/did he go?

　　g. I　bin-a-tsai na u lai,　goa tsiu beh likhui
　　　　he tomorrow if come I　then will leave

　　　　If he comes tomorrow, then I will leave.

　　h. tsit-e tsinghing (*u) pi　　　i　sianwe (*u) go　tsam
　　　　this class situation compared he think　　very bad.

　　　　'*This situation is worse than he thinks*' (from Margret See Gebauer).

As Cheng (1977, p. 165) says, these data show that negation or interrogation is impossible without 'modality', here **u** in the modality "it is an observed fact that ... does/did occur". Since **u** may also occur with conditionals but never with comparatives, Taiwanese exhibits the third step in the hierarchy.

As yet I have been unable to find a convincing example of a polarized auxiliary appearing in all four environments. This non-occurrence should, however, not be terribly unexpected, since the hierarchy predicts that this environment should be the least likely or most difficult for a polarized auxiliary.

If I have been successful in establishing that the NPI-affective interaction follows a graded hierarchy, then there remains the question of the source of this variation. Linebarger (1981, pp. 158–63) convincingly demonstrates the 'squishy' nature of NPI's themselves, providing a taxonomy of types: *independent expressions*, those freely occurring as scalar endpoints with their literal meanings outside the scope of affectives, e.g. (*not*) *read a verse*; *near NPI's*, those that may sometimes occur outside the scope of an affective with their literal meanings, e.g. (*not*) *know a thing about*; *true NPI's*, those that do not occur outside an affective environment, e.g. *not hold a candle to*. Yet, all of the polarized auxiliaries discussed here are intended to represent true NPI's and thus the variation in acceptability cannot stem from this source. Since a true NPI is being kept constant in a varying affective context, it seems fair to assume that something about the triggering context is changing. A possible source of this gradience would be in a varying scalar implicature. But if this suggestion is to be upheld, we must ask as Linebarger (1981, p. 140) does, "How can one operator be more or less downward-entailing than another?" Fauconnier (1976, 1979) emphasizes the differences among scalar reversers (downward-entailing environments for Ladusaw). He defines a scale reversing environment U⎯V as follows, Fauconnier (1979, p. 296):[4]

(17)   U⎯V is scale reversing iff

$$U\ f(x^*)\ V \rightarrow \forall x\ U\ f(x)\ V$$

where $f(x)$ represents an open proposition and $x^* \in X$ (the universe of discourse) is pragmatically the most probable value satisfying the proposition, i.e. is a (local) endpoint or extremum on a scale formed on X.

Definition (17), of course, is intended to predict the behavior of NPI's that correspond semantically to points, e.g. Mandarin **le-you**, *ever*. It will not necessarily apply to expressions that do not denote points, though expressions like German **brauchen** may really correspond to something like 'the point, situation of maximum necessity'.

In order to see how scalar implicature can vary with the different affective operators, let us consider negation. According to the scheme in (17), a sentence containing a negation will be assigned two interpretations, one from its literal meaning and one from its implicated meaning. For example, a sentence such as (18a) would receive interpretations roughly equivalent to (18b) and (18c).

(18) a. John didn't ever arrive on time.

b. There is no time John arrive on time.   (literal)

c. For all times John didn't arrive on time.   (implicated)

But for negation, these two interpretations will be intuitively and logically equivalent; the implicature will not produce 'new' readings. On the other hand, Ladusaw (1980a) and Fouconnier (1979, p. 298) have noticed that questions do not allow the implicated interpretation in most instances. Thus, (19a) can mean only (19b) and not (19c).

(19) a. John wondered whether Mary was ever married.

b. John wondered whether there was a time when Mary was married. (literal)

c. John wondered of every time whether Mary was married then. (implicated)

For comparatives the situation is still different. Fauconnier (1979, p. 299) argues that an endpoint-NPI in the scope of comparatives receives an interpretation only from the implicature; there is no acceptable literal meaning produced. Notice, for example, that *any* and *ever* in this environment correspond to universal and not to existential quantifiers; they are, for instance, compatible with *just, absolutely, nearly, almost*, numerals and 'amount relatives', which are possible only with the universal interpretation, and incompatible with *there is*, cf. Horn (1972) and Carlson (1981, p. 9).

(20) a. John is taller than just, absolutely, nearly anyone ever suspected.

b. John is stronger than any three people in his class.

c. John is stronger than any person there is in his weight class.

d. *John is taller than there is anyone in his class that ever suspected.

Conditionals occupy the middle ground in allowing both a literal and an implicated meaning. Thus, there is for some speakers ambiguity in the following sentences in just the way indicated.[5]

(21) a. If you'll eat any fish, you will be given the prize. (i.e. some vs. all)

   b. If John is ever courteous, he can become a diplomat. (i.e. once vs. always)

It is still unclear to me if the variation in the strength of the scalar implicature can be related to the failure of some NPI's to appear in the more 'inaccessible' affective environments. Nevertheless, it is striking that the two phenomena share obvious parallelism. It is also not surprising that auxiliaries are linked to polarity. Whether one accepts the claim in Akmajian *et al.* (1979) that AUX represents a universal category in natural language or not, it is reasonable to assume that auxiliaries often encode tense/aspect or modality, which presumably rely on sequences of time points, intervals, etc. These ordered elements could constitute the scale on which the implicature would depend.

University of Texas at Arlington

APPENDIX

I. *Negative Polarity Items Possible Only with Negation*

| − | Q | → | than | + |

Malagasy (Charles Randriamasimanana): **velively** (at all)

   *Nandidy ny mofo velively i Jeanne.
   past-cut the bread at all personal article Jeanne

Jeanne cut the bread at all.

Tsy nandidy ny mofo velively   i   Jeanne.
neg past-cut the bread at all personal article Jeanne

Jeanne didn't cut the bread at all.

*Nandidy ny mofo ve velively   i   Jeanne?
past-cut the bread Q at all personal article Jeanne

Did Jeanne cut the bread at all?

*Raha nandidy ny mofo velively   i   Jeanne, ...
if past-cut the bread at all personal article Jeanne

If Jeanne cut the bread at all, ...

II. *Negative Polarity Items Possible Only with Negations or Questions*

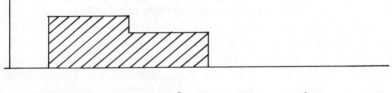

Italian (Filippo Beghelli) **mica** (at all)

*Io vado mica al cinema.
I go at all the movies

I go to the movies at all.

Io non vado mica al cinema.
I neg go at all the movies

I do not go to the movies at all.

Vai   mica al cinema?
(you) go at all the movies

Do you go to the movies at all?

*Se vai   mica al cinema, ...
if (you) go at all the movies, ...

If you go to the movies at all, ...

German **gar** (at all, even)

*Ich bin gar da gewesen.
I have ever there been

I've even been there.

Ich bin gar nicht da gewesen.
I have even neg there been

I've not ever been there at all.

Bist du gar schon da gewesen.
Have you even already there been

Have you even been there?

*Wenn du gar schon da gewesen bist, . . .
if you even already there been have

If you've even been there, . . .

III. *Negative Polarity Items Possible with Negation, Questions and Conditionals*

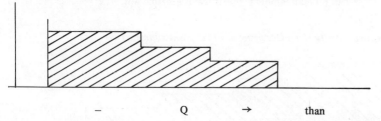

Latin (Kühner and Stegmann, pp. 639–40) **ullus, quisquam, quis** (any, some)

K/S say of **ullus,** 'The pronoun **ullus** = any is used at least in negative sentences as an adjective as **quisquam** is used as a noun'. (my translation). Their illustrations, however, are with conditionals.

sī quisquam est timidus, is ego sum.
if anyone is afraid it I is

Thai (Apiram Chaikijkarana and Rach Kulthamrong) **lə:ɟ** (right away, at all)

*chǎn ma lə:ɟ.
I come right away

chǎn mâj dâj ma lə:ɟ.
I neg get come at all

I didn't come at all.

khun ma lə:ɟ rý plà:w
you come or not

Are you coming right away?

thâ khun ma   lə:ɹ . . .
if you   come right away

If you come right away, . . .

* John ma   sǎɹ   bò:ɹ   kwà: ma   tæ̀:cháw   lə:ɹ
John come later more than come early   at all

John comes late more than he comes early at all.

English *so/that hot* (i.e. 'good')

     * That's so/that hot.
     That's not so/that hot.
     Is that so/that hot?
     If that's so/that hot, I'll take two.
     * This product is more popular than it's so/that hot.

IV. *Negative Polarity Items Occurring in all Four Environments*

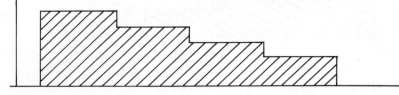

English (Bolinger 1977, p. 27) *dare, need, any, let on* (vs. *reveal*), *care to* (vs. *like*)

     ? John let on he knew./* I care to go.
     John didn't let on he knew./I don't care to go.
     Did John let on he knew./Do you care to go?
     If John lets on he knows . . ./If you care to go, . . .
     John knows more than he lets on./She goes more often than I care to.

German **überhaupt** (at all, ever)

     * Das ist überhaupt gelb.
     that is at all   yellow

     Das ist überhaupt nicht gelb.
     that is at all   not   yellow

     That's not yellow at all.

     Ist das überhaupt gelb?
     Is that at all   yellow

Wenn das überhaupt gelb ist, . . .
if   that at all   yellow is

If that's yellow at all, . . .

Die Lage   ist schlimmer als   wir uns überhaupt gedacht haben.
the situation is worse   than we   ever   thought have

The situation is worse than we ever thought.

Malagasy (Charles Randriamasimanana) **àry** (ever)

* Àry   tonga   i   Paoly
ever   arrived personal article Paul

Paul ever arrived.

Tsy àry   tonga   i   Paoly
neg ever   arrived personal article Paul

Paul didn't ever arrive.

Àry tonga ve   i   Paoly.
ever arrived Q personal article Paul

Did Paul ever arrive?

Raha àry   tonga   i   Paoly, . . .
if   ever   arrived personal article Paul

If Paul ever arrived, . . .

Toa   sarofran ny roharaha noho isay àry no-herverin   i   Paoly.
seems difficult the business than what ever passive-think personal article Paoly.

The matter seems more difficult than Paul ever thought.

French Grammaire Larousse (1964, p. 267) claims that **aucun, nul, pas un, personne,** and **rien** have a positive sense ". . . dans des phrase de coloration negative ou dubitative . . . ". Negative and dubitative sentences mean here sentences containing negatives, interrogatives, the second term of a comparison of inequality and such as **sans que** (without), **avant que** (before) and **si** (if). Fauconnier (1976) cites these examples with **jamais** (ever):

* Pinocchio a   jamais   menti.
Pinocchio has ever   lied

Pinocchio n'a jamais   menti.
Pinocchio has not ever lied

J'ignore   si elle est jamais allée en   Angleterre.
I not know if she has ever   gone to   England

Car   si une bête   a   jamais   proclamé   sa race,   c'était bien
because if a   beast has   ever   proclaimed his race   it's certainly

elle, par toute sa   beauté crassée et campée.   (from C. Audry,
he   by all   his   beauty soiled and nomadic
Derrière la baignoire)

Il a   travaillé plus que   tu (ne) l'as   jamais fait.
he has   worked   more than you neg have   ever   done

Fauconnier (1976, p. 122) also notices that the expletive negative in French does not suffice to trigger NPI's, cf. *Je crains qu'il ne fasse grand chose.* **Grand-chose** (much) is the NPI here.

NOTES

* I would like to thank Frank Heny for his valuable stylistic and editorial assistance as well as for his encouragement. My appreciation also goes to two anonymous referees whose lucid comments helped me clarify my ideas and avoid many errors. Responsibility for the final product remains, of course, mine.

[1] Although there is no time to pursue an analysis of PPI's, the suggestion I propose here would predict that *excellent* should become progressively more acceptable with questions, conditionals, etc.

[2] In this study I have limited myself to four operators: negation, non-negative yes-no questions, conditionals and comparatives. Both Wh- and negative questions seem more complex than these. At least, negative questions do not trigger NPI's in the same fashion as negative statements. The position of the *not* appears to be of crucial importance, cf. (1) and the sentence pair below.

(i)   * Didn't Mao die until 1976?

(ii)   Did Mao not die until 1976?

[3] The **yǒu** in **méiyǒu** may be omitted except sentence finally.

[4] Intuitively, (17) claims that if, for example, some proposition $f(x)$ *isn't true at the most probable value, x^*,* then it is also not true for less probable values.

[5] Many find a non-polarized interpretation of *ever* (i.e. always) quite difficult to accept. Cf. American Heritage Dictionary.

(i)   John is ever courteous.

BIBLIOGRAPHY

Akmajian, Adrian, Susan Steele, and Thomas Wasow: 1979, 'The Category AUX in Universal Grammar', *Linguistic Inquiry* 10, 64.

Baker, C. Leroy: 1970, 'Double Negatives', *Linguistic Inquiry* 1, 169–86.

Bills, Garland, Bernardo Vallejo and Rudolph Troike: 1969, *An Introduction to Spoken Bolivian Quechua*. University of Texas Press, Austin and London.

Bolinger, Dwight: 1960, 'Linguistic Science and Linguistic Engineering', *Word* 16, 374–91.

Bolinger, Dwight: 1977, *Meaning and Form*, Longman, New York and London.

Borkin, Ann: 1971, 'Polarity Items in Questions', *Papers from the Seventh Regional Meeting of the Chicago Linguistic Society*.

Carlson, Greg: 1980, 'Polarity *any* is Existential', *Linguistic Inquiry* 11, 792–804.

Carlson, Greg: 1981, 'Distribution of Free Choice Any', *Papers from the Seventeenth Regional Meeting of the Chicago Linguistic Society*, 8–23.

Chao, Yuen Ren: 1968, *A Grammar of Spoken Chinese*, University of California Press, Berkeley and Los Angeles.

Cheng, Robert: 1977, 'Taiwanese Question Particles', *Journal of Chinese Linguistics* 5, 153–85.

Cheng, Robert: 1978, 'Tense Interpretation of Four Taiwanese Model Verbs', in R. Cheng (ed.), *Proceedings of Symposium of Chinese Linguistics*, Student Book Co. Ltd., Taipei.

Cheng, Robert: 1980, 'Modality in Taiwanese', *Journal of Chinese Language Teachers Association* 40, 45–93.

Cheng, Robert: 1981, 'Time Relations in Chinese', Ms. University of Hawaii.

Comrie, Bernard: 1976, *Aspect*, Cambridge University Press.

Fauconnier, Gilles: 1975, 'Pragmatic Scales and Logical Structure', *Linguistic Inquiry* 6, 353–75.

Fauconnier, Gilles: 1976, *Etude de certains aspects logiques et grammaticaux de la quantification et de l'anaphore en français et en anglais*, Thèse pour obtenir le grade de docteur ès lettres, Université de Paris VII.

Fauconnier, Gilles: 1979, 'Implication Reversal in a Natural Language', in F. Guenthner and S. Schmidt (eds.), *Formal Semantics and Pragmatics in Natural Language*, Reidel, Dordrecht.

Grammaire Larousse, 1964, Librairie Larousse, Paris.

Horn, Larry: 1970, 'Ain't It Hard (Anymore)', *Papers from the Sixth Regional Meeting of the Chicago Linguistics Society*, 318–27.

Horn, Larry: 1972, *On the Semantic Properties of Logical Operators in English*, Unpublished Ph.D. dissertation UCLA (also 1976, Indiana University Linguistics Club).

Horn, Larry: 1978, 'Some Aspects of Negation', in J. Greenberg *et al.* (eds.), *Universals of Human Language IV*, Stanford University Press.

Jespersen, Otto: 1966, *Negation in English and Other Languages*, Munksgaard, Copenhagen.

Keenan, Edward and Bernard Comrie: 1977, 'Noun Phrase Accessibility and Universal Grammar', *Linguistic Inquiry* 8, 63–99.

Klima, Edward: 1964, 'Negation in English', in J. Fodor and J. Katz (eds.), *The Structure of Language*, Prentice-Hall, Englewood Cliffs.

Kühner, Raphael and Carl Stegmann: 1976, *Ausführliche Grammatik der lateinischen Sprache*, Verlag Hahnsche Buchhandlung, Hannover.

Ladusaw, William: 1980a, *Polarity Sensitivity as Inherent Scope Relations*, Indiana University Linguistics Club.

Ladusaw, William: 1980b, 'On the Notion *Affective* in the Analysis of Negative-polarity Items', Ms. University of Iowa.

Ladusaw, William: 1980c, 'Some *Any's* Mean Some', Ms. University of Iowa.

Ladusaw, William: 1980d, 'Affective *Or* Factive Verbs, and Negative-polarity Items', *Papers from the Sixteenth Regional Meeting of the Chicago Linguistics Society*, 170–74.

LeGrand, Jean: 1973, 'Sometimes, or = and', *Linguistic Inquiry* 4, No. 2.

LeGrand, Jean: 1974, '*And* and *Or*; some *Somes* and all *Anys*', *Papers from the Tenth Regional Meeting of the Chicago Linguistic Society*.

LeGrand, Jean: 1975, *Or and Any: The Semantics and Syntax of Two Logical Operators*, Unpublished Ph.D. dissertation, University of Chicago.

Li, Charles and Sandra Thompson: 1981, *Mandarin Chinese: A Functional Reference Grammar*, University of California Press, Berkeley and Los Angeles.

Li, Paul Jen-kuei: 1971, 'Two Negative Markers in Taiwanese', *Bulletin of the Institute of History and Philology* (Academica Sinica) 43, 201–20.

Linebarger, Marcia: 1981, *The Grammar of Negative Polarity*, Indiana University Linguistics Club.

Poutsma, Hendrik: 1926, *A Grammar of Late Modern English*, II.2, Noordhoff, Groningen.

Quirk, Randolph, Sidney Greenbaum, Geoffrey Leech, and Jan Svartvik: 1972, *A Grammar of Contemporary English*, Longman, London.

Wang, William S.-Y.: 1965, 'Two Aspect Markers in Mandarin', *Language* 41, 457–70.

GREG N. CARLSON

MARKING CONSTITUENTS

0. INTRODUCTION

The cross-linguistic investigation of auxiliaries reveals that certain types of meanings are expressed by members of that category with nothing short of amazing regularity.[1] Steele (1980) reports that one routinely finds tense, aspect, negation, modality, assertability conditions, question, and emphasis expressed in the AUX, to the exclusion of practically all other notions. While this may appear to encompass a fairly wide range of meaning, it is in fact quite narrow if one reflects on the range of possibilities, and linguistic theory should ultimately give an account of this. In a sense, we are confronted with a rather constant relationship between certain meanings and certain forms, and in the end will have to elucidate some principled connection between linguistic form and linguistic meaning. This runs counter to much in modern linguistics which emphasizes the arbitrary nature of language, both in terms of sound-meaning relations as well as whatever semantic content syntactic categories might hold. But, in the case of auxiliaries at least, there does appear to be semantic content to the category AUX, for not just anything is expressible as an auxiliary.

The question of auxiliaries, though, needs to be put in a larger setting that concerns what appears to be a very basic and very pervasive fact about language — that there are two distinct types of morphemes. Most, if not all languages exhibit in their vocabularies two quite different types of morphemes, variously referred to as lexical vs function morphemes, full words vs empty words, content words vs. particles, and so forth. I will henceforth use a variant of Fries' (1952) terminology and call them *lexical* morphemes and *function* morphemes, though the nature of the distinction to be presented below hardly coincides with his (and is, in fact, much closer to Sapir (1921, p. 88ff)). This distinction is basically familiar to all grammarians, having been made by Aristotle in the form of 'concepts' and 'grammatical meaning', used by Leibniz and the Port-Royal grammarians, and noted by virtually all modern linguists. One finds, for instance, this distinction coded into the structure of Chomsky's Standard Theory in *Aspects*. Other grammatical traditions, too, make similar distinctions; Bloomfield (1933, p. 199f) notes

F. Heny and B. Richards (eds.), Linguistic Categories: Auxiliaries and Related Puzzles, Vol. One, 69–98.

that Chinese has *full words* and *particles*. This is not to say, of course, that there is anything close to universal agreement on which morphemes should be included in which category. In spite of this lack of clarity, the general distinction between the meaningful lexical morphemes and the intuitively 'meaningless' function morphemes is one that is persistent enough and intuitively clear enough to be worthy of serious investigation.

What I wish to investigate here is the general nature of the category of function morphemes, a category I take to wholly include members of the Aux, and to present the outlines of a syntactic and semantic theory which elicidates the nature of the lexical-function morpheme distinction. I will then propose a connection between the syntactic account and the semantic account – a connection between form and meaning. I do not believe that any of the components of the account are original. I will be taking a number of ideas from various quarters, some quite traditional in origin, and others more modern, and fitting them together in what I hope will be a reasonably coherent and illuminating way.

1. FUNCTION AND LEXICAL MORPHEMES

Quite a large number of differences between these two classes of elements have been noted. Probably most basic is that the function morphemes are generally felt to be 'meaningless', or to be considerably more devoid of meaning than the lexical morphemes. But there are many more differences. Function morphemes may play purely formal or grammatical roles (as markers of case, or subordination, for instance), whereas lexical morphemes do not generally play such roles. The set of function morphemes in a language is a closed, finite class, whereas the set of lexical items is considerably larger (possibly unlimited) and open to ready expansion by virtue of language-internal processes such as derivation and compounding and extralinguistic processes such as borrowing and coinage. Function morphemes, further, do not enter into word-formation processes the way lexical items do (see Keyser and Postal (1976) for illustrations); they do enter into agreement processes (lexical items do not except as conditioning factors); function morphemes do not form 'anaphoric islands' the way lexical items do (Schwartz, 1978), which is closely related to the fact that function morphemes routinely coalesce with one another (e.g., French **du**), while lexical items do not. Function morphemes also tend to come in *n*-tuples graded for markedness, while lexical items tend not to. Function morphemes tend to be bound morphemes, while lexical morphemes tend to be free.

Lexical morphemes and function morphemes also differ considerably in the conditions under which they contribute meaning to the sentence. Basically, lexical morphemes contribute to the meaning if present in the sentence, but if absent do not contribute to the meaning (except as allowed for under whatever anaphoric processes the language might have). Function morphemes, on the other hand, oftentimes fail to make a contribution to the meaning when present. The phenomenon of spurious or expletive plurals, definite articles, conjunctions, past tenses, passives, negatives, pronouns, and so forth is well attested. On the other side of the coin, the absence of a function morpheme does not preclude the presence of the meaning it is generally held to bear. In various languages, such elements as conjunctions, complementizers, definite articles, and other deletable items may be omitted, under certain circumstances, without loss of meaning. In fact, much of transformational grammar has been concerned with the circumstances under which function items may be omitted, retaining meaning.

These properties serve to distinguish the two classes of items in at least a rough-and-ready way. They should not be construed as a series of tests to be applied which *define* the two classes; a definition of the distinction is one that ultimately falls out of a theory, and not out of a series of tests. If the tests are valid and reliable, the theory should explain why they work, but the tests cannot explain the theory.[2]

I will be arguing, largely on grounds of parsimony, that in general meanings seemingly associated with function morphemes should not be assigned to the morphemes themselves, but instead to the structures in which the morphemes appear. Lexical morphemes, on the other hand, do have meanings directly assigned to them, and do not associate themselves with a meaning by virtue of the structures in which they are found. I assume throughout that there is a distinction between inflectional and derivational morphology, and I will have very little to say about the latter. I take it that derivational morphemes are added in the lexicon, and the subsequent change of meaning becomes a part of the word's meaning. Inflectional morphemes, though added like derivational morphemes in the lexicon, make no contribution to the meaning; hence a word with an inflectional ending means the same as that word without it.[3] I further assume, at least for the moment, that polysynthetic languages like Eskimo, Nootka, and Shawnee have highly productive systems of derivational morphology (though we will see in the end that much of this productivity might be regarded as inflectional).

2. FUNCTION MORPHEMES AND MEANING

Let us consider for the moment a system of semantic interpretation in which the rules of interpretation operate compositionally on surface structures in the usual way, and in which each morpheme is assigned a meaning (we will treat any unit constructed by the derivational morphology as a single morpheme for our present purposes). Such a notion of how semantic interpretation should be accomplished is quite influential, even if not adhered to strictly. Saussure, for instance, recognizes two types of meaning, one borne by the morphemes, and the other borne by the structure. Morphemes, however, do not count as a part of the structure. Wells, in his account of Saussure's theories, explains, "Let us call a class of similar syntagms a pattern . . . . Now patterns have meaning, and the meaning of a syntagm is a function of the meaning of the morphemes contained in it and of the pattern to which it belongs" (Wells, 1947). This general notion is implicit in an 'Item-and-Arrangement' view of morphology (Hockett (1954)), and though it was exlicitly rejected in Chomsky (1965), arguments in transformational grammar based on such assumptions about meaning have been most influential. Katz and Postal (1964), in defending the claim that transformations cannot change meaning, argue for certain underlying forms in which there are meaning-bearing morphemes, even if they are wholly absent at the surface. They explicitly reject the notion that grammatical operations can be thought of as bearing the appropriate meanings. They note with regard to previous theories that:

Unlike the Lees and Klima treatment of negation, the underlying P-markers operated on by question and imperative transformations . . . do not contain morphemes which can be assigned the meanings which differentiate actives, questions, and imperatives. These differences must thus be attributed to the effects of the transformations, and the semantic component must be thought of as either operating on the derived P-markers or on the transformations themselves. Our theory of the way projection rules operate entails that this view of the question and imperative sentence types must be at least partly incorrect and that the rules for these phenomena should be formulated in a manner similar to that more recently provided for negative sentences. We claim that special question and imperative morphemes must occur in the underlying P-markers of question and imperative sentences respectively (p. 74).

There is undeniable appeal in a system of this type. In fact, I am quite sure it would be almost wholly accurate were it not for the presence of function morphemes. But these cause problems in three distinct ways. First, if they bear meanings, they appear 'lower' in the tree than they should; secondly, function morphemes may appear in different places in the structure and still make the same semantic interpretation in each place. Finally, they give rise to difficulties in deciding what to assign meanings to. Similar problems do not arise for lexical items.

As an example of the first difficulty, consider the case of the Latin conjunction marker **-que**. This element represents one of three ways in which Latin conjunction may be realized (the other two are zero and the placement of a conjunction between the conjoined constituents). In brief, **-que** is placed after the first word of the final conjunct unless that first word is a monosyllabic preposition, in which case it is placed after the second word of the final conjunct. Things are actually a bit more complex than this as we will see below, but this will do for now. Thus, suppose the PP **ob eas res** 'because of these things' were the last conjunct in a series of two more PP's. -Que would then be placed after the demonstrative **eas**, yielding the PP with the following structure (example from Hale and Buck (1966)):

$$_{PP} [_{ob} {_{NP}} [_{Dem} [[e\bar{a}s] que] {_N} [r\bar{e}s]]]]$$
because (of)   these-and   things

and because of these things

If we have a system of semantic interpretation which works strictly bottom-up, the meaning of **-que** cannot be incorporated at the level of encounter (in the unit [*e\bar{a}s que*]). At this level it *appears* to be conjoining the demonstrative with something else, when in fact the demonstrative is not conjoined. It is not at all clear that any type of meaning could be consistently assigned to **-que** at this level (using what variables and lambda's you like), since the unit [*e\bar{a}s que*] could be the first word of any type of larger unit, which would require that **-que** be assigned a possibly unlimited number of different meanings. A much simpler interpretation of **-que** could be given, though, if we were to somehow 'postpone' its semantic effect until a larger unit is encountered in the tree, namely one of the form $_A$ [AA]. Then it could be treated the same as English and the other Latin conjunctions (see Gazdar (1980) for one such possible treatment).

The notion that other function elements must likewise have their interpretations 'postponed' until a later point in the semantic interpretation is a common and persistent one. Case-marking, it is universally agreed, comes into play only at the NP level (and not at some lower level), in spite of the tendency for nouns to bear the case marking. Tense, typically a marking on verbs, is exceedingly often treated as meaningful at the sentence level (though perhaps only for the convenience of treating it so in a propositional calculus). Modality, too, receives similar treatment. Passive is commonly treated essentially as a property of sentences or other phrasal units in the tree, though often marked only on the verb. Bennett (1974) claims that plurality is relevant semantically only at the NP level, and not at any lower level. Verkuyl (1972) argues likewise for the mass/count distinction. Dowty (1979) analyzes the progressive aspect in English as a function applying to verb phrases, as does Carlson (1980) for habitual aspect marking. Causatives, too, are often analyzed as higher-level phenomena (Babby, 1981). Similarly, markers of nominalization, though often appearing on the verb, mark the whole phrase as nominalized (e.g., English 'running home').[4]

Arguments advanced in favor of these claims are not water-tight. Indeed, most of these treatments compete with other analyses which take the marking to be purely word-level phenomenon, and interpretable as such. However, one must account for the persistence of 'postponement' analyses in the face of the complications such modes of interpretation introduce into the system. I do not know of any systems of logic that work this way, for example, and I think most semanticists would agree that a reasonable goal of semantic interpretation would be to construct a system as close as possible to the 'ideal' system mentioned above. I think the less than ideal analyses are proposed because the data generally take us in that direction.

There is another matter related to these observations (again, we are assuming function elements are assigned meanings, and the meanings are combined with one another in accordance with the syntactic structure). This is that the same element can contribute exactly the same meaning, but at different places in the derivation. Consider English tense, once again. In a sentence like (1), the tense appears on the verb, under the VP node. In (2) and (3), on the other hand, it appears on the auxiliary, immediately dominated by the S node.

(1)   John *left* the party.

(2)   (But I tell you), John *did* leave the party.

(3)   *Did* John leave the party?

In (1), the tense marking, if treated as a part of the interpretation of the verb, contributes its meaning at the VP level. In (2) and (3), though, its contribution is not present until the S level. I have yet, however, to find any differences with respect to tense and its contribution between such examples.

For instance, it does not appear that (2) and (3) allow wider scope privilege to tense than (1), in spite of the fact that tense c-commands more material in the latter two structures. A similar example is that of Latin **-que** and its counterpart **et**, the latter of which stands between conjoined constituents, like *and*. They appear at different levels, yet the semantic contribution to the whole is the same. A similar point could be made about English contracted and uncontracted negatives. Likewise, in Norwegian and other Scandinavian languages, the definite article may appear either as an immediate constituent of the NP (like English *the*), or as a nominal suffix. In either case, the semantic contribution to the whole is the same. The system of interpretation under consideration does not account for this variability of placement accompanied by identity of semantic contribution.

Turning to the last problem noted above, that of what to assign meanings to, we find the system under consideration once again facing severe difficulties. There is first the problem of what to assign meanings to when an interpretation is signaled by two or more morphemes that must be simultaneously present. French negation, the discontinuous **ne** ... **pas** construction, is as clear a case as I can think of. Both **ne** and **pas**, under other circumstances, can contribute a negative meaning to the whole.

(4) a. *Pas* encore.

   Not yet.

   b. Il *ne* regarda plus le journal.

   He no longer looked at the paper.

In combination, though, they contribute a single negative meaning, and not two; (5) has only a single negative reading.

(5)   Je *ne* comprends *pas.*

   I do not understand.

It would appear to be an arbitrary decision in (5) to assign negative meaning to one and not to the other.

Or consider the Norwegian means of expressing the demonstrative *that*.

(6)   *Det* stort hus*et*
   the   large   house-the

   that large house

Both *det* and the nominal suffix *-et* alone can be used to signal definiteness.

(7) a.   Det stort hus

the large house

b.   Huset

the house

In combination with one another, though, they mean *that*. In similar fashion, Gordon (1972) notes that Old Norse could mark definiteness most redundantly in an NP.

(8) a.   þat it   helgi   sæ ti
the the holy-def seat def

the holy seat

b.   hafit   þat it   djupa
sea-def the the deep-def

the deep sea

But in this case, a number of definiteness markings add up to a single definite.

The notion of multiple marking, I believe, encompasses much of what traditionally is subsumed under the notions of concord and agreement. Case and plurality endings appearing on different elements of an NP, aside from the head noun, would be common examples. In English, one finds in some dialects multiple comparative and superlative markings, giving rise to 'more smarter', 'most greatest', and so forth. More subtly, the progressive *be . . . ing*, perfect *have . . . en*, and passive *be . . . en* may be looked upon (and in fact are routinely looked up) as instances of multiple marking. Such a notion may well extend to runaway negative concord, as exemplified by the Old English sentence (9).

(9)   Ac he ne sealde nanum nytene ne nanum fisce nane sawle.
and he neg give   no   beast neg no   fish no   soul

And he did not give beasts or fish souls.

See Note 7 for a brief discussion of the distinction between multiple marking and agreement.

The notion of multiple marking developed here is not unlike that of

Harris' (1945) 'discontinuous morpheme'. Discontinuous morphemes are well attested at the word level. Yokuts expresses its dubitative by the configuration **na'as** ... **al** surrounding the verb stem. Similarly, German exhibits a dependency between the prefix **ge-** and the endings **-en** and **-et** as in **gefangen** 'captive' and **geeignet** 'suitable'. In similar vein, Harris proposes that the Latin phrase **victrix bona** 'good victor (fem.)' contains the discontinuous morpheme ... **ix** ... **a** as a segment meaning 'female'. That is, he proposes that this discontinuous morpheme combines with the phrase **victr- bon-** 'good victor' to arrive at the suitable meaning. Aside from imputing a meaning to the discontinuous morphemes and some technical details of implementation, the notion of multiple marking advocated here is not unlike Harris'.

The appearance of a single morpheme or of multiple morphemes in a constituent does not by any means exhaust the possible ways for a semantic notion to be realized. Changes of word order, deviating from some background order, is commonly used in forming questions, as in English and Finnish, though in other languages the notion of question is conveyed by use of a particle (as in Japanese), multiple particles (as in Zapotec, noted in Fromkin and Rodman (1978, p. 336), or verbal inflections (as in Yavapai, Tuscarara, and Pawnee), and enclitics that attach to members of several categories (Latin **-ne**). However, in the case of inversion, no evident morpheme is present to assign a meaning to. Manipulation of suprasegmentals, too, is used to convey various notions, chiefly questions, but other notions as well, such as that of habitual aspect in Etsako (Elimelech, 1978) and the jussive in Ewondo (Redden, 1979). If indeed the intonation bears the meaning, where in the structure does it fit for the purpose of semantic interpretation?

Yet another occasionally used means of conveying a meaning is the use of reduplication, most commonly reduplication of a single word to convey iterative aspect, plurality, intensity, diminuition, continuousness, universal quantification, and a few other notions (Moravscik, 1978). Phrasal reduplication, as found in Engenni, also appears, but much less frequently (we will return to Engenni at some length below). Where the meaning is to be assigned in the case of reduplication is most problematic if one insists on assigning all meanings to some morpheme.

Finally, there are of course the huge numbers of cases where a meaning is present, though no morpheme appears to bear that meaning. Null pronouns, conjunctions, present tenses, case markers, and so forth abound. Aside from taking the dubious step of allowing for $\emptyset$ morphemes (and most languages would have to distinguish among a number of them), there is nothing whatsoever present in any form to assign meanings to.[5]

I can only conclude from the general pattern of the data considered that the notion that all morphemes bear a meaning (and that all meanings are borne by morphemes) is not a very elegant way of looking at natural language. What I have been doing is to essentially reproduce arguments against an Item-and-Arrangement morphology, though I have tried to divert attention away from the word level and towards the sentence or phrasal level.

One can gain a perspective on this array of facts if we no longer assume that meanings are directly associated with function morphemes. Let us assume instead that meanings associated with function morphemes are in fact a part of the structure of a phrase itself; the function morphemes reflect what that structure is by virtue of their presence, but in isolation are meaningless (unlike lexical items). Let us take an example to clarify this somewhat. Suppose we have a sentence of language X which contains the lexical items ABCD. Let us assume now that the notion of *question* is 'in the structure of' this sentence (we will make 'in the structure of' more precise below). Natural language has a number of ways of conveying that the notion of question is in that structure, which means that something is done to the form of the sentence to reflect this fact. We can simply change the intonation contour, for example, from ABCD to ABCD; we can invert: ABCD to BACD; we can add particles in various locations: PrtABCD, ABCDPrt, PrtABCDPrt, APrtBCD; we can inflect some word so that it takes on a new form: ABCD to ABC'D, where C' is a form of C (in fact a verb or an AUX). But in none of these cases do(es) the added elements(s) actually bear any meaning.

Let us now turn to discussion of ways in which the notion of a meaning being 'in the structure' can be represented.

3. REPRESENTATIONS OF STRUCTURAL MEANING

There are two current models of grammar which present as a fundamental part of them a means of representing how certain semantic notions can reside in the structure of a sentence. The first is derived from linguistic tradition, and involves the use of syntactic features on nodes. The second approach is much more closely allied with mathematics, and represents these meanings as correlated with functions mapping structures to other structures.

Let us consider the model from linguistic tradition first. The notion that labels on nodes in a syntactic structure are analyzable into features rather than being atomic wholes is a fundamental part of current linguistic theory. Much use is made of $\bar{X}$ syntax, where such features as [±N, ±V] and an n-ary 'bar' feature specify the composition of any given node (see, for instance,

Jackendoff (1977)). These features are occasionally augmented by features of another sort which serve to more finely distinguish among phrase types, many of which correspond to the presence of an inflectional morpheme within the constituent the feature appears on. The type of grammar outlined in Gazdar *et al.* (1981) is just one of many examples of grammars making use of such features.

By representing such things as tense, case, plurality, and so forth, as features on nodes on a par with the categorial features (also features on nodes), one represents the notion that function morphemes have meanings inherent in the structure in a very straightforward way once we provide for the interpretation of these structures. The general outlines of a means of interpreting structures with these features in them can be constructed with great facility. As we will want to allow features to also appear on nodes in the tree where they are not interpreted, we must distinguish places where features are interpreted from places where they are not. Intuitively, this requires that a feature be interpreted only in the presence of some other features. For instance, suppose plurality is a feature that appears on nouns as well as on noun phrases, but is only interpreted at the NP level and not at the N level. The interpretation of the feature [+pl] will not take place if on the same node as the features defining a noun, but will take place if on the same node as a set of features defining a noun phrase.

Let us call the syntactic node where interpretation of a feature f takes place a *propagating node* with respect to f. What we have yet to do is to make the connection between the presence of f on a propagating node (hence, the presence of the meaning of f in the compositional meaning of the whole), and the presence of the appropriate function elements in the syntax.

The basic fact to be accounted for is that the function morphemes always appear as a part of the constituent marked for f, and are not external to it. A plural NP, for example, is never marked by independently putting a particle at the end of the sentence; the particle will be a part of the NP itself. The system outlined in Gazdar *et al.* (1981) represents an elegant and principled means of accounting for this fact, and of providing structures for interpretation. The claim is that natural language syntax can be wholly accounted for by descriptive devices that are available within the theory of context-free phrase structure grammar. Let us take context-free rewrite rules of the usual sort as the device to be scrutinized.

In a set of CF rules, features of higher nodes may get 'passed along' to lower nodes.[6] This is at the heart of the $\bar{X}$ approach, but generalizes to function-morpheme features as well. For instance, the feature of plurality might get 'passed along' to other elements in the NP by such rules as the following schematic example.

$$NP_{[+pl]} \longrightarrow (Dem_{[+pl]}) \, (Adj^*) \, N_{[+pl]} \, .$$

This marks the head noun, as well as any attendant demonstratives (*these, those*), as plural in form (the actual *form* is specified in the lexicon). This might work well for English, but for other Germanic languages plurality marking gets passed along to the adjectives as well. The features might also be realized in other ways, for example as independent particles, or as inversions, or, perhaps, not at all.[7]

How features can get passed along and where they may end up requires, of course, some further specification. The Head Features Convention of Gazdar *et al.* is one plausible beginning (it ensures, in effect that the head of the phrase will get the feature if any of the words in the phrase do).[8] Other conventions may be required as well. For instance, Bill Ladusaw (personal communication) has speculated that features realized as particles that are immediate constituents of the propagating node may not in addition be realized as features on the head. There is, for instance, no example we know of where a relative clause is marked by a word like English *that* and, at the same time, by a verbal affix; a similar pattern is likely to hold for questions.

However, the basic claim that function morphemes can be appropriately instantiated by use of CF rewrite rules appears doubtful. I wish to discuss two cases mentioned above — the placement of the Latin enclitic -**que**, and the matter of phrasal reduplication in Engenni. The first proves awkward to handle in a set of CF rules, the latter perhaps impossible.

As mentioned earlier, the enclitic -**que** is adjoined to the first word of the final conjunct of a series (it may also appear in earlier conjuncts as well, but this does not affect the point at hand).[9] We find, for instance, the following (from Key (1866)).

(10) a. [Solis]   et   [lunae]   [reliquōrumque sīderum] ortūs
       sun   and   moon   other-and   stars   rising
       The rising of the sun, the moon, and the other stars.

    b. [A   cultū   prōvinciae longissime absunt] [minimēque ad
       From culture province   furthest   be-absent least-and   to

       eōs   mercatōrēs saepe commeant] [proximīque sunt Germānīs]
       them merchants often visit   near-and   are   Germany
       *They are furthest from the civilization of Roman Italy, are rarely
       visited by merchants, and are closest to Germany.*

c. [Duāsque ibi   legiōnēs   cōnscrībit]
   two-and   there   legions   enrolled

   . . . *and there he enrolled two legions.*

However, if the first word of the phrase is a monosyllabic preposition, the enclitic is attached to the second word of the phrase:

(11) a. in forōque

      and in the forum.

   b. ob eāsque rēs

      and because of these achievements.

A disyllabic preposition, though, will take **-que**.

(12)   interque eōs

      . . . and among them.

Let us assume that placement of *-que* is to be accomplished by a set of CF rules, a general version of which might be (let us restrict our attention to examples with two conjuncts):

$$X \longrightarrow {}_X [X \underset{[+\mathrm{conj}]}{X}] \quad \text{for any category } X.$$

Let us now consider the case where two NP's are to be conjoined, and assume that the NP expansion rule of Latin is something like the following (taken from Lapointe (1980)):

$$\mathrm{NP} \longrightarrow (\mathrm{Det})\, \mathrm{N}'$$
$$\mathrm{N}' \longrightarrow (\mathrm{AP*})\, \mathrm{N}\, (\mathrm{AP*})$$

In order to appropriately place **-que**, though, no such rules can be used, for one must know which of the optional elements is present in a particular derivation to know what the first word is. One could, of course, rewrite the rules in such a way as to make the optional elements obligatory:

$$\underset{[+\mathrm{conj}]}{\mathrm{NP}} \longrightarrow \mathrm{Det\text{-}que}\ (\mathrm{AP*})\ \mathrm{N}\ (\mathrm{AP*})$$

$$\underset{[+\mathrm{conj}]}{\mathrm{NP}} \longrightarrow \underset{[+\mathrm{conj}]}{\mathrm{AP*}}\ \ \mathrm{N}\ (\mathrm{AP*})$$

$$\begin{array}{l} \text{AP*} \\ \text{[+conj]} \end{array} \longrightarrow \text{Adj-que (Adj*)}$$

$$\begin{array}{l} \text{NP} \\ \text{[+conj]} \end{array} \longrightarrow \text{N-que (AP*)}$$

Of course, a similar set of rules must be devised for each category that enters into conjunction. The result is not something that is beyond the mathematical power of a CF set of rules, but one does have to give up a good deal of economy of description, namely, the ability to collapse rules that should be collapsed.

Matters become slightly more cumbersome when we consider the distribution of **-que** in PP's. Assume the PP rule to be:

$$\text{PP} \longrightarrow \text{P NP} \quad \text{(a simplication of Lapointe)}$$

We need two different rules to distribute the conjunction appropriately:

$$\begin{array}{l} \text{PP} \\ \text{[+conj]} \end{array} \longrightarrow \text{P-que NP}$$

$$\begin{array}{l} \text{PP} \\ \text{[+conj]} \end{array} \longrightarrow \text{P NP}$$

The first of these rules cannot be used, though, if the preposition is monosyllabic, and the latter cannot be used if the preposition is polysyllabic. Additional features must then be introduced to obtain the appropriate results; for instance,

$$\begin{array}{l} \text{PP} \\ \text{[+conj]} \end{array} \longrightarrow \begin{array}{l} \text{P-que} \\ \text{[+poly]} \end{array} \text{NP}$$

$$\begin{array}{l} \text{PP} \\ \text{[+conj]} \end{array} \longrightarrow \begin{array}{l} \text{P} \\ \text{[+mono]} \end{array} \begin{array}{l} \text{NP} \\ \text{[+conj]} \end{array}$$

But the features [+mono] and [+poly] are, in this case, features without morphological motivation, nor is this particular distinction generalized to other parts of the grammar.

There is a further observation which complicates matters considerably. If there are two conjoined PP's with the same monosyllabic preposition then the **-que** may be attached to the last preposition:

(13) a. haec [de sē] [deque prōvincia]
         these from himself from-and province

     b. [per senectūtem tuam] [perque eam]
         through old age your through-and it (fem)

It is not entirely clear to me that the grammar itself should account for such facts (as opposed to, say, some stylistic preference on the part of the Classical writers – Lewis and Short (1969) note that exceptions to this pattern may be found). But on the assumption that such facts are to be accounted for in the grammar, the proliferation of *ad hoc* features becomes even more burdensome. It might run something like the following for PP's conjoined, both with **de**.

$$PP \atop [+conj] \rightarrow {PP \atop [+de]} \quad {PP \atop {[+conj] \atop [+de]}}$$

$$PP \atop [+de] \rightarrow {P \atop [+de]} \quad NP$$

$$PP \atop {[+conj] \atop [+de]} \rightarrow {P \atop {[+conj] \atop [+de]}} \quad NP$$

$$P \atop {[+conj] \atop [+de]} \rightarrow de \; que$$

$$P \atop [+de] \rightarrow de$$

The feature [+de] would have to be supplemented by a unique feature for each monosyllabic preposition. Furthermore, these features could not appear in the same rules which make use of the features [±mono], since P's marked [+mono] cannot take -**que**. Hence, we require either a convention telling us which of two conflicting features to pay attention to, or a completely new set of PS rules duplicating much of the previous sets of rules.

    Such an argument can be generally advanced whenever any type of marker is to be placed after the second word of a phrase, as is found occasionally, especially in the placement of auxiliary elements. The placement of -**que** in Latin involves an extra problem because of the exceptional behavior of prepositions (and, of certain adverbial words, as well). In any event, the use of CF rules to accomplish the appropriate placement of Latin -que presents us with considerable loss of generality, even if such placement is well within the mathematical power of the system.[10]

The second case I wish to discuss is potentially more serious. This is the matter of phrasal reduplication in Engenni, a language of Nigeria in the Kwa goup. I rely entirely on the description given in Thomas (1978).

In this language, 'secondary aspect' is signalled by reduplication of certain *phrases* within the sentence. Habitual/intensive aspect, for instance, is signalled by repeating 'the final phrase of the clause' (which, from the examples given, appears to be the final immediate constituent of the S bearing the habitual/intensive meaning). For instance, the verbal phrase is repeated in the following example:

(14) a. ạdogbò ọ̀dàú syịna nị̀ ạdhu *su   nù   su   nù*
wreath of-odau pass def eye float def float def

It was Odau's wreath that used to float down first.

b. ò za   nì   na   ọ   sì̀   mọ́ni sise dhè *ẹnuma nà ẹnuma nà*
it stay cpl that he will be-able put finish money the money the

If he can really put down all the money . . .

In the case of repetitive aspect, it is either "the VP alone, or the VP and the NP$_o$ (= object NP: GNC) and the adverbial phrase, if present)":

(15)   à   í   *dyii êgwè imò   n'ọ̀bhò dyii êgwe imò   n'ọ̀bhò*
they so tie pl   children in hand tie pl   children in hand

So they kept on giving the children gifts. ('tie in the hand' is an idiom)

Distributive aspect in this language is realized by a different pattern of reduplication, where the subject NP and the final phrase of the clause are reduplicated (the subject NP is not reduplicated if the head of it is the inherently distributive **onyenye** 'each person').

(16)   *ạkìè ạkìè* kou dhe   in   nà kpòri ivìè *gbe   gbe*
town town steer finish they inc sing   song go-home go-home

Each town got their boat into place and went home singing.

In addition, if the object NP is a clause-final pronoun, the verbal phrase is reduplicated as well:

(17) *ògwè ògwè* za ta êtyì na ó *dhyomu bhà dhyomu bhà*
group group stay go place that it please them please them

Each group went on to the place they liked.

Such phrasal reduplication would require an enormous number of ad hoc features within a CF framework. From the examples give, it is impossible to tell if the process of reduplication is an unbounded one. However, the language does have NP-internal relative clauses and PP's which fall between the head noun and NP-final markers of definiteness. For instance, the following example is given:

(18) ẹdhyomù âno [na ina i kye ni êní bhue ni]
food this rel mother-in-law his give cpl us keep cpl

[na bha ùtòmù eva tóu dhịa] nà
rel they head two will-take eat the

the food which his mother-in-law had given them and which they were both going to eat

Presumably NP's containing relative clauses, too, would be reduplicated if in the appropriate position of structures requiring reduplication. If this process is indeed unbounded, the mathematical power of a set of CF rules is entirely overstepped since such rules are mathematically incapable of producing unbounded XX patterns (where XX indicates two identical strings)[11]. I cannot at this time make any such definitive claim. What is clear, however, is that at the very least an incredible number of ad hoc features would be required to obtain the bounded patterns exemplified.

The resulting feature proliferation militates strongly against a pure CF approach, and it would appear that a more powerful system must be permitted in order to represent more convincingly the nature of the realization of function elements in natural language. One way of doing this would be simply to add a class of transformations to the set of CF rules already in place — resulting in a transformational grammar. Such a system still represents the notion that function elements do not bear meaning themselves by retaining the assignment of features to nodes, and interpreting the features as indicated. I do not wish to elaborate on what the transformational component of such a grammar might look like, but I would suggest that any such transformational component would concern itself only with the appropriate realization of features on nodes, and need serve no other function. In other words, the transformational rules themselves are for the function elements, and the PS rules for putting the lexical items into structures.

There is, from a different tradition, a competing notion of how to represent some meaning as being a part of the structure of a sentence. Logicians, in giving the syntax of an artificial language, oftentimes distinguish between elements introduced in a rule to be operated on, and those syncategorematic elements that are added as the result of applying a rule.[12] Thus, for instance, conjunction of two elements A and B combines A and B by a rule which results in a sentence of the form [A & B]. The ampersand is *not* one of the elements to be combined, but is something that results from the application of the rule of conjunction. The meaning (in the interpretation) is not directly associated with the symbol &, but instead with the operation of putting A and B together in a particular way (namely, forming a sentence consisting of A followed by & followed by B). This particular distinction is carried over into Montague grammar, where certain elements in Montague (1974) are introduced syncategorematically that correspond to the function elements of the language (tense, determination, conjunction and disjunction, negation, relative clause marking). In these cases, the resulting meanings are associated with the operation of determining, tensing, etc., and not with the function elements themselves. For instance, *will*, *not*, and *or* are not assigned meanings, though in Montague's system they very well could have been. This does represent quite well the intuitive 'meaninglessness' of function elements and the notion that associated meanings are a part of the structure of the sentence itself. Just as the structure [$_S$NP VP] is mapped onto a particular type of semantic interpretation (namely, a function-argument interpretation), a structure such as [$_{S\,[+Neg]}$ NP VP] is mapped onto another type of interpretation, of a slightly more complex sort, by a different rule of interpretation. This rule will have, of course, a corresponding syntactic function of somehow marking the sentence as negative; the particular mode depends on the language (e.g., in French **ne . . . pas** would then be distributed appropriately; in English *not* or *n't* would be put in, etc.).[13]

There is no distinction between this approach and the transformational approach outlined above in terms of mathematical power, as both offer general systems very much in need of further constraint. Both could deal equally effectively with the facts about Latin and Engenni presented above. One area of partial divergence between the two approaches, I believe, concerns how each system would be able to handle the assignment of function elements in free word-order languages, such as Walbiri (and to a certain extent, Latin), provided the type of program outlined here is carried out. What is required under the present conception of function elements is a propagating syntactic node (e.g., an AP that is marked as a comparison, a sentence marked as a question, and so forth). In free word-order languages, though, there is often no such surface constituent since the words of a phrase may end up widely separated from one another, yet still bear appropriate 'agreeing' morphologically form. But in these languages, although the lexical items themselves have a fairly unconstrained order of appearance, the function morphemes have fairly rigid constraints placed on their order of appearance (for instance, the Aux may have to appear in second position). This is also reflected at the word level, as has been so often noted: prefixes stay at the front of words, infixes inside, and so forth. In order for a transformational approach to the marking of constituents to work, one must have constituents defined by the base rules to operate on. For a free word-order language, this entails setting up constituents in deep structures and then applying transformations to 'destroy' those constituents (as when, say, a determiner, and adjective, and a noun all become separated from one another). As is well known, 'scrambling' transformations become hard to write, and give less than convincing accounts of free word order.

It appears that a MG approach can avoid at least some of the problems that would be inherent in a tranformational approach. In a Montague-type grammar, the constituents are created and then combined with one another to form a larger constitutent (rather than being *re*-combined with one another as in a transformational approach). The scrambling can then take place in the process of combining constituents (this suggestion is due to Rich Larson). We introduce into the grammar a new syntactic function, let's call it 'Interleave', F_I:

F_I: If A is a constituent consisting of w_1, w_2, . . . , w_i, and B is a constituent consisting of w_{i+1}, w_{i+2}, . . . , w_n, then F_I (A, B) results in a constituent C consisting of any arrangement of w_1, . . . , w_n such that w_j always precedes w_{j+1} for $j = 1$, . . . , i, and w_k always precedes w_{k+1} for $k = i+1$, . . . , n.

The order of the elements of the constituents themselves is maintained, though the words themselves may end up scattered throughout some larger constituent.

Let us examine a brief example to show how this might work. Consider
the Walbiri sentence from Hale (1981):

(19)   Kurdu-ngku ka   maliki   wajilipi-nyi   wita-ngku
        Child-ERG   pres. dog   chase-nonpast   small-ERG
        The small child is chasing a dog.

(the N *dog* is in the absolutive case, which has $\emptyset$ marking)

Suppose also that F_I applies whenever two constituents are to be combined
with one another (they would have to both contain lexical items). Hence,
if a noun and an adjective are combined with one another to form, say, an
NP, they may go together in any order. But once they are put together in
a particular order, they must maintain that same relative order throughout.
For instance, we might have rules combining **kurdu** 'child' together with **wita**
'small (one)' to form the NP's **kurdu wita** or **wita kurdu**. Both may then
be marked for ergative case (let us take the former as it is relevant to the
example at hand), resulting in **kurdu-ngku wita-ngku**. Let us also further
suppose (probably contrafactually) that we have built up the Walbiri VP
maliki wajilipi 'chase a dog', and we are to combine the NP with this VP. The
only matter of relevant is that the words of each constituent retain their same
relative order. Among the possible combinations is the following:

(20)   kurdu-ngku maliki wajilipi wita-ngku.

We now have a sentence, which requires placement of a 'nonpast' marker
on the verb, and a present tense morpheme after the first word. These are,
presumably, accomplished by two fairly common functions in natural language. The first marks a feature on the verb, resulting in a lexically-added
suffix:

(21)   kurdu-ngku maliki wajilipi-nyi wita ngku.

And the second places an auxiliary element in second position in the sentence.

(22)   kurdu-ngku ka maliki wjilipi-nyi wita ngku (= (19)).

Thus, the Interleave function results in free scrambling of lexical items, but
maintains the strict order of function morphemes. It also does not require a
distinct level of syntactic representation where all the words of the sentence
are in some particular underlying order, as is required by a transformational

approach, and which appears to be at the root why transformations are not felt to be able to deal very effectively and insightfully with the scrambling of lexical items in a sentence. The same sort of observation as made by Lapointe (1980) bears repeating: that different languages may have different versions of the Interleave function. For instance, some languages may be able to scramble major constituents, but not lexical items out of them, or perhaps only certain lexical categories within a given phrase.

One final point before turning to the last section. Lapointe (1980) and, in effect, Hale (1981) both make use of a level of logical form in dealing with apparently broken-up constituents. The general program presented here (though not presented at nearly the careful level of detail found in Lapointe's dissertation) makes it possible to dispense with a level of logical form, at least as motivated by a need to have a form in which the dispersed items of a constituent are 'collected together' for interpretation. A level of logical form may well be a necessary component of the grammar, but until these other alternatives are investigated more thoroughly one should not assume that the phenomenon of free word order makes it a necessity.

4. FORM AND MEANING

Let us now turn our attention to the range of forms that certain semantic notions may take in natural language. Certain meaningful notions, such as 'past tense', 'question', 'plural', 'imperfective aspect', and so forth, take on a set of forms for the most part quite different from such meaningful notions as 'horse', 'visit', 'brown', etc. Let us take the meaning of the word *horse* as an example. As far as I know, or can imagine, the notion of *horse* is not expressed in any language as, say, a discontinuous morpheme, as an inversion of word order, as a reduplication, as a change in intonation, or as null. I exemplify what sentences from such languages might look like:

(23) a.   John rode cow (John rode mule = 'John rode a mule', etc.)
         John rode a cow.

    b.   John ip rode pip.
         John rode a horse.

    c.* John ip rode.

    d.* John rode pip.

(24) a. John rode cow.

    b. Rode John.
      John rode a horse.

    c. John rode.
      John rode.

(25) a. John rode cow.

    b. John John rode rode.
      John rode a horse.

    c.* John John rode.

    d.* John rode rode.

(26) a. John rode cow.

    b. John rode.
      John rode a horse.

    c. John rode.
      John rode.

(27) a. Cow is here.
      A cow is here.

    b. Is here.
      A horse is here.

    c. John saw cow.
      John saw a cow.

    d. John saw.
      John saw a horse.

Assuming these are not possible natural language ways of expressing the concept 'horse', I believe that the previous discussion actually offers us a fairly straightforward beginning in untangling this problem.

One of the most often-cited characteristics of inflectional morphology vis-à-vis derivational morphology is that inflectional morphemes do not change the category that a word belongs to. If inflections are looked upon as marking whole phrases rather than just words, a similar observation holds as well: they still do not change the category (with one possible exception to be discussed below).

The failure of the addition of an inflectional element to change category is suggestive of one notion of an *operation* found in mathematics. Anderson and Belnap (1975), following Curry, suggest that an operation is a type of function which takes terms and maps them to other terms. Addition, for instance, is an operation in this sense because it takes them (two numbers) and results in another term (another number). Hockett (1954) and Wall (1972) suggest something along the same lines but a bit more general than this. Wall, for instance, suggests that an operation is any function which converts "... one or a pair of things into another thing of the same kind". What is left open is, of course, how to define the relevant kinds.

Let us take this general notion (but not restrict ourselves necessarily to just one or a pair of things as input) and apply this to natural language. First of all note that category membership is retained under inflectional marking: a negative sentence is of the same syntactic category as a positive one, a comparative AP is of the same syntactic category as a positive one, a plural NP is of the same category as a singular one.[14] If we think of the syntactic functions that mark these categories appropriately (say, in the MG framework elaborated on above) with respect to the notion of *operation* in the sense of sameness of input and output, these functions are operations (as Frank Heny has pointed out to me). Compare this with the other syntactic functions which build up sentences. Adding a preposition to an NP results in a PP, not an NP; the addition of an NP to a VP results in an S, not another NP; combining a V and an NP results in a VP, not in another V. Functions which do this are not operations in the sense intended here.

On the semantic side, we find a similar pattern provided we accept the general notion that for each syntactic category there is an interpretation 'space' which defines the possible denotations of each category (for instance, S denotations are members of the set of truth values, VP's denote sets of entities, NP's denote sets of sets of entities, and so forth). It follows then that the meanings associated with the presence of function elements is such that they, too, represent operations. The denotation of conjoined VP's is of the same sort as the denotation of a non-conjoined VP. On the other hand, the 'meaning' of a function which puts a V and an NP together to

form a VP results in a meaning of a sort different from that of a V, or that of
an NP.

Some further discussion is necessary, but the basic connection between
form and meaning we arrive at is that if some meaning is expressed by means
of a syntactic operation, then that meaning when applied as a function to
the meaning of the operand must be an operation as well. The converse, that
syntactic non-operations are semantic non-operations does not hold. Thus,
meanings of function morphemes may be expressed lexically as well, but not
all lexical meanings are expressible in function-form. Let us illustrate this
briefly by returning to our 'horse' examples above, and show why *horse* could
not show up in any of the ways indicated (nor as an inflectional (as opposed
to a derivational) affix).[15] If 'horse' were expressed in the ways indicated,
some higher node in structure would have to be operated on by a syntactic
operation which is associated with the appropriate meaning, according to
what I have argued here — let's assume it's the VP for purposes of illustration.
This syntactic fact alone requires that the meaning of *horse* be something
which when applied to VP meanings results in VP meanings (e.g., from sets
to sets). But the meaning of *horse* is no such thing. In order for the meaning
of *horse* to be represented in that way, *it would have to mean something else*.
It couldn't mean what it does and contribute the required type of meaning.
This type of meaning would correspond to the meanings of VP adverbs,
meanings which, it seems plausible, do occur occasionally as verbal inflections.
For example, Redden (1949) notes that in Ewondo (a Bantu language) the
'Auxiliary' system includes the notions 'iterative', 'habitual', 'nearly', 'in spite
of', 'always', 'recently', 'first', 'properly', 'fast', all of which are potentially
representable as functions from predicates to predicates in the semantics.
Other languages exhibit other conglomerations of function elements in the
Aux or inflected on the verb. What has been said here in no way predicts
whether a given semantic operation will be realized lexically or as a function
element; the restriction is on what may not appear as an inflection or as
another function form.[16]

It would appear that further restrictions are necessary to account for the
regularity with which the notion of tense is marked functionally, but other
sentence-modifier notions (say, that of 'wisely' or 'luckily') are much more
rarely, if ever, instantiated functionally. The regularity of the appearance
of the functional marking of comparison, number, modality, aspect, tense,
case, conjunction, and so forth, as opposed to the unlimited number of other
possibilities requires some explication. One could, for instance, appeal to
some notion of utility: handy concepts that get used a lot that are semantic

operations tend to get marked functionally. Whether or not this is so, of course, is far from clear; equally unclear is the relevance of utility to linguistic structure. One other possible line of inquiry, along the lines of examination of substantive universals, derives from the general notion of markedness. Certain notions, such as singularity, present tense, third person singular, nominative case, positive degree, indicative mood, and so forth are very often not realized in any form whatsoever. In order for null realization to be detectable, there must be something for them to contrast with (plurality, past tense, second person, accusative case, comparative degree, subjunctive mood, etc.) — other members of the same semantic fields (however 'semantic field' is to be ultimately defined). The selection in any given language of what to express by function morphemes in the syntax, then, begins with the field which has an unmarked member (or rather, a potentially unmarked member); what any language adds to that and what particular distinctions will be made in the semantic fields containing unmarked members, is a matter of cultural taste, perhaps, and well beyond the bounds of linguistic theory.

5. CONCLUSION

The hypotheses presented represent but a first attempt to get at a fundamental organizing principle of language, the distinction between function and content morphemes. Obviously the specific hypotheses will require further refinement as we come to know more about language. For example, one matter that remains problematic concerns the process of nominalization, where phrases of one category are, apparently, turned into phrases of another category by an operation (?) which normally leaves an inflectional marking of some sort. It is not at all clear if a derived structure of $_{NP}[\ _X[\ \ldots\ ]]$ means that the category has been changed from an X to an NP, and it is not clear how this bears on the notion of operation discussed above. It also remains to be seen if nominalization has any effect on meaning. In work by Cocchiarella (1979), for instance, it has no effect on meaning (and hence can be a semantic operation); Thomason (1979), on the other hand, suggests there is a meaning-change.

Nevertheless, the general hypothesis advanced here about the connection between form and meaning seems amenable to empirical investigation, and if anywhere near correct, presents us with a fundamental principle of human language.

University of Wisconsin and Wayne State University

NOTES

[1] I am indebted to Barbara Abbott, Robin Cooper, Walter Edwards, Phil Fare, Frank Heny, Bill Ladusaw, Rich Larson, Andrew Sihler, as well as two very thorough anonymous referees for their ideas and their help in clarifying the problems with an earlier version of this paper. None are responsible for the shortcomings of this paper, and none necessarily agree with my conclusions.

[2] Prepositions are often included among the function words, although according to what I have said here they are not, since they combine with NP's (and possibly other elements such as S's and PP's) to form a constituent of another type, the P being external to the NP. Prepositions are indeed a closed class of words which do not undergo derivational processes, as are the other function words. There are, however, some differences which show that prepositions have affinities with lexical items as well. First, they appear routinely in compounding: *offshoot, push-up, instep, without,* etc. Other function words do not. Secondly, some prepositions appear also as members of other lexical categories, a common property of lexical items. *Near*, for instance, is also a verb and an adjective; *up* appears as a verb, as does *down*, and a number of others, especially in more colloquial speech. Finally, these words also appear to subcategorize for certain configurations, much the same as a verb or an adjective might. Jackendoff (1977) and others have argued for intransitive and transitive prepositions, and prepositions which take other PP's as complements as well as sentences. My own inclination is to believe that prepositions most often function as true lexical items, though they may, at times, take on function-word duties as well. *Of*, for instance would appear almost wholly to take on function-word status (this is reflected in the various proposals for having it transformationally inserted into configurations where a PP is not really needed, but an NP 'ought to' fit).

[3] I am assuming that both derivational and inflectional forms of words are constructed in the lexicon. The chief difference is that the forms created by the derivational morphology have rules of semantic interpretation associated with them which when applied to an input give a different output. Rules applied to create inflectional forms, on the other hand, have no effect on meaning (the identity mapping). Hence, all alternative inflectional forms will be accorded the same meaning in the lexicon – the meaning of the base form. As all the forms are created by rules in the lexicon, it's entirely possible that quite closely related rules may apply to create highly similar forms. English passive participles and deverbal adjectives are likely one such case, as are gerunds and verbal nominalizations (running the city vs. the running of the city).

[4] Edwin Williams (personal communication) has noted certain places in the lexicon which appear to be non-compositional. Such forms as *hydro-electricity*, appear bracketed the wrong way: it should be [hydro electric] ity. Similarly, such English nominalizations as *misuse, disproof*, signaled by devoicing, appear to have a nominalized part, *use* and *proof*, when in fact the whole verb *misuse, disprove* has been nominalized. If essentially the same types of operations are used in the syntax as we find in the lexicon, the position well articulated in Dowty (1978), such examples as *misuse* are to be anticipated, as the syntax is often non-compositional in this same way.

[5] I am not claiming that any meaning that may appear as one functional form (for instance, as an inflectional ending) may readily take on any of the other possible forms in other languages, or in the same language. Inversion, for instance, seems fairly limited

in terms of what notions it may signify; suprasegmental change, though, appears less restricted, though not nearly as free as affixation.

6 Pronouns, I assume, are realizations of bundles of features on NP's. It follows then that properties of pronouns (case, number, gender, person, plurality) are also properties of NP's. This appears to conflict with the fact that many of these properties appear as intrinsic properties of nouns (for instance, gender in French, German, etc.). There are a couple of fairly straightforward ways to resolve this apparent conflict. One way would be to require that all features on lexical items be instantiated, or the derivation will be ill-formed. So, to take an example, suppose one has a French NP of the form **un grand pere** and one applies a rule making everything feminine. Un[+fem] is instantiated as **une**, **grand**[+fem] is **grande**, but there is no form in the lexicon instantiating **pere** [+fem]. The derivation is thus ill-formed. In essence, this type of solution is one that could also be applied to words with defective paradigms.

A second type of solution passes features up and down the tree, both ways. (This is, in fact, the HFC.) What is required is complete homogeneity of feature composition between head and constituent.

A problem everyone must face, though, is the matter of 'false marking', for instance English *pluralia tanta*, and how to deal with the semantic interpretation of such forms. Note that one cannot simply claim that a word like *scissors* is marked [+singular] (even if it looks plural) because it behaves like a plural in all syntactic respects. Demonstratives agree with it, and so do verbs. We need to somehow distinguish between 'serious' plurals, and the purely formal plurals at the NP level. In this case, we need to specify what happens in the semantics in the presence of a false feature. It seems to me that many of the false features we find (subjunctives, plurals, passives, past tenses, genitives, perfectives, etc.) are the marked forms. Perhaps there is an automatic rule of interpretation which takes false marked forms and treats them as unmarked forms, so past tenses become present, subjunctives become indicatives, plurals singular, passives actives, etc. I have yet to investigate this area to see if this proposal is feasible.

7 Distinguishing between multiple marking and agreement in the abstract is a fairly simple matter. Consider two constituents A and B whose forms co-vary along some dimension when they are in certain structural configurations. This variance is connected with the presence of a certain semantic notion (e.g., feminine gender, plurality, etc.). Suppose that A and B are both dominated by a node C. If the semantic notion is applicable to A and/or B but not to C, it is agreement; if applicable to C, it is multiple marking. To take an example, plural agreement between English subject NP's and verbs (VP's) is agreement, because plurality is not a notion that applies to S's, though it is certainly applicable to NP's, and possibly to VP's as well. The obviously difficulty here is determining what 'applicability' is, which seems to be an empirical matter that will fall out of investigation of the semantics of natural language.

A notion of multiple marking as opposed to agreement does have some advantages. Agreement requires the presence of some primary constituent with a given property in order to determine the agreeing forms. In the absence of that primary constituent, a theory of agreement would appear to predict that no agreement markings should appear on the agreeing constituents. Just such a case is discussed in Gouet (1976) and Herschensohn (1978) where French NP's lacking overt nouns nevertheless show gender marking on the articles on adjectives in the NP. A theory of agreement requires a dummy N or an underlying N of some sort. Multiple marking, on the other hand, makes no such requirement; whatever is present that is appropriate will be marked. A similar type of situation is found in English in phrases like 'these nine' and 'those two', where the head N is absent.

[8] Greenberg (1963) notes that postnominal adjectives may bear all the marking to the exclusion of the noun as in Basque. This would appear to be in violation of the HFC.

[9] The following description of Latin -que is based on the discussion in Hale and Buck (1966), Lewis and Short (1969), Key (1866), and Kuhner and Stegmann (1955).

[10] Gerald Gazdar (personal comm.) informs me that more recent developments in the GPSG framework may be able to handle the data presented here. The two crucial notions are that of 'foot feature' and a separation of statements of dominance and linear precedence.

[11] This is stated somewhat loosely. See G. Pullum and G. Gazdar (1982), and the references cited there for a much more precise statement.

[12] Sue Schmerling has pointed out to me that Kenneth Pike used a system of this general type well before the advent of Montague grammar.

[13] Dowty (1978) distinguishes between lexical operations and syntactic operations, and notes that the types of operations used in the lexicon may be pressed into service in the syntax, and vice-versa. I think this point of view is basically correct, as we seem to find many syntactic correlates to the usual stock of morphological processes. For instance, prefixation may correspond to the placement of a particle at the beginning of a sentence, metathesis to inversion, and so forth. Dowty's basic claim is that the lexical operations are fundamentally for the derivational morphology, and only secondarily syntactic. This receives some mild support from Greenberg's (1963) proposed universal that languages with inflection (i.e., lexical operations used in the syntax) also are languages with derivation, but the presence of derivation does not entail the presence of inflection.

In addition, this general framework would appear to conflict with Partee's (1979) well-formedness constraint on the recursive rules in an MG framework.

[14] I conceive of these marking operations as being in actuality complexes of more primitive operations. Marking for tense, for instance, may require first the marking of the VP, then the marking of the V, then the marking of the word itself, then the application of a rule in the lexicon to segmentalize the feature, then the replacement of the featured form in the syntactic tree with the appropriate form from the lexicon. I am not rejecting the 'rule-to-rule' hypothesis (Bach (1976)), which requires that each syntactic rule have a corresponding semantic rule; rules are not to be confused with elementary sub-functions.

[15] What may appear in the form of an affix in the derivational morphology appears to be almost completely unrestricted; think of the 'combining forms' of English: *Sino-, hydro-, spatio-*, etc. If we look at a wider range of constructions, beyond the essentially concatenative affixation processes, I suspect that the range of expressible meanings is somewhat diminished. Reduplication of word portions, for instance, has an extremely limited range of meanings (Moravscik (1978)); $\emptyset$-derivation, too, appears quite restricted.

[16] To the extent that affixation in polysynthetic languages represents semantic operations, it is possible that one is dealing with inflection rather than derivation.

BIBLIOGRAPHY

Anderson, A. and N. Belnap: 1975, *Entailment: The Logic of Relevance and Necessity*, Princeton University Press.

Babby, L.: 1981, 'A Compositional Analysis of Voice in Turkish: Passive, Derived Intransitive, Impersonal, and Causative', in Harbert and Herschensohn (eds.), *Cornell University Working Papers in Linguistics*, Vol. 2, Department of Modern Languages and Linguistics, Cornell University.

Bach, E.: 1976, 'An Extension of Classical Transformational Grammar', University of Massachusetts (mimeo).

Bennett, M.: 1974, *Some Extensions of a Montague Fragment of English*, Unpublished Ph.D. dissertation UCLA, distributed by Indiana University Linguistics Club.

Bloomfield, L.: 1933, *Language*, Holt, Rinehart, and Winston, New York.

Carlson, G.: 1980, *Reference to Kinds in English*, Garland Publishing, New York.

Chomsky, N.: 1965, *Aspects of the Theory of Syntax*, MIT Press, Cambridge.

Cocchiarella, N.: 1979, 'The Theory of Homogeneous Simple Types as a Second Order Logic', *Notre Dame Journal of Formal Logic* **20**, 505–24.

Dowty, D.: 1978, 'Applying Montague's Views on Linguistic Metatheory to the Structure of the Lexicon', in D. Farkas, W. Jacobsen, and K. Todrys (eds.), *Papers from the Parasession on the Lexicon*, Chicago Linguistic Society, pp. 97–137.

Dowty, D.: 1979, *Word Meaning and Montague Grammar* (Synthese Language Library), D. Reidel Publishing, Dordrecht.

Elimelech, B.: 1978, *Tonal Grammar of Etsako*, University of California Publications in Linguistics, No. 87.

Fries, C.: 1952, *The Structure of English*, Harcourt, Brace, and World, New York.

Fromkin, V. and R. Rodman: 1978, *An Introduction to Language* (2nd ed.), Holt, Rinehart, and Winston, New York.

Gazdar, G.: 1980, 'A Cross-Categorial Semantics for Coordination', *Linguistics and Philosophy* **3**, 407–410.

Gazdar, G., G. Pullum, and I. Sag: 1981, 'Auxiliaries and Related Phenomena in a Restrictive Theory of Grammar', distributed by the Indiana University Linguistics Club.

Gordon, E. V.: 1927, *Introduction to Old Norse*, Oxford University Press.

Gouet, M.: 1976, 'On a Class of Circumstantial Deletion Rules', *Linguistic Inquiry* **7**, 693–7.

Greenberg, J.: 1963, 'Some Universals of Grammar with Particular Reference to the Order of Meaningful Elements', in Greenberg (ed.), *Universals of Languages*, MIT Press, Cambridge, pp. 73–113.

Hale, K.: 1981, 'On the Position of Walbiri in a Typology of the Base', distributed by the Indiana University Linguistics Club.

Hale, W. G. and C. Buck: 1966, *A Latin Grammar*, University of Alabama Press.

Harris, Z.: 1945, 'Discontinuous Morphemes', *Language* **21**, 121–7.

Herschensohn, J.: 1978, 'Deep and Surface Nominalized Adjectives in French', *Linguistic Inquiry* **9**, 135–7.

Hockett, C.: 1954, 'Two Models of Grammatical Description', *Word* **19**, 210–231.

Jackendoff, R.: 1977, $\bar{X}$ *Syntax: A Study of Phrase Structure, Linguistic Inquiry*, Monograph No. 2, MIT Press, Cambridge.

Katz, J. and P. Postal: 1964, *An Integrated Theory of Linguistic Descriptions*, Research Monograph No. 26, MIT Press, Cambridge.

Key, T. H.: 1866, *A Latin Grammar*, Bell and Daldy, London.

Keyser, J. and P. Postal: 1976, *Beginning English Grammar*, Harper and Row, New York.

Kuhner, R. and C. Stegmann: 1955, *Ausfurliche Grammatik der lateinishen Sprache*, Gottschalksche Verlagbuchhandlung, Leverleursen,

Lapointe, S.: 1900, *A Theory of Grammatical Agreement*, unpublished Ph.D. dissertation, University of Massachusetts at Amherst.

Lewis, C. and C. Short: 1969, *A Latin Dictionary*, Oxford University Press.

Montague, R.: 1974, 'The Proper Treatment of Quantification in Ordinary English', in R. H. Thomason (ed.), *Formal Philosophy: Selected Papers of Richard Montague*, Yale University Press, pp. 247–70.

Moravcsik, E.: 1978, 'Reduplicative Constructions', in J. Greenberg (ed.), *Universals of Human Language*, Vol. 3, *Word Structure*, Stanford University Press.

Partee, B. H.: 1979, 'Constraining Transformational Montague Grammar: A Framework and a Fragment', in S. Davis and M. Mithun (eds.), *Linguistics, Philosophy, and Montague Grammar*, University of Texas Press, Austin, pp. 51–102.

Pullum, G. and G. Gazdar: 1982, 'Natural Languages and Context-free Languages', *Linguistics and Philosophy* 4, 471–504.

Redden, J.: 1979, *A Descriptive Grammar of Ewondo, Occasional Papers in Linguistics*, No. 4, Southern Illinois University, Carbondale.

Sapir, E.: 1921, *Language*, Harcourt, Brace, and World, New York.

Schwartz, L.: 1978, 'On the Island Status of Lexical Items', in D. Farkas, W. Jacobsen, and K. Todrys (eds.), *Papers from the Parasession on the Lexicon*, Chicago Linguistic Society, pp. 326–35.

Steele, S.: 1980, 'Cross-Linguistic Equivalence: Theory and Application to Categories (especially Aux)', paper presented at the Fourth Groningen Round Table.

Thomas, E.: 1978, *A Grammatical Description of the Engenni Language*, Summer Institute of Linguistics, Publication No. 60, University of Texas at Arlington.

Thomason, R. H.: 1979, 'On the Interpretation of the Thomason 1972 Fragment', distributed by the Indiana University Linguistics Club.

Verkuyl, H.: 1972, *On the Compositional Nature of the Aspects*, D. Reidel Publishing, Dordrecht.

Wall, R.: 1972, *Introduction to Mathematical Linguistics*, Prentice-Hall, Englewood Cliffs, New Jersey.

Wells, R.: 1947, 'De Saussure's System of Linguistics', *Word* 3, 1–31.

ERIC J. REULAND

GOVERNMENT AND THE SEARCH FOR AUXES:
A CASE STUDY IN CROSS-LINGUISTIC
CATEGORY IDENTIFICATION*

0. INTRODUCTION

In this article I will discuss an issue which must be raised in connection with the research program underlying much interesting recent work by Akmajian, Steele and Wasow (cf. Akmajian, Steele and Wasow (1979), henceforth ASW, and Steele *et al.* (1981), henceforth SEA).[1] The goal of the program is to provide a framework in which the question of the similarity of categories across the grammars of particular languages can be provided with a 'substantive empirical basis': the framework uses cross-linguistic comparison to identify as equivalent, categories which are motivated in the first instance solely by language internal analyses. The treatment of the category AUX is intended to exemplify the general approach.[2]

Their guiding question is the following: suppose that in the optimal analysis of English clauses one has to make use of a category, to be labeled AUX; suppose moreoever, that in the optimal analysis of clauses in some other language, say Luiseño, one has to make use of some category that may be labeled ZED; is there now any principled way in which to decide whether AUX and ZED are to be identified? To put it differently: is there any empirical content to a proposal to identify them? They contend that such cross-linguistic identification must rest on some notional basis (cf. Lyons (1968) for some discussion of notional definitions, cf. also Greenberg (1963)). So ASW (p. 2) presents the following definition of AUX:

(1)   AUX is a category – i.e. distinct in its syntactic behavior from the behavior of other syntactic categories – labeling a constituent that includes elements expressing the notional categories of Tense and/or Modality.

In SEA, AUX refers to a set of constituents non-distinct under (2).

(2)   Given a set of language internal analyses, in terms of constituents, those constituents which may contain only a specified (i.e. fixed and small) set of elements, crucially containing elements marking tense and/or modality will be identified as non-distinct. (*footnote omitted*)

SEA argues, for a number of languages, viz. Egyptian Arabic, English, German,

99

*F. Heny and B. Richards (eds.), Linguistic Categories: Auxiliaries and Related Puzzles,
Vol. One*, 99–168.
Copyright © 1983 *by D. Reidel Publishing Company.*

Japanese, Luiseño and Lummi, that each of them contains a constituent meeting the requirements of (2). Moreover, it is claimed that in all of these cases these constituents possess some of a set of non-definitional properties as well, i.e. properties which are not necessary consequences of the definition. For instance, the category to be identified with AUX is a constituent occurring in first, second, or final position, which generally attaches to some adjacent element. Besides the elements mentioned in (2) AUX may include elements marking subject marking (sic), subject agreement, question, evidential, emphasis, aspect, object marking, object agreement and negation (SEA, p. 178). The restriction to first, second and final positions is meant to hold for the position of this constituent at the surface in any sentence, not simply on some abstract level from which strings of any variety are derivable (though the possibility is admitted that certain elements are transparent to the determination of these positions). In SEA the question is posed why these (and some other) characteristics should cluster together, i.e. what is AUX?

The most attractive hypothesis is considered this:

AUX is that part of the sentence which makes possible a judgement about its truth value That is, the presence of the piece of a sentence which we (= *Steele et al.*) have labelled AUX is a necessary (but not sufficient) condition for the sentence to be a "speech act" which expresses a truth value.

SEA attempts to derive some of the other properties mentioned above from this function of AUX. We return to this later. It is this hypothesis which if true would lead one to expect that every language will exhibit something which can be included in the equivalence class AUX. To put it more bluntly, but to my mind correctly, this hypothesis entails the universality of the category AUX. Conversely, then, the non-universality of AUX would entail the falsity of the hypothesis. I will argue in this paper, that AUX in the sense intended in ASW and SEA (differences aside) is not a universal category, or equivalence class. Hence the hypothesis cited is false in this form. In the final section however, I will discuss the possibility that some of its intuitive content might find a correct expression in some different way.

The argument will be carried out against the background of the theory of government and binding developed in Chomsky (1981b) and references cited there, with certain modifications as proposed and discussed in Reuland (1981a, b, c). In fact the argument will involve a comparison of the category AUX with the category INFL as it occurs in the rule S $\rightarrow$ NP INFL VP (where one may abstract away from the order of the constituents on the right-hand side) (cf. Chomsky (1981b) for discussion). There is a prima facie resemblance between AUX in the sense of ASW and SEA, and INFL in Chomsky's rule. There, too, the occurrence of INFL is linked to a very general consideration, viz. "that a clause at the level of logical form must contain a 'mood indicator' of some sort, namely, what we have called INFL, which may be finite or infinitival". Of course, there is a historical connection between AUX and INFL in Chomsky's writings. Given the existence of such connections it is perhaps not superfluous to introduce explicitly the terminological convention that AUX refers to the notion in ASW/SEA, and INFL to that in the Government Binding theory (henceforth GB). The similarity between AUX and INFL resides in the fact that both are in some respects linked to notions such as tense, mood, agreement, etc. and hence the question arises whether they can be identified.

Although there are important differences, presumably, between the theoretical assumptions implicit in ASW/SEA and those of GB, they do not preclude a discussion of this question in substantive terms. I will argue then that AUX and INFL cannot be identified: it will be shown that the category INFL does not meet Steele's notional requirements, which precludes identification. Further, it will be shown, that there are languages the optimal analysis of which depends on the availability of a category with the properties of INFL. Moreover, it will be argued that in these languages the set of constituents meeting the requirements of AUX do not form a natural subcategory of the set of realizations of INFL, i.e. AUX would never be arrived at on language internal grounds, and complicates the grammar if imposed. Hence, these languages do not exhibit a category identifiable with AUX. This entails that AUX cannot be universal, and the conclusion follows that the hypothesis proposed in SEA in that form is false.

In order to facilitate interpretation of the nature of the difference between AUX and INFL I will insert some brief remarks on the relation between the notional basis of a category and its extension. We saw that both INFL and AUX are provided with a notional basis, which is rather similar. Now, notional criteria are used to identify categories in the following way. Suppose, we have a language L_1 with categories justified on internal grounds, e.g. A (with members $a_1, a_2, \ldots$), B (with members $b_1, b_2, \ldots$), etc. and we have a language L_2 with categories C (with members $c_1, c_2, \ldots$), D (with members $d_1, d_2, \ldots$), etc. (also justified on internal grounds). The question is now which of the categories of L_1 is equivalent to which category of L_2. The role of notional criteria is that they enable one to identify specific members of some category of L_1 with specific members of some category of L_2. For instance, one finds that $a_2, a_3, a_5, a_7, a_{11}$, etc. notionally correspond with

d_4, d_9, d_{25}, d_{49}, d_{121}, etc. but no member of A corresponds to any member of C. One will conclude then that category A in L_1 corresponds with category D of L_2 and not for instance with C. However, either category may, and probably will, contain members for which no equivalence can be established with respect to members of the other category.

To phrase this differently, notional criteria can be used to establish the names (i.e. the cross-linguistic equivalence of syntactic classes, not their membership (cf. Lyons (1968)). For establishing the membership one needs to make use of 'formal criteria'. In fact there is no guarantee against the occurrence of discrepancies between different sets of notional criteria, given a grammatical theory with sufficient structure. Suppose we adopt some version of $\overline{X}$-theory, which specifies relations between syntactic categories. It is now clearly a condition of adequacy on sets of notional criteria that they do not identify some X^n with some Y^n without identifying X^0 with Y^0. But, of course, this condition is not trivially met; in fact it might enable us to reject certain sets of notional criteria as misguided. One can say that the more structure a theory of grammar has, the stronger is the empirical claim embodied in the selection of one set of such criteria over another. The issue regarding the equivalent of AUX and INFL, or the absence thereof, can now be represented in the following way within $\overline{X}$ theory. Assume two approaches which employ (explicitly or implicitly) notional criteria in such a way that they identify as S a single set of categories. If these two $\overline{X}$ approaches do not identify the head of S in the same way, then one of them must be wrong. To put it concretely: one cannot at the same time regard α and β as identical, maintain that $\alpha = \overline{\text{AUX}}$ and that $\beta = \overline{\text{INFL}}$, and that AUX $\neq$ INFL. The only option available for someone who wishes to maintain that $\alpha = \beta$ and AUX $\neq$ INFL is to deny that AUX/INFL is the head of α/β. To the extent that it can be shown that either AUX or INFL behaves as the head of α/β this option becomes untenable. Part of the ensuing argument will be devoted to showing that the head of S has the properties of INFL. I take it to be clear from this discussion that I do not reject the use of notional definitions, but rather want to stress, that as with any kind of criterion with empirical import, they do not provide us with a straight route to truth, but are themselves subject to empirical evaluation.

In order to be able to present a precise account of the differences between AUX and INFL it is necessary for us first to resolve an ambiguity hidden in the definitions of AUX as they are presented in (1) and (2). The ambiguity resides in what it means for a constituent to include, or crucially contain, tense and/or modality markers (for sake of brevity I will henceforth use the term 'tense marker' to refer to such elements, i.e. this term will include modality markers). For a category C in some language to be identifiable as an AUX, is it necessary that every realization of C in a sentence contain a tense marker? Or is it sufficient that among the realizations of C some contain a tense marker, but perhaps not all of its realizations? I will label these two ways of interpreting the requirement of containment *S-contain*, and *P-contain* respectively: If C *S-contains tense* then every Syntagm into which C is expanded contains a tense marker, while if C *P-contains tense*, then *tense* is a member of the Paradigm of C, viz. one of the alternative realizations of C.

This can be illustrated as follows. Suppose for some language one could motivate on internal grounds the rules given in (3).

(3) a.   S $\rightarrow$ NP C VP

b.   C $\rightarrow$ [± tense, ± AG]

If *tense* is to be identified with [+tense] then C would P-contain, but not S-contain *tense*, and, as a consequence, could not be identified with AUX if S-containment is the relevant notion. Although the ambiguity is nowhere clearly resolved in either ASW or SEA, there are indications that S-containment is intended.[3] For instance, the 'speech act' interpretation for AUX is compatible only with S-containment. Throughout both papers only sentences comparable in status to tensed sentences in English are used to exemplify AUX. In ASW gerunds and *to*-infinitivals are analyzed explicitly as not containing AUX, similarly in SEA (Chapter 4). Appendix A of SEA is an exception in that one AUX candidate in English contains the infinitival marker *to* as one of its realizations, and is not rejected off-hand; however, it is not unequivocally adopted.[4] Given these indications I will assume that *includes* in (1) and *containing* in (2) are to be read as *S-contains* and *S-containing* respectively. I will argue that this leads to incorrect results if the head of S is identified with AUX and hence is required to S-contain *tense*, etc.; only *P*-containment can be demanded. One of the central ideas carrying the argument is that one can identify in English and Dutch some constituent as the head of *S*. It is then argued that this constituent must be INFL, not an AUX. It should be noted that this issue is to be distinguished from the issue whether there is a category of auxiliaries in English or Dutch distinct from the category of verbs. As far as this issue is concerned it could very well be the case that all traditional auxiliaries are actually main verbs, and yet in the optimal grammar one must assume a position outside the VP (an *S*-daughter),

which at the surface is always occupied by a verb, with properties different
from those of the ordinary V-position with the VP. So, the point to be made
here is different from the one made in Pullum (1981). There it is argued
that there is no separate class of auxiliaries in English, leaving one with the
possible outcome that AUX would be essentially a slot for introducing a
finite verb. Pullum draws the conclusion that if this route were taken the
case that AUX exists independently of V would just crumble away. This
conclusion would surely follow if the only categories in the grammar were
lexical categories, or projections thereof. To the extent that grammars provide
insights by also using categories consisting of grammatical formatives which
must be applied to members of lexical categories, Pullum's conclusion does
not follow.

The question as to what the properties of the head of S are derives its
import from the theory of government. The central notion of government
theory is the relation between the head of a construction and its dependents
(cf. for extensive discussion Chomsky (1981b) and the references cited there).
Much of my argumentation will hinge on what to my mind is the core of the
theory of government, which will play an important role in this article. This
idea of government (for more discussion and instantiations cf. Reuland
(1981a, b, c)) is that no constituent in the domain of a head can be governed
by a constituent outside that domain. Whenever we find a configuration of
the form:

(4) $[_{Y}n \ldots Y^0 \ldots [_{X}n \ldots Z^n \ldots X^0 \ldots] \ldots]$

with Y^0 and X^0 heads of Y^n and X^n respectively, and Z^n some constituent, it
is impossible for Z^n to be governed by Y^0, regardless of whether it is actually
governed by X^0. Conversely, I claim here that any position within some X^n
which is not in the domain of the head can be governed by a head outside this
domain. The only position meeting that requirement is the position of the
head of X^n, viz. X^0. So, if in (4) Y^0 is the head nearest to X^n, i.e. if Y^0 and
X^n are separated by $\bar{Y}$-boundaries only, then X^0 will be governed by Y^0, but
not conversely, since government requires c-command (the extended notion
of c-command discussed by Reinhart (1976) is assumed here).

This approach to government, which I will make precise in (5) and (6)
below, separates out two effects of 'being in the domain of a head'. The first
effect is that a constituent in the domain of a head, such as Z^n in (4) which
is in the domain of X^0, cannot be governed by a constituent outside that
domain; i.e. it cannot be governed by Y^0. The second effect is that of being

governed by that head. The separation of these effects, reflected in the phrase 'regardless of whether it is actually governed by X^0, derives its import from the claim that it is indeed possible for some constituent Z^n to be minimally c-commanded by some head without being governed by the latter; as a result such a constituent will end up ungoverned. The realization of this possibility depends on properties associated with the category of the head; these reflect the fundamental distinction between categories which are, and those which are not proper governors in the sense of Kayne (1981a, b), Chomsky (1981b), and much other recent work. This distinction is manifested syntactically in the fact that only proper governors unconditionally allow extraction of an element in their domain (by Wh-movement, or NP-movement). Extraction out of the domain of a head which is not a proper governor is possible only when, besides the usual conditions on movement rules, some special condition is satisfied. For instance extraction out of the subject position of tensed clauses (the domain of Agreement) may depend on deletion of the complementizer (the 'that-trace effect'). Likewise, if preposition stranding is to be admissible the PP may have to be within the VP (cf. Pesetsky (to appear), Weinberg and Hornstein (1981), Kayne (1981a, b), Chomsky (1981b)). It is currently assumed that the relevant difference between the two kinds of governors is that the proper governors are the lexical categories, i.e. they are positively specified for at least one lexical feature: [+N, −V] (=N), [−N, +V] (=V) and [+N, +V] (= A). The category P(reposition) is not a lexical category in this sense, being specified as [−N, −V]. Thus, the relation of proper government is not a purely structural relation between a head position and a complement position, but is a relation holding only if the head meets certain requirements. In the same vein, I will be assuming that the relation of government is not purely structural. Only the opacity with respect to outside governors is purely structural. The opacity is induced by any head. This structural relation is made precise as the notion of a *governing domain*:

(5) b is in the **governing domain** of a iff

    (i) $a = X^0$ (X = N, A, V, P, Comp, INFL),

    (ii) a and b are contained in X^i and a is the head of X^i,

    (iii) there is no c such that (a) $c = Y^0$ and (b) c and b are contained in Y^i and c is the head of Y^i, unless Y^i contains a.

It is the governing domain of a, a being some head, which is opaque to outside government. Only if a is a lexical head in the sense discussed above will it be the case that the set of positions in the governing domain of *a* automatically coincides with the set of positions governed by *a*.

In this paper we are primarily concerned with INFL, as the head of S, and with its properties as a governor. The properties of INFL as a governor will depend in part on its feature content. Unless it is [+F] for some relevant feature F, INFL, like P will never itself be a lexical governor. The feature content of INFL is not, in fact, a straightforward matter. Here I will simply put forward some relevant considerations and on the basis of these will adopt a tentative hypothesis.

A standard proposal in the literature is that clauses are either tensed or tenseless, and either do, or don't contain an agreement marker. The values for tense and agreement are both taken to be realized on the inflection of a clause. Hence we find that INFL $\longrightarrow$ [±tense (AG)]. It is usually assumed that AG may only appear if INFL = [+tense]. In the next section, on NP-ing constructions in English, it will be argued however, that the choice of AG is actually independent of the value of the tense parameter. Hence the rule should read INFL $\longrightarrow$ [±tense, ±AG]. That is, the theory must be constructed so as to allow tenseless finite clauses. In fact, it can be argued that the theory must make this option available anyhow, given the opacity phenomena in certain tenseless clauses in Turkish (cf. George and Kornfilt (1981)) and the properties of the inflected infinitive in Portuguese (cf. e.g. Rouveret (1979) and Zubizarreta (1980)). Both are argued to be finite and tenseless.

In addition it has been proposed that AG is actually a nominal element (cf. Chomsky (1981b), Reuland (1980c) and references cited there). As such it is taken to be a nonmaximal projection in a nonargument position. It might be seen as more or less comparable to a clitic. If this is correct, AG can be regarded as an abbreviation of the feature complex [+N, −V], that is, a Nominal element. It is then tempting to try to do away with AG in the feature analysis of INFL. Clauses where AG is present simply contain an inflection realized as [±tense, +N, −V]. However, the case where AG is absent does not seem to find a natural representation under this proposal, i.e. [±tense, −AG] cannot be represented as [±tense, −[+N, −V]]. Rather, if one set of options is to be represented as [±tense, +N, −V] one would expect the full set of options to be given by [±tense, ±N, ±V]. I would like to suggest now, that such a view of the set of realizations of INFL is not at all implausible.

It is fairly obvious that it is the choice of the inflection which to a large extent determines the way a subordinate clause is to be construed. If the verb bears participial inflection, the clause can appear as an adverbial or attributive modifier, but cannot for instance appear in argument position. If the verb bears a finite inflection, the clause appears in argument position, unless some specific choice of a clause introducer facilitates its occurrence in another type of position. *To*-infinitivals occur in argument position but also as attributive modifiers. Very roughly then, participial clauses seem to exhibit adjectival characteristics, finite clauses nominal characteristics, and *to*-infinitivals look as if they contain a preposition in the Inflection position with concomitant characteristics (cf. Reuland (1979) for more discussion, mainly based on Dutch).

It is quite natural, now, to assume that the adjectival/adverbial character of a clause with participial inflection reduces to its INFL having the relevant features, i.e. to INFL being realized as $[-\text{tense}, +\text{N}, +\text{V}]$. Similarly, the fact that *to*-infinitivals contain a preposition-like marker (which as we will see, does indeed crucially behave like a preposition in Dutch, as well as in English) can now be straightforwardly made to follow from the fact that there is a prepositional option for INFL, viz. $[-\text{tense}, -\text{N}, -\text{V}]$.

As matters stand, the hypothesis that the general rule for expanding INFL, is given by INFL $\longrightarrow$ $[\pm\text{tense}, \pm\text{N}, \pm\text{V}]$, is still tentative. It is not clear that all values it specifies are indeed realized. If some of its values turned out to be never realized this would naturally require explanation. Certainly it seems clear that some feature combinations are far more common than others. For instance, $[-\text{tense}, +\text{N}, -\text{V}]$ with $[+\text{N}, -\text{V}]$ realizing agreement seems to be far less common than its tensed counterpart. Similarly, it can be argued that English contains tensed participial clauses ($[+\text{tense}, +\text{N}, +\text{V}]$), as in [*while walking in his garden*] *Rudy devised some new tricks* (cf. Reuland (1980c) for discussion), but again this seems to be a marked property. An extensive discussion of these issues would lead us beyond the scope of this article. Hence, I will not pursue them here. For the purpose of this article I will in general adopt the idea that INFL is realized as $[\pm\text{tense}, \pm\text{N}, \pm\text{V}]$ though I will often use the more conservative notation $[\pm\text{tense}, \pm\text{AG}]$. Importantly, any specific point made, could have been made on the basis of the assumption that this notation is in fact correct, and that other realizations of INFL have to be specifically stipulated and do not fall out as consequences of such a general schema. The general schema has been adopted since it seems to be conceptually so much simpler.

Notice that it is a consequence of the proposed representation of the $[+\text{AG}]$ option that a $[+\text{AG}]$ INFL would appear to be a proper governor. For INFL when it is $[+\text{AG}]$ contains $[+\text{N}]$: $[+\text{tense}, +\text{N}, -\text{V}]$, and in terms of the discussion immediately above (5) this makes it close to being a proper governor. We shall see directly, when proper government is precisely defined (in (7)), that in fact this is not true, since it has no complements of its own. There is yet another possible barrier to AG in finite clauses governing material such as the subject in a purely structural way. Since the AG is in a sense 'seg-mentalized' with respect to the *tense* feature, it might well be that AG itself does not really c-command that material. Hence, some additional requirement must be met if AG is to govern the subject position and cause (nominative) Case to be assigned. For sake of concreteness I will adopt a generalization of a proposal by Stowell (1980). In order to account for existential constructions in English such as *there are three men in the room*, Stowell proposes that (nominative) Case is first assigned to *there*, and then floats off to *three men*. He implements this proposal by arguing that the rule Move α be generalized so as to also cover Move Case. This idea can be generalized over all cases of nominative Case assignment to the subject of finite clauses. In finite clauses [+N, −V] in INFL is independently realized as AG as proposed above. I will assume now that AG is assigned Case under conditions to be discussed below, but anyhow, when the clause is tensed. It is this Case which floats off to the subject position. This Case movement brings about coindexing between AG and the subject. This coindexing will now be taken to be the necessary requirement on government by AG. I.e. the subject NP is governed by AG iff this NP is in the governing domain of AG (= the governing domain of INFL), and is coindexed with AG.

This discussion of government is summarized and slightly extended in (6).

> (6)   *a* governs *b* if
>
>   (i) *b* is in the governing domain of *a*, and
>
>   (ii) *a* is [+N] or [+V] (viz. *a* = N, A, V, a preposition cosuperscripted with a verb, or a suitable value of INFL: the lexical, or **structural governors**), or
>
>   (iii) (i) holds and *a* = P and *b* satisfies a strict subcategorization feature of *a*; or
>
>   (i) holds and *a* = AG, *a* is coindexed with *b* by Move Case.

It follows from (6) that the prepositional INFL, lacking features, does not govern the subject. Yet it creates an opaque domain with respect to an out-side governor. As a consequence, the subject position is ungoverned. Hence, it is realized as PRO (cf. the discussion of the binding theory below). Participles realize the option [±tense, +N, +V]; hence, in this case INFL is a structural governor of the subject position. Yet the subject of participial clauses is PRO as in [*PRO walking in his garden*] *Rudy devised some new tricks*. Following Chomsky I will assume that the rule R of Affix Hopping is available in both syntax and phonology. If it applies in the syntax, the result is that at S-structure the PRO-subject is only governed by the trace of the inflection. Hence, it is not governed by a lexical feature in the sense of (6). Yet, this trace of inflection will prevent a governor outside its domain from governing the subject. Thus, the latter is ungoverned and realized as PRO as required. It should be noted that under this approach the PRO-drop parameter is specifically associated with the conditions under which AG, i.e. a segmentalized nominal inflection, governs the subject, and whether it can move into the VP. Other types of inflection may undergo R freely, independent from this parameter.

I mentioned that one of the characteristics distinguishing between proper (or lexical, or structural) governors on the one hand, and prepositions and Inflection on the other, was that only proper governors allow extraction of their complement without special conditions. In the framework adopted this is represented in the following way: a constituent moved by Move α leaves a trace; this trace must satisfy the empty category principle (ECP). The ECP requires that a trace be properly governed under (7) (cf. Chomsky (1981b, p. 274)).

(7)   *b* is **properly governed** by *a* iff *b* is governed by *a* (*a* a *structural governor*) and *b* is in the complement of *a*.

Below, we shall see that not only the first, but also the second clause of this definition is quite crucial. In particular, INFL has no complements, and hence is not a *proper* governor even when it is by (6 ii) a *structural* governor.

Given this approach to government, the question whether the head of S has the properties of AUX or those of INFL receives an immediate empirical interpretation: Is it only in tensed (or comparable) clauses that an NP outside the VP is in an opaque position with respect to outside governors, or does this hold true of tenseless clauses as well? Although the question is formulated in general terms, it will be obvious that the NP position involved in the question is that of the subject NP. In order to see that this is the relevant question to ask, consider the structure ... $[_{VP}V[_{\bar{S}}[_S NP^* \text{ INFL VP}]]]$ ... (for ease of reference I will follow the practice in Chomsky (1981b) of singling out some relevant constituent by marking it with '*'). In a structure where Comp is absent nothing but the presence of INFL prevents NP* from being governed by the matrix verb (notice that I have not introduced any notion like that of being an absolute barrier to government, cf. Chomsky (1981a), and Chomsky (1981b), where $\bar{S}$ is such a barrier). Nothing else is needed in the framework defined by (5): INFL, being the head of S, sets up an opaque domain barring government of NP* by V. Suppose now, that only AUXES are possible heads of S. In that case we would expect NP* to be governed by the matrix verb whenever the S is tenseless. For if there is no *tense* there is by definition no AUX. If AUX is head of S then S lacks a head and we would expect 'exceptional government/Case marking' to be the rule in tenseless sentences — and not only in English but generally. To put this in another way: we would expect there to be no difference between tenseless full clauses and small clauses, clauses consisting of a subject and an NP, AP, or PP predicate (like α in *I consider* [α *John ill*]). There are, however, essential differences between tenseless full clauses and small clauses, with respect to government of the subject position by the matrix verb. These differences are precisely those which one would expect under the assumption that full clauses do, and small clauses do not contain INFL (cf. Stowell (1981) for more discussion of small clauses). It will be one of the main descriptive aims of this article to show that opacity phenomena show up in tensed and tenseless full clauses alike. This in turn will show us that even tenseless full clauses contain a realization of INFL. This is so, because the presence of INFL in a clause is the only possible source for opacity of the subject position with respect to outside governors. Since, as we saw, the difference between INFL and AUX is that INFL P-contains tense, but AUX must S-contain it, opacity phenomena in tenseless clauses not only show that they have a head, viz. INFL, but also lead to the conclusion that the head of S in general is to be identified with INFL rather than with AUX in the languages for which the argument holds. Hence AUX is not a universal category.

A specific hypothesis about the relation of INFL (or AUX for that matter) to S, or a specific proposal as to what is the core of a theory of government, cannot be supplied with absolute proof. At best it can be shown that they are consistent with some body of known facts, and in addition provide insights not previously available; it is the interest of these new insights which ultimately justifies their adoption. We shall show now that there are interesting insights made available under the approach to government advanced above, together with the hypothesis that INFL rather than AUX is the head of S.

1. NP-*ING* CONSTRUCTIONS IN ENGLISH

The first type of clause to be investigated is the NP-*ing* construction in English. Examples are given in (8).

(8) a. The girls kept house for John, *he* being a bachelor.

    b. The hunchback hated nice people being hanged.

    c. The architects favored each other being placed upon the investigations committee.

(8a) represents the 'absolute nominative' construction, (8b, c) the ACC-*ing* construction (Cf. Horn, 1975). Since it appears to be uncontroversial that these constructions are not tensed in the sense required for their head to be identifiable with AUX, I will not argue that point here. Horn (1975) shows that ACC-*ing* constructions are clauses, arguments along the lines of Williams (1975) support that contention. See Reuland (1980c) for a full discussion. The point which is relevant here, is that they must be analyzed as *finite* tense-less clauses, and in order for the argument to go through the domain of their head must be opaque to outside governors. Tensedness relates to the possibility of time reference independently from the matrix clause. Finiteness is related to agreement; since agreement markings are often realized by null formatives, in general the question whether there is agreement in a construction is only meaningful in so far as it can be answered on the basis of certain formal characteristics of the way the subject NP is governed by some verb form. In this vein, the question whether NP-*ing* clauses are finite reduces to the question whether the subject NP is governed on the basis of principle (6iii, second clause). This I will argue to be the case.

If one wants to assess in which way some NP is governed, several factors enter into the considerations. One factor is the Case which has been assigned. A second source of evidence, is how NPs in that position behave with respect to the binding theory. Thirdly, the behavior of that position under extractions plays an important role. In order to facilitate discussion I will give a brief statement of the relevant principles.

Case is assigned by the principles given in (9):

(9) a.   NP has objective Case if it is governed by V.

   b.   NP has oblique Case if is is governed by P.

   c.   NP has nominative Case if it is governed by AG.

The main features of clausal structure are given in (10).

(10) a. $\bar{S}$ → (Comp) S.

   b.   S   → NP INFL VP (possibly separated by adverbial material).

   c.   VP   → V ... where ... contains the material subcategorized for by V.

   d.   INFL → [± tense, ± AG].

   e.   Comp → ± Wh.

The expansion of INFL in (10d) expresses the fact that clauses are tensed or tenseless, and may be either finite (when [+AG] is present) or non-finite (when the option [−AG] is chosen). Of course, the usual assessment is that these properties are not independent, i.e. [+tense] always goes together with [+AG], and [−tense] (as in infinitival clauses) goes together with [−AG]. Here I will argue that these parameters may be independently fixed.

The essentials of the binding theory are given in (11) (cf. Chomsky (1981b)).

(11) a.   an anaphor is bound in its governing category,

b.   a pronominal is free in its governing category,

c.   an R-expression is free.

The notion of a governing category is given in (12).

(12) b is a governing category for a if and only if b is the minimal category containing a, a governor of a, and a SUBJECT (accessible to a).

The notion of binding referred to in (11) is A-binding: being coindexed with a c-commanding constituent in an argument position (argument positions are the base NP positions in S or NP, not operators, INFL, etc.). If an argument is not bound it is free. R-expressions are the referential expressions: non-pronominal non-anaphoric NPs and variables, i.e. the Case marked traces left by Wh-movement, etc. The term SUBJECT in the definition of governing category in (12) refers to the most prominent nominal element in an S or NP. In finite clauses the SUBJECT is AG, in non-finite clauses it is the traditional subject (the notion of accessibility does not play a role in this paper, so for discussion I refer to Chomsky's book). Since adjectives and nouns are governors, but not Case assigners, it is possible for an NP to have a governing category without being Case marked (its only grammatical value is then *trace of NP-movement*). PRO, the realization of NP in control structures, is a pronominal anaphor. Therefore it is subject to both principles (11a) and (11b) of the binding theory. As a consequence PRO must be ungoverned; otherwise a conflict arises, yielding ungrammaticality (but cf. recent work by Koster for an alternative view of some instances of PRO).

The third factor mentioned, extraction, is relevant because of the possible occurrence of ECP effects (the definition of ECP has been given above definition (7). If we find ECP effects, this may give us an indication that a certain position is not governed by a lexical governor.

All this has provided sufficient background to proceed with the actual discussion of these NP-*ing* constructions. Any analysis of the absolute nominative construction must account for the following properties: apparently the subject has nominative Case;[6] the subject may not be a lexical anaphor, the subject may be optionally realized as PRO; extraction from these constructions is impossible. The last property is shared with all clauses in non-subcategorized positions; therefore it can be kept out of our considerations. The fact that the subject may be lexical entials that there must be some principle by which it is assigned Case; the fact that it may not be a lexical anaphor, illustrated by the ungrammaticality of structures such as *the rabbits kept chasing the cats, [$_\bar{S}$ each other following closely]*, shows that this Case must be assigned in such a way that the Nominative-*ing* construction itself comes out as the governing category of the subject. For, *each other*, being an anaphor, must be bound in its governing category. In the example given *each other* is free in the $\bar{S}$ adverbial clause, but it is bound in the matrix clause, viz. the latter contains suitable antecedents. Therefore, in order to account for its ungrammaticality one must assume that the $\bar{S}$ *each other following closely* is the relevant governing category of *each other*. Given the definition of *governing category* in (6), this entails that the construction must contain both a SUBJECT, distinct from the subject, and a governor. The following hypothesis yields precisely the required results: -*ing* is a realization of AG; i.e. in tenseless clauses AG is optionally present; if present it is realized as -*ing*.

Thus the structure of the absolute nominative construction can be represented as in (13).

(13)   ... [$_\bar{S}$ $\emptyset$ [$_S$NP [INFL [AG-ing]] VP]] ....

Case assignment and government by AG is based on application of the rule Move Case, mentioned earlier, which floats the Case off AG onto the subject NP. The grammar must contain some principle assigning nominative Case to AG in tensed clauses. In order to account for nominative assignment in (8a) this principle will have to be modified. So we will adopt the formulation in (14).

(14)   AG has nominative Case

   (i) if it cooccurs with tense, or

   (ii) if it is ungoverned.

Since AG in (13) is ungoverned (and the clause tenseless) (14 ii) applies and nominative is assigned to *-ing*. If Move Case applies, the subject receives this Case, and as a consequence it may be lexical. If it is a lexical anaphor it is governed in S. Since *-ing* is AG, it is the SUBJECT of S. Hence S is the governing category of the subject; therefore if that is an anaphor it must be bound in S. This condition cannot be met, hence the ungrammaticality. On the other hand if the subject is a pronoun it may be coreferential with an NP in the matrix clause; this also follows from the result that the S in (13) is the governing category of the subject.

In tensed clauses in English the subject may never be PRO, but in NP-*ing* constructions PRO is generally admissible. This I will take to follow from a stipulated difference between *-ing* and the realization of AG in tensed clauses. In tensed clauses AG = PRO, and hence cannot retain the Case assigned by (14) since PRO may not have a governing category. Hence Move Case has to apply. In *-ing* clauses AG is nominal but not PRO; hence Case can be retained. Therefore Move Case need not apply. If Move Case does not apply, there is no coindexing between NP and AG, therefore NP is not governed, and hence it may be realized as PRO. Thus the relevant properties of nominative-*ing* constructions have been derived (using only independently established principles) from the hypothesis that *-ing* = AG, from the extension of the nominative rule in (14 ii), and from the stipulation that *-ing* ≠ PRO.

Notice, that it is precisely the hypothesis that *-ing* is a realization of INFL which plays a crucial role in establishing the connection between the properties of this construction and the general theoretical principles explaining them. Hence, I take the analysis as evidence in favor of this hypothesis. We will now show that the essential features of this account are also essential in providing a general account of the properties of the constructions in (8b, c), the ACC-*ing* constructions.

Any grammar of English must provide an explanation for the following properties of these constructions: (1) the NP in subject position has objective Case; (2) this NP (and other NPs) may undergo long Wh-movement; (3) it may not undergo NP-movement (e.g. when the matrix verb is passive); (4) the governing category for the subject position is the matrix clause; (5) quantifiers such as *every* in this position strongly favor a narrow scope interpretation with respect to a Wh-item extracted from object position; (6) the subject NP is optionally realized as PRO. This collocation of properties is quite remarkable: (2), (3), and (5) are shared with tensed clauses; (1) and (4) are shared with infinitival complements of verbs such as *believe*; (3) and (6),

finally, are shared with infinitival complements of *want*-type verbs. Property
(1) is exemplified by one case of (8b). Property (4) is exemplified by (8c),
where *each other* takes *the architects* as its antecedent. Property (2) is illustrated in (15).

(15)   Who would you hate [*t* being elected president]?

Property (3) is illustrated in (16) and contrasted with the complement of an
exceptional Case marker (which happens to be the same verb with a slightly
different meaning).

(16) a.   I understand [John behaving foolishly].

  b.* John was understood [*t* behaving foolishly].

  c.   I understand [John to behave foolishly].

  d.   John was understood [*t* to behave foolishly].

The examples in (17) illustrate property (5).

(17) a.   What do you expect everyone to eat?

        Answer: (i)   Well, the caviar!

             (ii)   Well, Bill meat, Johnny fish, and Cindy caviar!

  b.   What would you hate everyone eating?

        Answer: (i)   Well, the caviar!

             (ii) * Well, Bill meat, Johnny fish, and Cindy caviar!

I.e. the unacceptability of (17bii) as an answer to (12b) shows that the NP-
ing construction lacks a wide scope reading for *everyone* in subject position.
Properties (3) and (5) together show clearly that the relation between the
matrix verb and the subject of the complement in ACC-*ing* constructions
must be considerably different from that in constructions involving exceptional Case marking. In fact, it suggests an ECP effect. I will now show, how
these and other properties follow from the theory developed so far (with a
slight modification), in conjunction with the hypothesis that the structure
of ACC-*ing* constructions is essentially identical to that of nominative-*ing*
constructions. The relevant structure is given in (18).

(18)   ... [$_{VP}$ V [$_{\bar{S}}$ $\emptyset$ [$_S$ NP* [$_{INFL}$ [$_{AG}$-ing]] VP]]] ....

In the text I will now be using NP* to refer to the subject (the ACC) of the ACC-*ing* construction.

Property (1) follows from the theory developed so far, in the following manner: -*ing* being nominal (since it is AG) it is visible to rules of Case assignment. Comp is $\emptyset$, so AG is governed by the matrix verb since, by assumption, it is the head of S. (It is the only item within S which may be governed by a governor outside S.) Hence it will receive objective Case from V; objective Case is the only Case available, since (14) is inapplicable (for -*ing* is governed by V). When -*ing* has been assigned (objective) Case, this Case optionally floats off onto NP* (in this respect the situation is fully comparable to that in nominative-*ing* constructions); as a consequence NP* will be assigned objective Case. (It must be noted that property (1), though compatible with the theory presented, is also compatible with immediate Case assignment by V to NP*.)

Property (6) follows without further stipulation from this account: as in the nominative-*ing* constructions, -*ing* may optionally retain its Case. If it does, NP* is ungoverned: it is not governed by AG, since this would require the coindexing brought about by Move Case, and it is not governed by the matrix verb either, since the presence of -*ing* as a realization of INFL precludes this. When NP* is ungoverned, as a result of the non-application of Move Case, it must be PRO.

Property (3) is derived in the following manner. If the matrix verb is passive, it does not assign a θ-role to its subject. So the subject must derive this role from another position. The only position available is the subject position of the complement. We must then take it that the matrix subject has been moved to its surface position (i.e. the position of *John* in (16b)) from the complement subject position. This movement leaves a trace, indicated in (16b). This trace is not governed. It cannot be governed by *understood*, since the presence of -*ing* precludes this. It cannot be governed by -*ing* either, since -*ing* can only be a governor by virtue of having a Case to assign; but it has no Case. (If -*ing* were to govern NP* one still would find a violation of ECP, since AG is not a *proper* governor.) Since these are the only possibilities, the sentence is necessarily ungrammatical.

The possibility of long Wh-movement out of the subject position is not incompatible with this account: here, the trace does not give rise to a violation of the ECP, since, on the assumption of successive cyclic movement, the NP-*ing* construction being an $\bar{S}$, its COMP will contain a trace coindexed with the trace in subject position, and as a consequence the ECP will be met (cf. Reuland (1980c) for a discussion of the nature of the mechanism involved).[7]

On the other hand, it is impossible to construe the quantifier *everyone* in (17b) as having wide scope with respect to *what*, although such construal is possible in (17a). This difference follows under the assumptions entertained: *-ing* being a realization of AG, it is a governor, but not a proper governor. As a consequence, the trace left by QR applying at the level of logical form is not properly governed. Unlike what happens in long Wh-movement, the raised quantifier does not pass through COMP; so COMP will not be coindexed with the trace of the quantifier, and the ECP will be violated (cf. May (1978) and Kayne (1981a) for discussion of QR).

Property (4), finally, follows from the consideration that *-ing*, though a governor and a SUBJECT, is not a *governor in the complement*. It can only be a governor by virtue of having a Case to assign. Since Case is assigned by the matrix verb, *-ing* can only be a governor of the ACC in the minimal category containing both *-ing* and the matrix verb, which is the matrix clause. Hence, in the case of ACC-*ing* constructions the governing category of the ACC is the matrix clause.

The conclusion is that the subject of NP-*ing* constructions behaves as if it governed by Agreement; the hypothesis that *-ing* realizes Agreement explains this behavior. So, NP-*ing* constructions will have to be analyzed as tenseless finite clauses. In the beginning of this section it was said that in order for the argument to go through, it would still have to be shown that the domain of the head of these constructions is opaque to outside governors. And in fact this follows from the possibility of examples such as *I would hate* [$_{@}$*PRO going to that party*] besides *I would hate* [$_{@}$*Bill going to that party*]. Here and henceforth I use @ to cover S, and $\bar{S}$ boundaries and both S and $\bar{S}$ together. The possibility of PRO in the first example shows that it is in an opaque domain with respect to government by *hate*. Under the theory of government adopted, this implies that @ has a head. Only on the basis of the hypothesis that @ is clausal is it possible to explain the phenomena discussed. Yet @ is tenseless, but finite, as we saw. So we have to conclude that in this case we have an S, the head of which has the properties of INFL; not those of AUX. This is what we set out to argue.[8]

Given this result one might wonder about the status of the infinitival marker *to*. Is it, too, a realization of INFL, and therefore a possible head of S? This issue will be discussed in the next section.

2. THE INFINITIVAL MARKER *TO* AS A REALIZATION OF INFL

In the linguistic literature one finds a quite general reticence regarding the precise nature of the infinitival marker *to*. The analysis in Chomsky (1973) where *to* is represented as an alternative sui generis to Aux as such seems quite representative. Chomsky (1973) is therefore compatible with the opinion of ASW that infinitivals lack an AUX. On the other hand, the literature generally agrees that *to* occurs outside the VP, i.e. the structure of infinitival clauses is taken to be basically the one given in (19).

(19)   [$_{\bar{S}}$ COMP [$_S$ NP* to VP]] .

For most authors (19) is motivated mainly because *to* is in the residue of the clause after VP-deletion. This still does not clarify its status. I will now claim that infinitival clauses contain a realization of INFL, and that in fact INFL is realized as *to*. On the conceptual level this follows Chomsky (1981) who claims that any clause must be characterized as either [+ tense] or [−tense] and that it is the category INFL which carries such features. So, infinitival clauses being [−tense] must contain an occurrence of the category INFL.

However, given the theory of government adopted, the claim that infinitival clauses S-contain INFL has further theoretical consequences: given that INFL is the head of S, this hypothesis will enable us to explicate the notion of $\bar{S}$-deletion in terms of independently needed principles. To the extent that this explication is successful, it constitutes independent motivation for INFL as the head of infinitival clauses, and as a consequence, against having only AUX in the strict sense acting in the capacity of head of S.

The proposal that exceptional Case marking in the complement of *believe*-type verbs, or exceptional government in the complement of raising verbs requires a process of $\bar{S}$-deletion, originates in the On Binding framework, where it is stipulated in the theory of government that certain boundaries, viz. NP and $\bar{S}$ constitute absolute barriers to government. I.e. it is never possible for any governor to govern across such a boundary. This is exemplified in the sentence *John tries* [$_{\bar{S}}$ [$_S$ *PRO to write a paper*]] . PRO is not governed by *tries* because of the intervening $\bar{S}$-boundary. In order to derive the proper result in *John believed* [$_@$ *Bill to be a fool*] and *John seems* [$_@$ *t to be an idiot*] Chomsky proposed that in these examples @ does not contain an $\bar{S}$-boundary, but rather only an S-boundary. Under the assumption that all clausal complements are derived from $\bar{S}$ at D-structure, it must be taken to follow that exceptional government requires that some rule delete the $\bar{S}$-brackets around the complement. However, a rule deleting only bracketing, not involving the terminal string is quite unprecedented. So, any account in which $\bar{S}$-deletion can be explicated in terms of principles which are needed anyhow, can be taken to constitute progress. Notice now, that under the theory of government adopted here it is not a property of boundaries that they are opaque to government, but rather one of domains of heads. Thus the opacity of the complement of *try* implies the presence of a head in that complement. Given now the assumption that all infinitival clauses contain a realization of INFL, the opacity of the complement of *try* follows without stipulation. And in fact, this can be generalized to all Germanic languages having a cognate of *to* in the capacity of an infinitival marker. In all of these cases presence of a cognate of *to* in principle implies that the subject of the complement cannot be governed by the matrix verb. On the other hand, it also follows from the definition of government presented in (5, 6) that INFL does not cause its subject to be governed unless it meets specific requirements, for example that it contains AG, where AG realizes the [+N, −V] option. By taking *to*-infinitivals to realize the option [−tense, −N, −V] we simply make it follow from the principles of government that in *to*-infinitivals the subject is ungoverned: in this case INFL does not contain a positive specification for any lexical feature, hence none of the clauses in (6) implying government applies: INFL is not a structural governor, i.e. INFL cannot simply govern the constituents in its governing domain, since (6ii) is not satisfied; and, taking a *to*-INFL at its face value, viz. that of a preposition in the position of INFL, we also see that (6iii) is not satisfied: *to* is not AG, and the subject is not subcategorized for by *to*.

The general prediction is now that no exceptional government is possible unless something happens; the interest of the analysis, of course, resides in what we claim can happen. The basic idea, due to Kayne (1981a, b) (cf. Reuland (1981b) for somewhat more discussion) is that the possibility for exceptional government in some language is linked to the possibility of preposition stranding, i.e. the possibility for prepositions to act as structural governors governing blindly any position in their governing domain (as in (6ii)). Kayne proposes that a preposition governed by a verb may acquire a superscript from the latter. A preposition with a superscript in a sense inherits its governing properties from the relevant verb, i.e. it governs like a verb. This accounts for the possibility of P-stranding under Wh-movement.

In order for P-stranding under NP-movement to be grammatical, a narrower link between verb and preposition is required (cf. Weinberg and Hornstein (1981)). In fact, under the binding theory in Chomsky (1981) NP-movement is only possible, if the resulting trace does not have Case, since a Case marked trace is a variable and must be bound by an element that is not in an argument position (a variable being an R-expression in the sense of (11), a coindexed item in an argument position would violate the requirement that R-expressions be free). So, if one is to derive *John was depended on t* from *e was depended on John* one has to assume not only that *on* assigns Case like a verb, but actually that *on* assigns the Case of the verb form it is associated with, viz. no Case if the verb appears in participial form (under the assumption that participles are not Case assigners). This assumption is also necessary if the passive rule proposed in Chomsky (1981) is to be adopted (cf. (20)).

(20) (I) [NP, S] does not receive a θ-role.

    (II) [NP, VP] does not receive Case within VP, for some choice of NP in VP.

If the derived position of *John* is to be a non-θ-position, as required, *t* may not be in a Case position in the above examples; so, *on* really must assign the Case of *depended*, rather than some Case of its own. I will refer to this kind of relation between a verb and a preposition as *reanalysis*. Notice that the occurrence of reanalysis is dependent on specific properties of the items involved in the construction. Thus reanalysis does not take place in *e was given a book to John* between *given* and *to*, preventing **John was given a book to t*. Nor does does it apply between *wanted* and *for* in *e was wanted for John to come* preventing **John was wanted (for) to to come*.

The relation between exceptional government and preposition stranding as I conceive it is now based on the contention that the infinitival marker *to* is at the same time a realization of INFL and a preposition: it is a preposition in the position of INFL, realizing the option $[-\text{tense}, -N, -V]$, as proposed earlier. The phenomenon of $\bar{\text{S}}$-deletion, resulting in exceptional government and/or Case assignment, can now be explicated as the result of reanalyzing *to* with the verb of the matrix clause. This kind of reanalysis must be assumed to be in the grammar anyhow; what we are proposing is that it takes over the job performed by the principle of $\bar{\text{S}}$-deletion. The contention that *to* as an infinitival marker is a preposition, follows of course straightforwardly from the fact that not only *to* in English, but also its cognates in Dutch (**te**), German (**zu**), and Frisian (**to**) are homophonous to prepositions. Below, we will see that the contention that Dutch **te** is a preposition plays an important role in the explanation of a number of remarkable properties of Dutch infinitival constructions. The relevant property of *to* is that, being a preposition it does not structurally govern unless it bears a superscript.

Assuming the assignment of superscripts to depend on idiosyncratic properties of the matrix verb, we derive the following picture: *try* in *John tried [PRO to be honest]* does not assign a superscript to *to*. As a consequence *to* is not a structural governor. Since a preposition which is not a structural governor governs only positions for which it is strictly subcategorized, and since there is no reason to assume *to* to be strictly subcategorized for the NP position occupied by PRO on its left, PRO is not governed, as required. Consider now *Bill believed John to be a hero*. I assume that *believed* is marked so as to assign a superscript to the *to* in its complement; if *to* bears the superscript I take it to be subject to obligatory reanalysis in the sense given above, i.e. it assigns the Case assigned by the matrix verb. Given the fact that it assigns Case structurally, and not just to subcategorized positions, it follows that *John* in the above example will get its Case from *to* which in a sense mediates to government by *believe*. As a consequence, when *believe* appears in the form of a passive participle, and therefore does not assign Case, *to* in the complement will not assign Case either; therefore the subject of the complement has to move. If the matrix verb is a raising verb, such as *seem*, the same reasoning applies: *seem* is intransitive, and as a consequence the infinitival marker *to* in the complement does not assign Case after reanalysis either, but is rather a structural governor only.[9]

The advantages of this account which in turn argue that infinitival clauses possess an INFL, which is realized as *to*, are the following: first, the opacity of the subject position with respect to outside governors can be made to follow from the general structure of the theory, instead of being stipulated; second the phenomenon of $\bar{S}$-deletion can be explicated as an instance of a more general process. Notice that the latter explication is crucially dependent on the assumption that *to* is both in the position of the head of S, and a preposition. It must be in the position of the head of S, since otherwise it would not be governed by the matrix verb, which is needed for superscript assignment, and it must be a preposition, since otherwise the effect of superscripting, i.e. that of the preposition 'mediating' the government by the verb, would not follow as an instance of a general process relating prepositions to verbs.

The hypothesis that infinitival clauses are not headless, in conjunction with the approach to government advanced, also helps explain the general difference between infinitival clauses and small clauses. Small clauses are constructions involving a subject predicated by a constituent which does not contain a verbal head, but for instance a PP or an AP. Given the straightforward assumption that INFL is necessarily realized on a verb, small clauses, lacking such a verb, cannot contain INFL. Since it is the presence of a head which is the source for opacity of the subject position, we will expect that

small clauses exhibit the opposite pattern to infinitival clauses, viz. that the
subject cannot be PRO. This is indeed the case, as has been discussed in
Stowell (1980b) and Chomsky (1981b). The relevant cases are illustrated
in (21).

(21) a. I consider [John/*PRO [$_{AP}$ ill]].

b. I imagined [Rudy/*PRO [$_{PP}$ in the closet]].

The view that small clauses are characterized by headlessness also accounts
in a straightforward manner for a fact which Chomsky (1981b) derives in a
different way, viz. that there are no verbs which subcategorize for an NP
followed by a small clause in the way that *persuade* subcategorizes for an NP
followed by an $\overline{S}$. Since Case assignment requires adjacency in English, the
V in *V NP [NP* XP]* could not assign Case to NP*; yet NP* cannot be PRO
since it would be governed by V, V being a structural governor. More could
be said. Here, however, it suffices to note that small clauses and infinitival
clauses exhibit precisely the differences we would expect them to under the
theory proposed, and hence the theory derives support from this behavior.

A final consideration supporting the theory advanced is provided by
strict subcategorization. In Chomsky (1965) strict subcategorization was
introduced as a local relation. In Bresnan (1970) it was argued that the
complementizer of a subordinate clause must be available for strict subcategorization by the matrix verb. As a consequence the locality requirement
cannot be sisterhood. Actually, matrix verbs do not only subcategorize for
complementizers, but also for INFL of a subordinate clause; i.e. apparently
certain verbs may require a *to*-infinitival complement while not admitting
an *-ing* complement, and the other way round. Other verbs are special in
admitting bare infinitival complements. This would seem to introduce further
latitude in the admissible subcategorization frames. It is striking, however,
that the INFL of the complement clause may only play a role in the strict
subcategorization if the Comp of the complement is empty. Since COMP is
the head of $\overline{S}$, which if present would block government of the downstairs
INFL by the matrix verb, we see, that apparently the matrix verb may
subcategorize for a specific choice of INFL only when it governs INFL. Thus
the set of admissible strict subcategorization frames finds a natural restriction
precisely under the approach advanced (cf. Reuland (1981a) for some more
discussion).

We conclude that in an optimal grammar it is inevitable to analyze *to* in
infinitival clauses, just as *-ing* in NP-*ing* constructions, as a realization of the

head of S, viz. INFL. Hence the head of S cannot be AUX in these cases either. Therefore, this section constitutes another argument to the effect that the head of S does not S-contain *tense.*

3. ON THE STATUS OF *AUX* IN DUTCH

The next subject of our investigations is the status of the AUX, or INFL, in Dutch. Discussion of this is necessary because Dutch might seem to present a prima facie counter example to the claim in ASW and SEA that AUX is a universal category, and hence might seem to warrant the conclusion that this claim is false in a more elementary way than I have been arguing so far. Current analyses of Dutch either imply that there is no separate constituent at all outside the VP as a bearer of tense, modality, agreement, etc., or else, if they employ an element like INFL outside the VP, are hardly committed to that position.[10] So, generally, the features associated with AUX in ASW and SEA, are thought of as features on the main verb of the clause in Dutch, base generated in the VP, if a VP is assumed at all. Traditional auxiliaries are then analyzed as main verbs taking sentential complements (Evers (1975)). I will set out to argue that this view of Dutch in which it constitutes a simple counter example to the claims in ASW and SEA is incorrect. I think that there is good evidence that there is an Aux-like constituent in Dutch (I use this as a term neutral between AUX in the technical sense and INFL in the technical sense).

There are two kinds of evidence in favor of such an Aux-like constituent in Dutch. One kind of evidence is essentially neutral to the main point we want to establish with respect to the claims in ASW and SEA. This is evidence based on the phenomenon of VP-preposing in Dutch. It simply shows that there must be a position outside the VP containing tensed auxiliaries, hence arguing for a structure of Dutch which is much closer to that of English than what is usually assumed. This evidence will be reviewed in an appendix to this article.

The second kind of evidence is based on opacity phenomena in infinitival clauses; this evidence is directly connected to the issues treated in the preceding section. The logic of the arguments is similar. The facts are more striking. There are phenomena in Dutch infinitival clauses which seem to defy any reason. They will, however, turn out to be not at all surprising given the analysis of INFL proposed earlier, the theory of government adopted, and properties of Dutch prepositions which have to be assumed for independent reasons. Since this kind of evidence shows that tenseless clauses in Dutch must be taken to contain an Aux-like constituent as their head, it shows at the same time that Dutch contains INFL, and not AUX as the relevant category.

3.1. Control Structures in Dutch

One of the characteristic facts about Dutch infinitival constructions is that there appears to be a conspiracy against preverbal complement clauses containing an infinitival verb. The question to be answered is: Why?

The standard case of this conspiracy is illustrated in (22).

(22) a.* dat [$_S$ Annamaria [$_@$ PRO de mollen te vangen] belooft
        that   Annamaria   the moles to catch   promises

    b. dat [$_S$ Annamaria e_i belooft [$_@$ PRO de   mollen te vangen]$_i$
        that   Annamaria   promises   the moles to catch

    c. dat [$_S$ Annamaria [$_@$ PRO de   mollen e_i] belooft   te vangen$_i$
        that Annamaria   the moles   promises to catch

      that Annamaria promises to catch the moles

Given the arguments in Koster (1975) to the effect that Dutch is an SOV language underlyingly, and the fact that in cases like (22c) all material of the complement turns up to the left of the matrix clause, except for the verb, (22a) must be taken to be a base structure of Dutch. However, as an S-structure, (22a) is ungrammatical as indicated. The complement either has to undergo extraposition yielding (22b), or lose its verb with inflection yielding (22c). It is assumed that this results from the application of a rule of V-raising, first discussed by Evers (1975), which moves the verb out of the complement to a position on the right of the matrix verb. It must be noted that tensed complements too are preferred in extraposed position. However, with intonational help they can be retained in the base position, whereas infinitival clauses like (22a) are beyond salvage. This indicates that the principles involved are different. Hence, tensed complements will be ignored.[11], [12]

I will show now that this conspiracy follows from the theory of government given in the introduction, in conjunction with the hypothesis that, as in English, the infinitival marker **te** is a preposition in the position of the head of the clause, i.e. is a preposition realizing INFL; no further assumptions are needed: **te** just behaves like any other preposition in preverbal position.

Crucial in the explanation is the behavior of prepositions under stranding in Dutch. Unlike French and German, there is a possibility of preposition stranding in Dutch, but unlike English, preposition stranding is rather limited. For instance, there is never stranding under NP-movement. Given the account of preposition stranding we are assuming, we must regard this as resulting from the fact that prepositions never reanalyze with a verb in the sense that they never assign the Case of that verb.

Even where there is preposition stranding it never involves extraction of an ordinary lexical NP. The only items that can be extracted are the members of a special class of so-called [+R] pronouns (cf. Van Riemsdijk (1978) for discussion of the basic features of preposition stranding in Dutch). As far as Wh-movement is concerned, extraction is limited to the single lexical item **waar** 'where'. This fact is illustrated in (23)/(24).

(23) $\begin{cases} \text{* Welk boek} \\ \text{* Wat} \end{cases}$ heb je $10 voor t betaald?

   $\begin{cases} \text{Which book} \\ \text{What} \end{cases}$ have you $10 for   paid

   Which book/what have you paid $10 for?

(24)   Waar heb je $10 t voor betaald?
       Where have you $10   for   paid
       What did you pay $10 for?

The trace in (24) precedes the preposition, given the fact that in PPs containing such a +R pronoun this pronoun always precedes the preposition. This is illustrated in (25).

(25)   Je   hebt $10 daarvoor betaald. (* voordaar,   * voor dat)
       you have $10 therefor paid   forthere   for   that
       You have paid $10 for that.

Limited though this type of stranding is, it is still further restricted as to the environments in which it is allowed. Preposition stranding in Dutch can never take place in positions to the right of the D-position of the verb. So, although there is in Dutch a principle by which many PPs including nearly all subcategorized PPs are allowed freely in positions on the right of the S-final verb, wh-movement with stranding is impossible from that position. Compare (24) with (26).

(26) a. * Waar   heb   je $10   betaald t   voor?
       Where have you $10   paid   for

What have you paid $10 for?

   b. Je   hebt $10   betaald voor   dat   boek.
       you have $10   paid   for   that book

You have paid $10 for that book.

This restriction appears to hold without exception. In general stranding seems to be best from positions adjacent to the verb, but since there are exceptions to this descriptive generalization, this is presumably not the relevant factor. In fact the general picture appears to be much like in English, viz. that stranding is possible only from positions inside the VP (Cf. Weinberg and Hornstein (1981)).

Thus, stranding is possible from positions governed by the verb (viz. at D-structure; at S-structure this government may be mediated by a trace of the verb, if it has been moved). Continuing to follow Kayne's theory of preposition stranding along the lines indicated earlier, I will claim that the verb assigns a superscript to the preposition of a PP it governs, and that the difference between positions in which stranding is possible and positions in which it is not, is representable as the difference between positions in which the preposition receives a superscript and those in which it does not. The difference between Dutch and English as regards the choice of extractable items can now be viewed as a difference in the effect of superscripting: in English after superscripting a preposition assigns Case like a verb, it is a structural Case assigner (and also a structural governor); in Dutch, after superscripting, a preposition does not become a structural Case assigner, it merely becomes a structural governor; it only governs like a verb. This stipulated difference between Dutch and English as to the effect of super-scripting accounts for the fact that in English it is possible to extract items requiring Case marking, whereas in Dutch the extractable items are non-argument expressions, which consequently do not require Case marking.

That this is the relevant difference is indicated by the fact that the extractable items in Dutch, such as **waar** 'where', **daar** 'there', are quite similar to their English cognates in that in their other uses they are simply adverbials. Hence, it is perfectly reasonable to regard them as non-arguments in all their uses. In that case, we can block extraction of all arguments from the domain of prepositions by the suggested interpretation of superscripting, namely by having the Dutch preposition never assign Case structurally. The fact that extraction is possible only out of the domain of a superscripted preposition is due to the ECP. The ECP (cf. (7)), requires that the trace be in the complement of a proper governor, the proper governors being the lexical heads and prepositions cosuperscripted with a verb, i.e. precisely the heads which blindly govern any position in their governing domain. To predict that movement, even of [+R] elements, will be restricted as observed, it will be enough that prepositions ordinarily govern positions on their right, verbs positions on their left, and that in PPs with a [+R] pronoun the relevant trace is on the left of the preposition, which the preposition cannot govern unless it governs in the manner of a verb, i.e. blindly. This it can only do after superscripting. And superscripting will only occur if it is to the left of a governing verb. For a more precise discussion I refer to my (1981b), but for the purpose of this argument the present account suffices.

This property of prepositions in Dutch now yields an explanation of the conspiracy. Consider the representation of the underlying structure of (22) given in (27).

(27)   dat $[_S$ NP $[_{VP}$ $[_@$ PRO $[_{VP}$ NP V$-]-$te] V$-]$INFL]

The notion V$-]-$INFL employed here should be taken to represent the fact that INFL is a bound morpheme which must always be realized on the verb it governs. The notation should not be taken to imply that the merge between verb and INFL has taken place, but only that at some level this merger must take place, and the fact that INFL may not be stranded. I.e. if INFL moves the verb moves along. Thus, following Chomsky's account of the PRO-drop parameter, and since Dutch is not a PRO-drop language, I will assume that this merger (Chomsky's rule R) takes place after S-structure.

Given the theory of government adopted, **te** will be governed by the matrix verb if and only if **te** is the head of @. PRO will not be governed by this verb if and only if @ has a head. Since (27) is a control structure, we must assume that @ has a head. Why now the conspiracy? The conspiracy follows if **te** has the same status as *to* in English, viz. that it is a preposition and realizes INFL, i.e. it is in the head position of @. Recall that in Dutch a preposition governed by a verb receives a superscript, and then *governs like a verb*. But if **te** governs like a verb, i.e. it governs not only positions it is strictly categorized for, but simply any position it minimally c-commands, PRO will be governed. Viz. PRO will be governed by **te** if and only if **te** is in a position where it receives a superscript from a verb. But if PRO is governed, the result is a violation of the binding theory, which requires that PRO be ungoverned: PRO may not be assigned a governing category. As a consequence, the structure is out, unless something happens. The fact that something must happen explains the conspiracy.

What happens, is also explained by this account. Extraposition of @ has the effect of moving it to a position on the right of the matrix verb. This position is the one in which stranding is excluded. This we accounted for by saying that a preposition does not receive a superscript in that position; i.e. it is in a position not governed by the matrix verb. Hence, if @ moves into that position, **te** will not be governed by the matrix verb either; thus it does not receive a superscript, and hence is not a structural governor. Therefore, PRO remains ungoverned, as required (cf. (6iii)).

It is easily seen that applying the rule of V-raising has the same effect. It removes **te** (along with the verb), placing it in a position on the right of the matrix verb. The effect of this is, that the position of INFL in @ is now occupied by a trace, viz. trace of INFL. Notice, that under the assumption that before movement the head of @ had the structure $[_{INFL} [_P te] \ldots]$, the trace is indeed that of INFL, not that of P. Since the definition of a governing domain does not depend on the head having lexical content, the domain of this trace of INFL is still opaque to outside governors; hence PRO will not be governed by the matrix verb. INFL being empty PRO is not governed by INFL either. Notice moreover, that no stipulations have to be made about non-inheritance of governing properties. In fact, one has to assume that a trace inherits the governing properties of its antecedent, since otherwise the direct object of a verb that has undergone movement could not be assigned Case. Since **te** has been moved to a position on the right of the matrix verb, it does not receive a superscript, hence is not a structural governor, and therefore the trace of INFL is not a governor by inheritance either.

A final remark on this subject: as one sees from (22c), the verb moves along with **te**. The reason for this is, as I mentioned above, the fact that INFL may not be stranded: it forms a morphological unit with the verb. One might wonder then, what the structure after V-raising looks like. Of course, the answer to this question depends on the structure after merging of the V and INFL in general. The structure in (28) seems to me technically correct, in that it represents the right properties, without further stipulation.

(28)   dat $[_S$ NP $[_{VP} [_@$ PRO $[_{VP}$ NP $e_i]$ $e_j]$ $e_k]$ $[_{INFL}$ +tense $V_k]$ $[_{INFL}$ te $V_i]_j]$.

To obtain (28) one may assume that the verb is first raised into some verbal position within INFL, and then moved along with the latter. Thus, the moved constituent simultaneously binds two positions within the complement clause. It is only this property of (28) which seems to me essential.

Summarizing: The opacity of the subject position of control structures with respect to the matrix verb is explained on the basis of the hypothesis that this position is in the domain of some other head, which cannot be anything else but the head of S. This head is then identified with the infinitival marker **te**. And this identification, in turn, makes it possible to deduce the conspiracy from the binding theory. **Te** being a preposition, it is turned into a structural governor whenever it is the head of a constituent within the VP. Hence, in those positions it governs any position in its governing domain, including the subject position of its clause. Since this position has to be PRO, **te** has to move to a position in which it is not turned into a structural governor; hence, either extraposition of the whole clause, or V-raising has to occur, since both have the effect of moving **te** to a position in which it does not receive a superscript. Since this explanation crucially depends on infinitival clauses having a head with certain specifiable properties, and since **te** would not qualify for being an AUX in the sense of ASW and SEA, the conclusions drawn earlier on the basis of evidence from English are supported by the evidence from Dutch.

3.2. *Non-control Structures in Dutch*

This section is devoted to **te**-infinitivals as complements of verbs that do not assign a thematic role to their subjects, the so-called raising verbs. The θ-theory as formulated in Chomsky (1981b), incorporates the requirement that each argument bears one and only one θ-role, and that each θ-role is assigned to one and only one argument. An argument is assigned a θ-role on the basis of the position occupied by itself, or any of its traces. Any subcategorized position is assigned a θ-role by the relevant head; moreover, in general, verbs assign a θ-role to their subject. Raising verbs, such as *seem, appear*, etc., however, don't. This entails that their subject position cannot be occupied at D-structure, since the NP in subject position must have a θ-role. The raising verb does not meet this requirement, hence the subject must be able to obtain its θ-role from another position. But this implies that it must bind a trace, somewhere, from which it can inherit this θ-role. This in turn implies that it must have been base generated in a different position, since otherwise it simply does not have a trace to inherit this θ-role from. Thus the subject of a raising verb is either a non-argument such as the counterparts of *it* in some of its uses, or **er** 'there', or else the subject has been raised out of the complement by NP-movement. For independent reasons, obviously only the subject position of the complement is a possible source. Clearly, this notion of a raising verb has to be sharply distinguished from that of a V-raising verb in Dutch.

The question to be treated in this section is how these raising verbs in Dutch behave with respect to the conspiracy; i.e. how do NP-raising and V-raising interact? This is an interesting question for reasons which can be summarized as follows: If a raising verb can only have an argument expression as its subject when that argument expression has been raised from the subject position of the complement, it follows from the ECP that the latter position must be properly governed. The only proper governor that is available is the raising verb itself. However, the trace is in the domain of the inflection of its clause; hence it cannot be governed by the raising verb upstairs. Therefore, there is a dilemma. Notice, that this dilemma is a consequence of the theory of government adopted in conjunction with the assumption that infinitival clauses have a head. The important feature of these constructions is now that under certain conditions they exhibit a behavior, which is different from that of control structures. This difference in behavior will be explained on the basis of the hypothesis that the inflection of the complement of a raising verb is involved in a restructuring process with the inflection of the matrix clause, whereas in control structures this is not the case. It will be claimed that this restructuring process has the effect of freeing the way for the matrix verb to properly govern the trace in the subject position of the complement. The logic of the argument is then that if infinitival clauses did not have a head causing opacity of the subject position there would be no necessity for such a marked process to be incorporated in the grammar at all. Hence, that the theory entails a dilemma is corroborated by the obligatory occurrence of a marked process in the cases for which the dilemma is predicted

Consider now (29), which represents the D-structure of a sentence where the matrix verb is a raising verb, and the complement a **te**-infinitival.

(29)   dat $[_S$ e $[_{VP}$ $[_@$ NP* $[_{VP}$ NP V$-]-$te$]$ blijk$-]-$t$]$.

The verb **blijken** 'appear' does not assign a θ-role to its subject; therefore, the latter position must be empty at D-structure; this is indicated by *e*. By the θ-criterion NP* must be either a lexical argument expression or PRO at the level of D-structure. For neither value is (29) an admissible S-structure. By virtue of the argument in the previous section te will receive a superscript from **blijken**, and hence PRO is impossible, being governed by the inflection **te**. NP* cannot be lexical, since in order to be lexical it must have Case, which it cannot get from **blijken**. This is so for two reasons: **te** prevents NP* being governed by **blijken**; and moreover, **blijken**, being intransitive, would not assign Case even if it were to govern NP*. Of course, **te** cannot assign Case either. In order for NP* to get Case it has to move to the *e*-position. This yields the derived structure in (30).

(30)   dat $[_S NP_i^* [_{VP} [_@ t_i [_{VP} NP V-] -te] blijk-]-t]$.

In this structure t_i violates the ECP. Although **te** will become cosuperscripted with **blijk-**, and hence will govern t_i, the second clause of the requirements for proper government is not met: t_i is not *in the complement of its governor* **te**. (That is t_i is not (contained in) a constituent associated with a strict subcategorization feature of its governor, since INFL does not strictly subcategorize for any item.) It is true that t_i is in the complement of **blijk-**, but it cannot be governed by the latter, because the presence of INFL **(te)** precludes this. So, it ends up in the area between government and proper government. Hence the structure is out.[13]

Application of V-raising would not help to make the subject properly governed, nor would extraposition, since the effect of both of these rules is that of making the subject position of the complement ungoverned by moving the offending **te**-INFL to a nonsuperscripted position. Because the rule of extraposition is not involved in the derivation of a grammatical output I will not consider the effect of extraposition here separately. The reason that, except for some marginal cases, the complements of raising verbs don't extrapose is that extraposition would preclude proper government of the subject trace. The structure resulting from applying V-raising is given in (31).

(31)   dat $[_S NP_i^* [_{VP} [_@ [_{NP} \Phi]_i [_{VP} NP e_j-]-e_k] blijk-]-t [te V_j]_k]$.

Here, $[_{NP} \Phi]_i$ corresponds to t_i in (30). But it can no longer be construed as a trace, since it is ungoverned: It is in the domain of e_k, which is a head but not a governor. Under the contextual definitions of the null categories given in Chomsky (1981b), an ungoverned null NP cannot be anything else but PRO. So, technically, (31) violates the θ-criterion. Φ being technically PRO, it cannot act as a trace of NP*. Hence, NP* cannot inherit a θ-role from Φ.

Since it is not in a θ-position, it simply has no θ-role. This violates the requirement that every argument must have one.

The alternative we considered above was that the subject of the complement was PRO. If PRO moves we have essentially the same situation as in (31): the structure is out for the same reason. If PRO is not raised the structure violates the conditions on control. With e instead of NP_i^*, there would be no violation of the θ-criterion in (31). This e might be replaced by some dummy subject at S-structure. The subject of the complement is then simply PRO. However, it will be uncontrolled, since a dummy subject is not a possible controller (cf. the discussion in Chomsky (1981)), and the arbitrary interpretation is not available in these cases. Hence the structure is also out under this option. This is then the dilemma: the *structure* is out under all available options.

Yet the *sentence* given in (32) is grammatical.

(32)   dat   Annamaria de mollen blijkt   te   vangen
        that Annamaria the moles   appears to   catch

   that Annamaria appears to catch the moles

Hence, if our theory is correct, its structure must be different from that in (31). The minimal difference which would be consistent with its grammaticality is the absence of a trace of INFL in the complement clause. That is, as a structure (31) is out only by a narrow margin, viz. the presence of the trace e_k, of INFL, which blocks government of the subject position by **blijk-**. I will claim now, that the grammaticality of (32) is brought about by a special process, involving the trace of INFL in the complement of raising verbs, and, as a consequence the whole string of verbs resulting from V-raising in these structures. The process is restructuring. Its first step is the elimination of the trace e_k under the condition that it be adjacent to the INFL of the upstairs clause. Elimination of the trace e_k deprives the complement of its head. Hence its subject is now in the governing domain of the next head up, which is the matrix verb **blijk-**. This verb is a proper governor; moreover, the subject is in its complement. Therefore a trace in this position does not violate the ECP.

I will now show that there is an independent reason to assume the existence of a restructuring rule in Dutch operative in the cases where our theory both requires, and prohibits the existence of a local relation between the subject of a complement and the matrix verb. The argument showing that there is restructuring in these cases will be based on a condition on restructuring proposed by Kayne. Its logic will be as follows: if Kayne's condition cannot be met, restructuring should be impossible. If restructuring is impossible, the trace cannot be eliminated. Hence the structure should be out. Hence, if we find that in general raising structures and control structures pattern alike, but that wherever Kayne's condition cannot be met, the control structures are in, but the corresponding raising structures are out, this shows that raising structures do, and control structures don't involve restructuring.

At present, grammatical theory does not yet provide for an articulated subtheory of restructuring. Developing one would lead us outside the scope of the present article. However, it seems to me that the approaches to restructuring taken in Kayne (1981a, b) and Chomsky (1981b) are essentially correct. My underlying assumption as to the nature of restructuring is that it is essentially a default procedure; one of a set of procedures available in the periphery of the grammar in order to 'save' structures that are out because of conflicts between the core modules arising from the way certain parameters are set. It seems to me worthwhile to pursue a view of restructuring under which it basically involves the elimination of an occurrence of some empty category, the presence of which blocks a grammatical parsing. Superficially the most characteristic features of the restructuring, at least in some cases, is that some string of constituents starts behaving as if it were a (lexical) unit. This is in principle to be derived as a necessary consequence from the application of the principles of grammatical theory, viewed as a parsing mechanism, to the remainder of the structure.

After this digression, let us return now to the structure under consideration. As I said, Kayne (1981a, b) formulated a condition on restructuring, which in certain cases can be used as a diagnostic. The condition is that *constituents involved in restructuring must assign Case in the same way*. It is not clear to what extent this condition can be taken to apply to all kinds of restructuring. I will assume that it does apply to all kinds of restructuring between heads (in fact this is the only kind Kayne discusses). Kayne's condition precludes restructuring between a verb and a preposition if the latter assigns oblique Case, to give an example. So, in languages in which all prepositions assign oblique Case there will be no restructuring between the two categories. From this Kayne derives the fact that in languages in which the oblique Case system has not been lost for prepositions, there is no preposition stranding, since the possibility of preposition stranding is based on some form of restructuring. In the case of raising structures Kayne's condition will be seen to block restructuring between a participle and a full verb. Given the current theory of lexical categories, verbs are specified

[−N, +V] and participles are [+N, +V], like adjectives. So, participles are not Case assigners. It is assumed that where they seem to assign Case, Case is actually assigned by virtue of the presence of an auxiliary, such as *have* or *be*, or their equivalents in other languages. Hence, we will expect that if it is the case that in order to derive a grammatical result in raising structures, restructuring must apply, and if it is the case that this restructuring must involve the matrix verb and the complement verb, the matrix verb may not assume participial form, even if this form would be required on the basis of other aspects of the structure. After the relevant examples I will give a derivation showing that this is precisely the result which obtains.

The contrast between raising structures and control structures with the matrix verb in participial form is illustrated in (33).[14]

(33) a. dat   Annamaria de mollen heeft beloofd te   vangen.
         that Annamaria the moles   has   promised to   catch

     that Annamaria promised to catch the moles

   b.* dat   Annamaria de mollen heeft/is gebleken te   vangen.
        that Annamaria the moles   has   appeared to   catch

     that Annamaria (has) seemed to catch the moles

We see that the matrix verb may assume participial form, if required by the auxiliary, when it is a control verb as in (33a). If it is a raising verb, as in (33b) the structure is out. There are no trivial explanations for the un-grammaticality of (33b). **Blijken** is not defective, since in other positions it does appear in participial form if required (cf. (34)).

(34)   Het is   gebleken dat   Annamaria de mollen gevangen heeft.
        it has appeared that Annamaria the moles caught   has

     It (has) appeared that Annamaria (has) caught the moles.

The fact that (33b) contains a compound tense, cannot be the relevant factor either, since (35) where the auxiliary is **zullen** 'will', which requires an infinitive, is grammatical.

(35)   dat   Annamaria de mollen zal blijken te kunnen   vangen.
        that Annamaria the moles   will appear to be able to catch

     that Annamaria will appear to be able to catch the moles

Any theory will have to account for the fact that a raising verb may not appear in participial form when it has an infinitival complement. We will see now, that under the present proposals this fact follows from the result that in such raising constructions there must be restructuring, in conjuction with Kayne's condition.

As I stated earlier, the first step in the restructuring process is that the trace e_k in (31) is eliminated under the condition that it be adjacent to the INFL of the matrix clause. Whether this is really deletion of the trace or a matter of merging it with the higher INFL is not relevant to our present purposes. I assume it to be merger. The requirement of adjacency is introduced in order to account for the fact, already noted in Evers (1975) that no material may be shifted to the right in the subordinate clause in such a way that it intervenes between the downstairs verb and the upstairs verb (cf. also Van Riemsdijk (1978)). Thus the rule eliminating the downstairs trace of inflection converts (31) into (36).

(36)   dat $[_S \text{NP}^*_i \ [_{VP} \ [_@ \ [_{NP} \ \Phi]_i \ [_{VP} \text{NP} \ e_j]] \ e_1] \ [_{INFL} \text{blijk}_1 -t]$
$[_\alpha \text{te V}_j]]$.

Now Φ in @ is governed by **blijk**-, or rather by its trace. We have to assume, of course, given this particular execution of the rule merging **blijk**- with its INFL -t, that the trace e_1 does not keep the downstairs trace of INFL from being adjacent to the upstairs INFL. Because of the adjacency requirement on restructuring the merger precedes the elimination of e_k in (31). As a consequence Φ is construed as the trace of NP*, since it is properly governed by the verb. This step, however, must be followed by another restructuring. Consider the status of $[_\alpha \text{te V}_j]$, the constituent moved out of the complement. The elimination of the trace e_k has essentially the effect of severing the ties of α with the downstairs clause as far as its status as INFL is concerned. That is, in control structures both the INFL part and the Verb part of the moved constituent are related to their respective Base positions. In (36) only V_j can be associated with its original position. What this implies is, that the constituent labelled α is not representable as INFL. Another way of saying this is the following: in the standard case S-structure represents all the information necessary to factor it into D-structure and Move α (Chomsky, 1981b). This is not true for (36). So, given the current theory, (36) cannot be the proper S-structure. What this comes down to, is requiring that a verb associated with INFL at D-structure must be associated with INFL at S-structure. The only INFL available for α to become associated with is the

INFL of the matrix clause, **blijkt**. Thus the second step in the restructuring process is that α restructures with INFL. In fact it restructures with that INFL, which was instrumental in the elimination of its original INFL position. This restructuring cannot be detected in the simple cases. However, as noted Kayne's condition on restructuring predicts a direct effect when the reanalysis should involve a participle, viz. that it is impossible. And if reanalysis is impossible the theory predicts that the sentence is ungrammatical. What is predicted is therefore precisely the contrast between (33a) and (33b). How? Consider the S-structure of (33b). As will be shown in the Appendix, the auxiliary **heeft** (or **is**) can be base generated in INFL position. This auxiliary requires a participle. The participle is base generated in the main verb position of the clause. Clearly, given the adjacency requirement on the INFL positions, if the first step is to take place, the participle must have been removed. The relevant pre-S structure is therefore as represented in (37).

(37)   dat $[_S$ Annamaria $[_{VP} [_@ t_i [_{VP}$ de mollen $e_j]]$ $e_1]$
       that   Annamaria   the moles

$[_{INFL} \begin{Bmatrix} \text{is} \\ \text{heeft} \end{Bmatrix}$ gebleken$_1$ te vangen$_j]$
       has   appeared to catch

So, **te vangen** should restructure with **heeft** or **is** in order to associate with inflection. However, the participle **gebleken** intervenes in the string. In principle, restructuring involves contiguous strings, with the exception of intervening arguments perhaps; **gebleken** must therefore take part in the process. Now it is required that elements involved in the restructuring assign Case in the same manner, and participles are not verbs, they are not $[-N, +V]$, and are not Case assigners. Since the other participants in the restructuring are verbs, neither of them can be restructured with **gebleken** by Kayne's principle. So, restructuring of verbs cannot take place across a participle. This establishes what we set out to argue, viz. that the impossibility of having the matrix verb in participial form is a diagnostic of restructuring. Thus the essential contrast between (33a) and (33b) is that in (33a) the application of V-raising is in itself sufficient to guarantee a grammatical output. In (33b) besides V-raising also restructuring is needed. In fact, the analysis proposed so far explains more than the ungrammaticality of (33b). It also explains why sentence (38) is much better than (33b).

(38) ? dat Annamaria de mollen heeft blijken   te kunnen   vangen
      that Annamaria the moles has   appear (sic!) to be able to catch

As (38) shows, replacing the participle **gebleken** with the infinitive **blijken**, even with an auxiliary which in other cases requires a participle, apparently almost solves the problem. In fact, it is so good, that it can hardly be treated as marginal. Given the theory, the infinitive **blijken** should not block restructuring, and as we see, it does not.

How do we get (38)? There are two possibilities, between which I will not decide here. The first possibility is that it is simply an instance of a principle of core grammar taking precedence over a rule in the periphery. The principle of core grammar is the one requiring restructuring, the rule of the periphery is the rule according to which the auxiliaries **hebben** 'have' and **zijn** 'be' require a participle. Given the conflict, the latter rule is simply relaxed in certain environments.

The second possibility is based on the analysis of participles proposed in Van Riemsdijk (1983) (cf. also Den Besten (1981)). Van Riemsdijk proposes that participles constitute an instance of category neutralization. I.e. they are not [−N, +V], like verbs, nor [+N, +V] like adjectives. Rather they are simply [+V]. This proposal can be combined with a very interesting idea recently advanced by Evers (1981). This idea is that verb forms must be characterized for tense, i.e. all verb forms are either [+tense], or [−tense]. Since one of the contributions of INFL to a verbal form is that it characterizes that form as [±tense], one can say that by severing the tie with INFL one gets verb forms which are no longer so characterized. Thus, movement followed by the first step of the restructuring process gives rise to sequences of verb forms as in (39a), when a participle intervenes, where (39a) expresses the feature composition of the segments.

$$(39)\ \text{a.}\ \begin{bmatrix} @\,\text{tense} \\ -N \\ +V \end{bmatrix} \begin{bmatrix} - \\ - \\ +V \end{bmatrix} \begin{bmatrix} - \\ -N \\ +V \end{bmatrix} \quad \text{b.}\ \begin{bmatrix} @\,\text{tense} \\ -N \\ +V \end{bmatrix} \begin{bmatrix} @\,\text{tense} \\ -N \\ +V \end{bmatrix} \begin{bmatrix} @\,\text{tense} \\ -N \\ +V \end{bmatrix}$$

The purpose of the restructuring is now to mark the final segment as @ tense (where @ expresses the fact that either value will do, if only the segment is marked). This can be achieved by having the feature @ tense spread across the boundaries. So, restructuring comes down to the spreading of features across word boundaries. But if this were so, the feature [−N] would also not be kept from spreading, and adding [−N] to the second segment obliterates the property distinguishing it from a true verb form, viz. that it lacks [−N] (cf. (39b)). Hence, it simply becomes the appropriate nonfinite verb form, **blijken**. There are a number of potential empirical differences between the two proposals, discussion of which I will defer to another occasion, since they do not concern the main issue of this argument.[15]

Summarizing, we have found the ungrammaticality of a raising verb in participial form with an infinitival complement is greatly reduced by replacing this participle with an infinitive. This indicates that there is restructuring of the verbs in raising constructions; otherwise there would be no explanation for the fact that Kayne's condition is relevant to the string of verbs resulting from V-raising in NP-raising constructions, but not in control constructions. The necessity for restructuring in these non-control structures in turn follows from the assumption that at D-structure they contain a realization of INFL, just like control structures, but that it has to disappear.

In a sense, what the non-control cases tell us, is the mirror image of what the control structures told us. The raising cases give us insight in the role played by the category INFL in tenseless complements, by showing what has to happen if for some reason it is not permitted. Since the consequences of removing INFL from tenseless clauses are considerable, as we have seen, the argument shows that INFL plays a crucial role in tenseless clauses, and hence that the optimal grammar of Dutch must have that category available. Since the argument involves tenseless clauses, it shows that this Aux-like category is an instantiation of INFL rather than of AUX.

3.3. *Bare Infinitivals in Dutch*

The diagnostic for restructuring in the case of raising verbs was the occurrence of an infinitive in a position where one would have expected a participle. This phenomenon of Infinitive for Participle, which I will abbreviate as IPP, is not only obligatory in non control te-infinitivals, but also in the so-called bare infinitivals in Dutch.

In this section I will argue that bare infinitival complements, contrary to what is suggested by their name, contain a realization of INFL at the level of D-structure, just like the non-control verbs of the previous section. Only, it is a different realization of INFL. The logic of the argument will be similar. It will be based on the obligatoriness of V-raising, coupled with the obligatoriness of IPP. The obligatoriness of IPP will again be taken as a diagnostic for restructuring, and the necessity for restructuring will be taken to be the reflection at S-structure of the presence of INFL at D-structure.

This contention will be supported by the existence of a contrast between these constructions and constructions where for independent reasons the complement must not be analyzed as an S, and hence must lack INFL.

Bare infinitival constructions appear as complements of perception verbs, causatives and auxiliaries. The term 'auxiliary' here is to be understood in its traditional sense, as referring to verbs such as **kunnen** 'be able/can', **zullen** 'will', **moeten** 'must', **mogen** 'may', **willen** 'want', the temporal **hebben** 'have' and **zijn** 'be' (which require a participial complement) etc. The reader should realize that in Dutch these verbs are much less clearly a separate category than in English: they exhibit verbal inflection in their person endings, although it is irregular, and appear in non-finite forms. In Evers (1975) they are treated as main verbs, taking a sentential complement in the base structure. Here, it will be argued that this is only correct for some of their uses. It will be shown that certain contrasts between perception verb complements and the complements to auxiliaries follow immediately from the assumption that auxiliaries may take non-sentential complements, viz. VPs. In the Appendix I will show that this assumption is necessary apart from phenomena of V-raising. As I did in the previous section, in my representations I will simply anticipate the result of the Appendix.

For the purpose of this argument, the causatives do not form a separate category, as they basically behave like the perception verbs. The first task is now that of providing an answer to the question why there is obligatory V-raising out of bare infinitival complements of perception verbs. This is a fact any analysis of Dutch must explain. It is illustrated in (40).

(40) a.* dat   Annamaria $[_@$ Patrick   de   ratten   vangen]   zag
        that   Annamaria   Patrick   the   rats   catch   saw

     b.   dat   Annamaria $[_@$ Patrick   de   ratten e_i]   zag vangen$_i$
        that   Annamaria   Patrick   the   rats   saw catch

     that Annamaria saw Patrick catch the rats

As I said, the matrix verb of a bare infinitival complement obligatorily undergoes IPP. This is shown in (41).

(41) a.* dat Annamaria $[_@$ Patrick de   ratten vangen]   gezien heeft
        that Annamaria   Patrick the rats   catch   seen   has

     b.* dat   Annamaria $[_@$ Patrick de   ratten e_i]   heeft gezien vangen$_i$
        that   Annamaria   Patrick the rats   has   seen   catch

     c.   dat Annamaria $[_@$ Patrick de   ratten e_i]   heeft zien   vangen$_i$
        that Annamaria   Patrick the rats   has   see   catch

The form **gezien** is the past participle of the verb **zien** 'see', the form occurring in (41c) is identical to the infinitive.

I will show now, that these properties of perception verb complements can be derived from the same principles as discussed in the previous section. The only special assumption is that the value of INFL in bare infinitivals is [−tense, +N, −V], rather than [−tense, −N, −V]. Instead of as **te** (or perhaps rather '**te-___-en**') as in the latter case, it is realized as **-en**. Since there is a clear difference in Dutch between the bare-infinitival form, and the verb stem the term 'bare infinitival' is somewhat of a misnomer. However, I will continue to use it here.

Motivation for regarding the realization of INFL in this construction as nominal is provided by the other uses of the the affix **-en**. Namely, virtually any infinitival verb form can be used as (or is homophonous to) a noun, appearing with the full range of determiners, adjectives, genitive formation on the subject, **van**-insertion (= *of*-insertion) on the direct object, etc. In fact, this is not a phenomenon specific to Dutch, the infinitive may be used as a noun quite generally in Germanic languages. That there is reason to identify the verbal and the nominal uses of the infinitival form on some level, is shown by the fact that e.g. in the older stages of English the infinitive exhibited Case marking. This property of the infinitive to bear Case marking survives in the two forms of the infinitive in present day Frisian.

On the basis of the assumption that this realization of INFL is nominal we arrive at a representation of (40) at the level of D-structure as in (42).

$$(42) \quad \text{dat } [_S \text{ NP } [_{VP} [_@ \text{ NP* } [_{VP} \text{ NP } V{-}]{-} [_{INFL} \text{ -en}]] \text{ } V{-}]\text{-INFL}]$$
$$\begin{bmatrix} +N \\ -V \end{bmatrix}$$

Unlike what is the case in **te**-infinitivals, the subject of the complement of perception verbs is lexical, and hence must have Case (cf. Evers (1975) for an argument showing that NP* must be in the complement). However, because of the presence of INFL NP* is not governed by the upstairs verb. So, it cannot get Case from the latter. It cannot get Case from INFL either. Although INFL is nominal, it is not AG (but see below p. 141); hence it is not able to transmit Case on the basis of Move Case. Since these are the only ways for NP* to get Case, and neither of them can apply, NP* cannot be lexical. But in fact, other values for NP* are also excluded. Since INFL has the lexical feature [+N], NP* is not only in the governing domain of INFL, but also actually governed. Hence it cannot be PRO. In order for NP* to be realized as the trace of NP-movement it should be properly governed. This is also impossible, for the same reasons discussed in the previous sections. Again, there is no value at all for NP*. Hence, in order to derive a grammatical output, V-raising and the ensuing elimination of the trace of INFL have to apply, together with the other consequences of restructuring. After V-raising and restructuring the representation can be taken to be as in (43).

(43)   dat $[_S$ NP $[_{VP}$ $[_@$ NP* $[_{VP}$ NP $e_i]]$ $e_j]$ $[_{INFL}$ $[_{INFL}$ heeft]
          $[_V$ zien$]_j$ $[_V$ vangen$]_i]]$.

The direct object of **vangen** now has Case, mediated by the trace e_i, and the subject of the complement, NP* is governed by the trace e_j of **zien**, and has Case mediated by this trace. Although the theoretical status of transmission of Case and government by a verbal trace is not clear, the existence of some such process must be assumed for any language with verb movement of the kind exemplified here. Here I will not anticipate theoretical problems which might be found with a simple notion of Case assignment by traces of verbs, and hence I simply talk about verbal traces as governing, assigning Case, or mediating Case assignment, etc. We see that basically the reason for restructuring in perception verb complements and in non-control **te**-infinitives is the same. In both constructions the subject of the complement must enter a local relation with the upstairs verb. This is precluded by the presence of INFL, hence the trace of INFL brought about by movement, has to disappear. Hence the downstairs verb in its new position is no longer associated with INFL, and has to associate with the nearest INFL. This it does by restructuring with the verb associated with this INFL. If a participle intervened, this restructuring would be blocked. Hence (41b) is ungrammatical, and the application of IPP is necessary, yielding (41c).

The necessity of restructuring interacts in a very interesting way with the option of passivizing the matrix verb in the bare infinitival construction: it effectively blocks it. This explains the ungrammaticality of both options in (44).

(44)   * dat   Cecilia$_i$ $[_@$ t_i een·lied $e_j]$ e_k is $\begin{Bmatrix} \text{gehoord}_k \\ \text{horen}_k \end{Bmatrix}$ zingen$_j$

         that Cecilia   a   song   was hear(d)   sing

   that Cecilia was heard to sing a song

Given the theory proposed in Chomsky (1981) the position which *Cecilia* occupies at S-structure, must be a $\bar{\theta}$-position, by virtue of the θ-criterion. It can be a non-θ-position only by virtue of the passive rule, which states that the subject of some verb is not assigned a θ-role if some NP in its complement cannot be assigned Case. So, **Cecilia** can only be in a non-θ-position if t_i is not in a Case position. It is in a non-Case position if it is governed by a participle, viz. **gehoord**. However, we know that it is essential in order for t_i to be properly governed, that @ does not have INFL. Hence, **zingen** must restructure. Restructuring of **zingen** with **is** is impossible since **gehoord** intervenes. Hence, IPP must apply. The effect is now, that restructuring can proceed. However, e_k is not linked to a participle anymore. Rather it is linked to **horen**, which is an infinitive. Hence, t_i is in a Case position, since it is governed by e_k, which transmits the Case of **horen**. But now, the passive rule cannot apply. So, (44) violates the θ-criterion: both **Cecilia** and its trace are in a θ-position, and hence **Cecilia** will be assigned two θ-roles. It also violates the binding theory, since under the binding theory as formulated in Chomsky (1981b) a Case-marked trace is a variable. Variables, being R-expressions must be argument free. However, t_i is argument bound by **Cecilia**; hence clause (11c) of the binding theory is violated.

Thus, the theory advanced explains the fact that NP-movement under passive is impossible out of bare infinitival complements in Dutch. We must now remedy a slight complication in this argument. The reason why there has to be restructuring in bare infinitival complements is that otherwise the subject of the complement (NP* in (42)) cannot get Case. That it cannot get Case from the matrix verb is straightforward. It is less clear that it cannot receive Case from INFL. Recall that the analysis of NP-*ing* complements in English is based on the assumption that there the matrix verb assigns Case to the realization of INFL, which is -*ing*. Then this Case floats off to the subject. What I am assuming there is that -*ing* realizes the $[-\text{tense}, +N, -V]$ option of INFL, in fact the same option as we find realized in Dutch bare infinitivals. The question is then why in Dutch there is no Case assignment to the subject as a result of Case floating off the nominal INFL: the Case assigned to INFL by the matrix verb. As far as I can see, the relevant parameter is whether $[-\text{tense}, +N, -V]$ is taken to realize AG or not.

As I said in the introduction, the status of AG is presumably comparable to that of a clitic. It is also a truism that in most Indo-European languages finiteness goes together with tensedness. That is, it is safe to assume that in the unmarked case $[+N, -V]$ only realizes AG if it co-occurs with $[+\text{tense}]$. It is reasonable then, to assume that there is a cost associated with interpreting $[+N, -V]$ as AG if INFL is $[-\text{tense}]$. If this cost is comparable to that associated with restructuring, or perhaps higher, we will expect that the conflict involving complement clauses with a tenseless nominal INFL will be solved depending on circumstances.

In Dutch, for instance the INFL of the complement is virtually adjacent to the INFL of the matrix clause, since Dutch is head-final. Hence restructuring between the two Inflections with the consequences we discussed is feasible. English is not head-final. The order of the relevant constituents is given by [$_S$ NP INFL V [$_@$ NP -ing VP]]. Here, *-ing* is separated from the INFL of the matrix clause by the string *V NP*. So, string-adjacency between INFL and the position of *-ing* cannot be attained, and even if English were to develop a version of V-raising, elimination of the trace of INFL in the position of *-ing* could not take place. Since the 'Dutch' option is out anyhow, analyzing *-ing* as AG is the only option available in English. This does not answer the question why the 'English' option would be out for Dutch.

Thus, so far the story is simply that there is a conflict arising from the choice of a nominal tenseless INFL in Dutch and English alike, and that there is parametric variation as to whether a nominal INFL in this structure can, or cannot function as AG. Only in English could the parameter not have been set so as to exclude *-ing* in NP-*ing* complements because the alternative, viz., restructuring is out for structural reasons. Structurally, Dutch would have been compatible with either setting. However, there are facts which show that only one option is in fact available. The parameters for that language must be set so as to account for the fact that bare infinitivals in Dutch never appear with a PRO subject, either before, or after V-raising. We don't find sentences like * **dat ik** [$_@$ **PRO komen**] **hoorde** 'that I come heard' or * **dat ik** [$_@$ **PRO** e_i] **hoorde komen**$_i$ 'that I heard come'. (In Reuland (1980c) and Reuland (1981b) I discussed the reason why the English counterparts are impossible. It is quite different: there, the null Inflection elements cannot retain Case, hence the subject will be governed.) These examples are ungrammatical because the nominal INFL will cause PRO to be governed. In this construction type, V-raising does not help. After V-raising PRO will still be governed by the trace of the inflection. (Recall that we have to assume that a trace in some sense inherits the governing properties of its antecedent since verbs appear to govern precisely the positions governed by their trace.) V-raising in **te**-infinitivals is fully consistent with this assumption, since crucially, the **te** + V moves to a position in which it is not turned into a structural governor. Hence the trace here has nothing to inherit. In the case of nominal INFL, the impossibility of PRO in the domain of its trace simply follows from the assumption that it behaves like any other trace, viz. that it inherits the governing properties of its binder. Eliminating the trace, of course, immediately yields a governed PRO. Therefore the structure is out under any way of construing it.

There is one more option in bare infinitival complements which should be mentioned. It is illustrated by the example in (45).

(45) a. dat   Cecilia [$_@$ een liedje e_i] hoorde zingen$_i$ / heeft horen
         that Cecilia   a   song   heard   sing   has   hear

         (* gehoord) zingen$_i$
            heard   sing

         that Cecilia heard a song sung

   b. dat [$_S$ NP [$_{VP}$ [$_@$ PRO [$_{VP}$ NP e_i] e_j]   hoorde zing$_i$-en$_j$

   c. dat [$_S$ NP [$_{VP}$ [$_@$ NP$_h$ [$_{VP}$ t_h e]   ]   [hoorde zingen]

The structure can be characterized as having somewhat passive-like properties within the complement. I.e. the interpretation is passive, and also one can introduce an agent in the complement in the form of a *by*-phrase (**door** NP). Both for the reasons reviewed above, concerning the impossibility of PRO-subjects in bare infinitivals, and because of the possibility of agentive *by*-phrases, the representation in (45b) must be wrong. NP-movement within the complement might seem to pose a problem since there is no passive morphology on the verb associated with the VP of the complement. Hence, one might wonder why t_h is not a variable with the ensuing violation of the binding conditions and the θ-criterion. I suggest that the solution may be found in the restructuring. As is shown by the obligatoriness of the application of IPP, there is restructuring in these constructions. The only supplementary assumption needed to derive these examples is that under restructuring **hoorde zingen** optionally becomes a single verb. As such it has only one Case to assign, which will be realized on the most prominent NP in the complement, viz. NP$_h$. The trace t_h in the VP of the complement will not have Case now, so it can be NP-trace. It can be properly governed by the trace of **zingen** under the assumption that it still transmits government. Although there may be problems with θ-theory as it stands, which would lead us far beyond the scope of this article, this way of viewing the construction seems to me promising, and basically correct.

This concludes the discussion of bare infinitival complements of perception verbs. The conclusion is, that all their properties follow from the assumption that they are clausal with a nominal INFL, in conjunction with the proposals about government, and restructuring formulated earlier. The basic cases follow without any further stipulations whatsoever; the construction of (45) follows with a quite minimal stipulation.

In the introductory paragraph of this section I stated that there is a contrast between the behavior of bare infinitivals as complements of perception verbs, and as complements of the members of the class of traditional auxiliaries. In fact, these auxiliaries exhibit a quite intriguing behavior. This can be described as follows: In a structure with a finite form of an auxiliary preceded by a complement containing one verb, the conspiracy does not apply, i.e. V-raising is simply optional. In a structure in which the auxiliary is preceded by a complement in which there is an auxiliary preceded by an infinitival complement, the conspiracy does apply, i.e. there is obligatory V-raising. This is illustrated in (46) and (47).

(46) a. dat   Patrick   de   mollen   vangen   kan
        that Patrick   the   moles   catch   can

     that Patrick can catch the moles

   b. dat   Patrick   de   mollen e_i kan   vangen$_i$
       that Patrick   the   moles   can   catch

Here we see that the auxiliary **kan** and the verb of the complement **vangen** may appear in either order. The grammaticality of (46a) can be compared to the ungrammaticality of (40a).

Consider now (47).

(47) a.* dat   Patrick   de   mollen   vangen   kunnen zal
       that Patrick   the   moles   catch   can   will

   b. dat   Patrick   de   mollen e_i e_j zal   kunnen$_j$ vangen$_i$
       that Patrick   the   moles   will can   catch

     that Patrick will be able to catch the moles

Here, apparently, the complement structure of auxiliaries has the same properties as that of perception verbs. The base order cannot be retained, and V-raising must apply. The fact that under the relevant conditions, the structure exhibits IPP, shows that there is restructuring going on. This is illustrated in (48).

(48) a.* dat   Patrick de   mollen vangen gekund   heeft
         that   Patrick the moles   catch   been able   has

     b.* dat   Patrick de   mollen heeft   gekund   vangen
         that   Patrick the moles   has   been able   catch

     c. dat   Patrick de   mollen heeft   kunnen   vangen
         that   Patrick the moles   has   be able   catch

     that Patrick has been able to catch the moles

This pattern of data is identical to that in (41). By comparing (48) with (49) we see that IPP is only possible when **gekund** has an infinitive in its complement. With an NP complement as in the next example, there is no IPP.

(49)   dat Patrick dit   gekund   heeft/ heeft gekund/ *heeft kunnen
         that Patrick this been able has/   has   been able/ has be able

     that Patrick has been able to do this

So, (49) patterns like (46), with optional movement of the verb.

The question is now: Why is restructuring obligatory in (47/48), and why is movement optional in (46/49)? Since movement is a prerequisite for restructuring in the system developed so far, we can also phrase this question as: Why is restructuring obligatory in (47/48) and why isn't there restructuring in (46/49).

The answer to this last question can be introduced by looking at another difference, viz. the difference between (40) and (46/49). That is, the difference between a construction containing a perception verb and its complement and a construction containing an auxiliary and its complement.

In all cases discussed so far, we have seen that the reason for the restructuring resides in the fact that the INFL of the complement blocks government of the subject of the complement by the matrix verb, together with the circumstance that the only way for a grammatical output to be derived requires government of this subject by the matrix verb. Since the only reason for restructuring is the necessity to eliminate (a trace of) INFL, it is a natural move to analyze the cases where there is neither restructuring, nor any other indication of the conspiracy (such as obligatory movement, or extraposition) as involving a complement lacking INFL. Since the presence of INFL is always linked to an S containing a verb, a complement with a V lacking INFL cannot be an S. If it contains a verb, it can only be a VP. As a consequence, these considerations lead us to analyzing (46) as (50).

(50)   dat [_S Patrick [_{VP} de   mollen   vangen] kan]
         that   Patrick   the   moles   catch   can

that Patrick can catch the moles

In (50) there is no necessity for restructuring, or even simple V-raising. Every NP is locally governed. The fact that, as we saw in (46), the verb may be optionally moved to the right of the matrix verb, can be simply accounted for by the assumption that the verb **vangen** has a free ride on V-raising. The rule is around in the grammar, is optional as any instance of the rule Move α, and hence **vangen** may move, but need not. The representation in (50) still leaves open the question what is the exact position of **kan**. The simplest proposal seems to be that it is base inserted in the INFL position and stays there. I don't know of any counter evidence to this. Moreover, this structure is fully consistent with the facts about VP-preposing to be discussed in the Appendix.

The differences between perception verbs and what I called the 'traditional auxiliaries' can now be made to follow from the hypothesis that the traditional auxiliaries can be base inserted in the INFL position, whereas perception verbs (and all other verbs as well) can only be base inserted in the main verb position of a clause, i.e. within the VP. In fact, I will propose that the modal auxiliaries can be base inserted in the INFL position only when INFL is [+tense]. The temporal auxiliaries **hebben** 'have' and **zijn** 'be', can also be inserted in an INFL marked [−tense]. Under this proposal Dutch actually comes out quite similar to what English looks like under certain analyses. In Dutch, however, the auxiliaries also possess infinitival and participial forms. I will take it that these forms are base inserted in the main verb position within the VP. Crucially, if an auxiliary is inserted in the main verb position of the VP it does not take a VP complement; rather it is a main verb then, and takes a clausal complement.

Consider (48) again. **Heeft** is in the [+tense] INFL position of the matrix clause; **gekund** is in the complement of **heeft**; since **heeft** is in the INFL position, **gekund** must be in the main verb position of the VP; hence, **gekund** has a clausal complement, containing **vangen**. I will assume now, that all modal auxiliaries are raising verbs, although this assumption is not without its problems. (I don't think that these problems, and their possible solutions will crucially affect the main features of the analysis I am proposing.) Under this assumption, the structure of (48) is to be represented as (51).

(51)   dat [$_S$ e [$_{VP}$[$_@$ Patrick [$_{VP}$ de mollen vang-]-en] [$_V$ gekund]]
        [$_{INFL}$ heeft]]

Since the subject of @ must be assigned Case, which it cannot get in its base
position, it has to move to the empty subject position of S, leaving a trace.
This trace must be properly governed. Hence, as in all other raising cases
the verb and the INFL of the complement have to move, leaving a trace of
INFL. This trace has to be eliminated, as in the other cases. As a consequence,
we find restructuring. The result of restructuring is given in (52).

(52)   dat [$_S$ Patrick$_i$ [$_{VP}$ [$_@$ t$_i$ [$_{VP}$ de   mollen e$_j$]] e$_k$]
        that   Patrick   the moles

        [$_{INFL}$ [$_{INFL}$ heeft] kunnen vangen]]
        has   be able catch

Here the trace t$_i$ of **Patrick** is properly governed by the trace of the verb
kunnen, viz. e$_k$ (of course, since **kunnen** is a raising verb, it does not assign
Case to its complement, so there is no problem with the binding theory; cf.
Chomsky (1981b) for this property of raising verbs).

The differences between perception verbs and auxiliaries are thus explained
on the basis of the assumption that auxiliaries can, and perception verbs
cannot be base inserted in the INFL position. The fact that in constructions
with three (and more) verbs like those exemplified in (47/48) and (41)
Auxiliaries and perception verbs pattern identically, follows from the fact
that there are only two positions in each sentence in which a verb can be
inserted, the main verb position and the INFL position. As a consequence, as
soon as a complement structure contains more than two verbs, the lowest of
these verbs must be in a different S than the others. This S must have a subject position and an INFL position, which will interact in such a way so as to
necessitate V-raising and restructuring.

A final note on the temporal auxiliaries **hebben** and **zijn** should be added.
It has been observed, that the participles in the complement of such verbs do
not obligatorily participate in V-raising (Den Besten (1980)). Den Besten
derives this from the fact that participles are not full verbs. Notice, that the
participle staying behind is always the most deeply embedded verb in the
complement structure. The facts are illustrated in (53).

(53) a. dat Annamaria de mollen *gevangen* beweert te hebben
        that Annamaria the moles caught   claims to have

b. dat   Annamaria de   mollen beweert te hebben *gevangen*
    that Annamaria the moles claims to have   caught

that Annamaria claims to have caught the moles

These facts follow from the assumption mentioned earlier, that **hebben** may
be inserted in the INFL position even when the latter is [−tense]. Since **te**
hebben is in the INFL position, it is possible to move INFL without stranding
a bound morpheme. Hence, there is no obligation for the main verb to tag
along. Therefore, the participle may stay behind. Thus, participles are involved
in the conspiracy and in the restructuring process only if they themselves
have a complement requiring restructuring. If, as in (53), they constitute the
most deeply embedded element of the complement structure, they are never
obligatorily involved. The optional variation in (53) is then simply due to the
fact that they may have a free ride on V-raising internal to the complement,
and then optionally go along as INFL moves.

The conclusion to be drawn from this discussion of bare infinitivals is
again that even tenseless clauses must be analyzed as containing a realization
of INFL. It is only this assumption that enables us to derive the various
properties of this construction. What it adds to the results already obtained
on the basis of **te**-infinitivals is the following: The contrast between the
control constructions, viz. the constructions in which the subject of the
complement ends up ungoverned at S-structure, and all cases where the
subject of the complement must end up governed at S-structure (all raising
constructions and the perception verb complements) cannot be that in the
latter type of cases INFL is simply absent at all levels of representation.
The explanation of the differences between the traditional auxiliary verbs
and the perception verbs crucially depends on the fact that auxiliaries in
INFL position have a complement which lacks inflection at all levels of
representation, whereas perception verb complements and those of auxiliaries
in main verb position have INFL at the level of D-structure, and it is only
restructuring which allows them to lack it at S-structure. Under an analysis
in which these complements were described as lacking INFL throughout,
at every level, one would expect them to behave like the structures containing
only an auxiliary and a main verb. And this is precisely what they don't do.

4. CONSEQUENCES

4.1. *Possibilities for Extending the Analysis*

I have been dealing with the Dutch infinitival constructions at some length and in considerable detail in order to be able to show how important the thesis is that infinitival clauses in Dutch are headed, and hence that the grammar of Dutch must make use of the category INFL, rather than of the category AUX. Thus the grammar of Dutch bears on the question which motivated this investigation, viz. whether AUX is a universal category. Like the infinitival constructions in English discussed in the previous sections, the Dutch infinitives demonstrate that AUX is not universal.

A second reason why I went into detail was that I think that it is important to demonstrate the results one can obtain on the basis of the formation of restrictive theories in linguistics. And moreover, in order to demonstrate the importance of a concept such as core grammar as distinct from the periphery. The function of the notion of core grammar is not to shove aside recalcitrant data, but rather to enable one to develop theories which can in principle be generalized across languages, since the distinction provides us with the means to abstract away from certain properties of languages in order to show how similar those languages are with respect to others. And, as importantly, it provides us with the means to explain the idiosyncratic properties of these languages as strategies to overcome conflicts between the core modules arising from parameters being fixed in certain ways.

This is illustrated, for instance by the way we analyzed the ACC-*ing* constructions in English, and the way in which it is possible to relate these to the bare infinitivals in Dutch. Like the Dutch affix -en, the English affix -*ing* is originally a nominalizing element. So English exhibits a similar problem to the one we observed in Dutch: What value is there available for the subject of a complement with a nominal INFL, where INFL $\neq$ AG. Since the INFL of the matrix clause cannot be adjacent to the INFL of the complement clause in English restructuring, as in Dutch, cannot apply. For English there were two ways out: either treating the complement as a full NP, with concomitant Genitive marking on the subject (with the disadvantage that this would block the possibility of Wh-extraction), or reinterpreting the offending nominal element -*ing* as the one nominal element that can occur in that position without a conflict ensuing, namely Agreement.

The account presented here, linking V-raising out of control structures to the facts about preposition stranding, which makes it an instance of unsuccessful exceptional Case marking, also extends to German, since it links the fact that in German, zu-infinitivals do not have to move, to the fact that in German there is no preposition stranding. The latter, in turn, follows from the connection established by Kayne between the possibility of preposition stranding and the loss of oblique Case assignment by prepositions (Kayne

(1981a, b)). This, again, might present us with a reason why in Frisian, although there is preposition stranding, there seems to be no conspiracy in to-infinitivals comparable to that in Dutch. In Frisian, there are two forms of the infinitive, one ending in /schwa/, the other ending in /schwa//n/. The latter form appears when an infinitive is in the domain of the infinitival marker **to**, and when it is in the domain of a perception verb. It looks as if the infinitive is assigned Case. (See my (1981c) for more discussion along admittedly different lines, and examples.) When a preposition assigns Case it is not amenable to superscripting (cf. my (1981b) for discussion). So, in Frisian, one would expect that the preposition does not become a structural governor. Hence the conspiracy does not apply. Although, this suggests an analysis for Frisian, on the basis of the principles assumed in this article, a more careful analysis of Frisian might yield a different result. I have only added this, in order to show what kind of considerations might guide further research.

4.2. *Consequences for the Theory of AUX*

On the basis of the analyses given in Sections 1, 2, and 3 we must conclude that both English and Dutch contain an Aux-like category, i.e. outside the VP. This category P-contains *tense* (i.e. *tense* in the sense of ASW and SEA) but does not S-contain it. As a consequence, this category is to be identified with INFL, but not with AUX. Hence, the conclusion appears to be justified that AUX is not a universal category. Returning to the main issues raised in the introduction, we have to conclude now that the hypothesis must be false, that the presence of a member of a category equivalent to AUX is a necessary condition for a sentence to be a 'speech act' which expresses a truth value.

One might still ask, for a language in which INFL is the head of S, whether it could be possible to maintain, nevertheless, that traditional tensed sentences in such a language contained a member of the category AUX. That is, can the category AUX be incorporated in the grammar of a language in which INFL is the head of S. One possibility would be to replace the rule expanding INFL, viz. INFL $\longrightarrow$ [$\pm$ tense, $\pm$N, $\pm$V], by a rule separating the cases meeting ASW's conditions for AUX, from those that are mere Inflections. The only way I can conceive of achieving this is by replacing the former rule by the rules INFL $\longrightarrow$ $\left\{ \begin{matrix} \text{AUX} \\ [-\text{tense}, \pm\text{N}, \pm\text{V}] \end{matrix} \right\}$, AUX $\longrightarrow$ [+tense, $\pm$N, $\pm$V]. But clearly, this way of introducing AUX is a standard case of a missed generalization in a feature system, by imposing an unwarranted hierarchical structure.

Splitting up the category INFL into two disjoint categories, INFL' and AUX would lead to even less desirable consequences. If we are to retain the basis for the explanations arrived at in the previous sections we must assume at least that those items which we claimed to be realizations of the category INFL in infinitival clauses are still heads. But this entails that INFL' and AUX are categorially different heads, and hence their projections would have to be categorially different as well. I.e., the one category S, which is $\overline{\text{INFL}}$, would be replaced by two different, and unrelated categories, viz. $\overline{\text{INFL}'}$ and $\overline{\text{AUX}}$. This obviously would lead to significant loss in descriptive and explanatory adequacy elsewhere in the grammar. It is a solution which one would never have arrived at on the basis of language internal considerations. Hence it is not a feasible way of rescuing the universality of AUX.

Summarizing: If we stick to a definition of AUX which keeps as close as possible to its notional basis, we obtain a category which is an arbitrary subset of the set of heads of S. We arrive at one of the results the logical possibility of which was pointed out in Section 0, one of the dangers implicit in the use of notional definitions. Moreover, we find that INFL even in its tensed realizations lacks the positional restriction which ASW and SEA introduce as important non-definitional properties of AUX. Limiting our attention to Dutch and German, we see that it is obvious that INFL in these languages does not meet the positional conditions on AUX in the manner required by SEA. That is, not even the finite verb in subordinate clauses can be said to be limited to either first, second, or final position. In fact there is no *n* such that the finite verb can be said to occupy the *n*th position. This is illustrated in the examples of (54) (taken from Den Besten and Edmondson (1981); the fact is mentioned in SEA, Appendix B, without conclusions being drawn).

(54) a. weil   er nicht **wird** haben kommen können (4th position)
          because he not   will   have   come   can

  because he will not have been able to come

b. (Ich glaube) dass sie ihn **wird** treffen wollen.
    I believe   that she him will   meet   want

  (3th position from the right)

  I believe that she will want to meet him

For Dutch one finds examples like (55)

(55)   dat Jan   Cecilia   die   sonate **schijnt** te hebben willen   laten
         that Jan. Cecilia   that   sonata seems   to have   wanted let

         uitvoeren in het Concertgebouw op   een gebarsten viool
         perform   in the Concertgebouw on   a   cracked   violin

         (7th position from the right)

         that Jan seems to have wanted to let Cecilia perform that sonata
         in the Concertgebouw on a cracked violin

In fact, still more material could be added on the right, and also any of the PPs on the right could as well be shifted to the left of the tensed verb.

The reason why this restriction is so important resides in its being linked to their hypothesis about AUX discussed earlier, viz. that it is the presence of AUX which makes it possible to assign a truth value to a sentence; or, phrased differently, the presence of AUX is a necessary condition for the sentence to be a speech act. Now, the argument they give explaining why the position of AUX should be subject to positional restrictions of the kind stated is crucially dependent on the 'speech act' version of the hypothesis about AUX. The basic intuition underlying their argument presumably is that AUX, being an operator on the sentence, must be assigned a positionally defined scope. Assuming that the correct way of phrasing the hypothesis about AUX is the one referring to 'speech acts', we might have an explanation for the failure of subordinate clauses in Dutch and German to contain a constituent meeting the positional requirements mentioned: although subordinate clauses may have truth values, there is certainly no justification for analyzing them as being 'speech acts', 'speech acts' being associated with root clauses only. Consider, however, where this leads us. The problem posed by Dutch and German disappears, since subordinate clauses (not only here, but in general) do not contain AUX. Actually, this is in keeping with the speculations in SEA, Chapter 4.

However, we face another version of the problem instead: there is still no way for AUX to be identified with INFL, since INFL occurs in both subordinate clauses and root clauses, whereas AUX is restricted to root clauses only. Further, as we saw, the carrier of tense in root clauses is INFL, but it should be AUX according to the basic hypothesis of the program. Thus, one would be led to the position that S $\rightarrow$ NP AUX VP (or equivalently) in root clauses, and S $\rightarrow$ NP INFL VP in subordinate ones. But in fact, given $\overline{X}$ theory, this implies that a root S differs categorially from a subordinate S. This is an unacceptable result for obvious reasons. Moreover, AUX and INFL being different categories, their obvious internal similarities for the values they share, and the fact that they share values at all, would be represented as completely accidental. So, one may conclude that there is something fundamentally amiss in the program as conceived; the question is: What?

It is, of course, possible that there simply is no real issue: AUX is just a spectre vanishing upon proper investigation. However, given the results of the program so far, it is more likely that a real issue exists. That there is a sense in which AUX plays a role in universal grammar. If this is so, there is only one conclusion possible: it is the conception of AUX which led astray, viz. AUX is not a category, but a relation between categories. E being the label of the initial category of the grammar, as in $E \rightarrow X^n \ \bar{S}, \bar{S} \rightarrow COMP \ S$, $S \rightarrow NP \ INFL \ VP$, AUX in the intended sense must be conceived of as a grammatical function of INFL with respect to E. Using the traditional notation for grammatical functions (Chomsky (1965)), we arrive at AUX being [INFL, E]. The properties ascribed to AUX by ASW and SEA can now be understood as conditions on INFL if it is to count as 'The AUX of E'. Thus, investigation of AUX can proceed.

APPENDIX

Throughout this article I have been assuming that there is a position in Dutch, outside the VP, directly associated with INFL – let us say that it is the INFL position itself – in which auxiliaries can be base inserted. This claim is not uncontroversial, as I stated earlier. Yet, it was on the basis of this claim, coupled with the assumption that main verbs (only) cannot be base inserted in this position, that we were able to derive the differences with respect to V-raising.

In this appendix I will show that there is independent evidence for the claim that auxiliaries can, and main verbs cannot, be base generated in a position outside the VP. Since it only concerns differences between tensed auxiliaries and tensed main verbs, the evidence does not directly bear on the main topic of this article: it is compatible with the hypothesis that the head of S is INFL, but also with the hypothesis that it is AUX. Indirectly, it is relevant, however, since it provides the basis for the explanation for the differences between auxiliaries and main verbs given in Section 3.2. The argument showing that there is an auxiliary position in Dutch outside the VP, is based on the phenomenon of VP-preposing. The reader is also referred to Zaenen (1979), who arrives at a comparable conclusion on the basis of similar data.

The term, 'VP-preposing', is actually a bit misleading since the construction may be is base generated, and also may perhaps involve smaller V-projections contained in VP too. The name is entrenched, however, and as far as the present discussion goes, nothing much hinges on these issues. So I will use it. The phenomenon itself is illustrated in (1).

(1) a. Jan zal waarschijnlijk nooit zulke goede gedichten schrijven.
Jan will probably   never such good poems   write

Jan will probably never write such good poems.

b. Zulke goede gedichten schrijven (dat) zal Jan waarschijnlijk nooit.
such good poems   write   that will Jan probably   never

Write such good poems John probably never will.

(1a) represents the unpreposed version: in (1b) the sequence *zulke goede gedichten schrijven* has been preposed. A concomitant difference in (1b) is of course the inversion between the subject and the (finite) verb in the residue, but this is a general process whenever some constituent other than the subject is in first position (the result of the rule V-second). Between the proposed sequence and the residue, there is an optional occurrence of **dat**, a so-called *d*-word, in Comp position (cf. Koster (1978)). Koster notices that all major constituents can be followed by such a *d*-word in sentence initial position. In fact this can be strengthened by requiring that only maximal projections can be followed by a *d*-word. This explains the ungrammaticality of (2), when **dat** is present: V, which has been preposed alone, is not a maximal projection.

(2) Schrijven (* dat) kan Jan zulke gedichten niet, maar voordragen
write   that can Jan such poems   not but   recite

(* dat) kan hij ze   wel.
that can he   them certainly.

Write such poems John can't, but recite them he certainly can.

All this can be taken as an indication that the preposed string in (1b) is a V-projection, and moreover, given the contrast between (1b) and (2), is a maximal V-projection, i.e. a VP. The fact illustrated in (3) supports that view. Here we see that those constitudents which are traditionally analyzed as sentence adverbs, viz. **waarschijnlijk** 'probably ' and **niet** 'not', may not occur in the proposed constituent.

(3)   (* waarschijnlijk) (* nooit) zulke gedichten schrijven (dat) zal Jan
probably   never such poems   write   that will Jan

Given the differences between VP-preposing and preposing of nonmaximal V-projections we will limit ourselves to VP-preposing proper in the discussion below. (Preposing of non-maximal projections seems to be felicitous only when a contrastive interpretation is possible, suggesting that it is subject to some specific conditions of its own.)

The relevance of VP-preposing to the point we wish to establish resides in the following fact: a constituent can undergo VP-preposing only if it is in the complement of what is traditionally categorized as an auxiliary verb. This would be quite surprising if there were no categorial difference between the complement of auxiliaries and the complement of main verbs. But, in fact, the verbs allowing VP-preposing are precisely the verbs not requiring V-raising (and/or restructuring) when their complement is a simplex clause; i.e. their complement does not contain INFL at D-structure. The difference with respect to VP-preposing between the complements of traditional auxiliaries and those of main verbs is illustrated by the differences between (4) and (5). The examples in (4) are grammatical; the highest verb is an auxiliary.

(4) a. Zulke gedichten schrijven (dat) { wil / zal / mag / moet/hoeft } Jan niet.

such poems write that { wants / will / may / must/needs } Jan not

b. Zulke gedichten geschreven (? dat) heeft Jan nog nooit.
such poems written that has Jan yet never

Written such poems John hasn't yet (done).

c. Door Dries naar de ondergang gevoerd (dat) is het land   nog niet.
by Dries to the ruin led that is the country not yet

Led to ruin by Dries the country hasn't yet been.

All the examples in (5), where the highest verb is a main verb, are ungrammatical.

(5) a. * Mooie gedichten (te) schrijven (dat) schijnt Jan nooit.
nice poems to write that seems Jan never

b. * Zulke gedichten uit (te) geven (dat) helpt Jan Cecilia niet.
such poems to publish that helps Jan Cecilia not

c. * Zulke liederen zingen (dat) hoort Jan Cecilia nooit.
such songs sing that hears Jan Cecilia never

As I said, this difference would be surprising under an analysis in which auxiliaries take the same kind of complements as main verbs do, viz. clausal complements. On the other hand the difference would be expected under an analysis in which (a) auxiliaries take VP complements and main verbs S̄-complements, provided (b) the constituent moved were not simply required to be *in* the complement of the verb which 'stays behind' but had to be *identical to* that complement. If we wish to use this data to support the hypothesis that Dutch has auxiliaries taking VP complements, then the second requirement, (b), is important. Fortunately it does not need to be stipulated since it follows if the binding theory is extended to empty V-projections.

To see that this is so, we return to the facts which led to the V-raising analyses in Sections 3.2. and 3.3. We begin with the verbs of (5). As is suggested by a comparison of (6) with (7), V-raising has to apply to all the verbs of (5). This will be sufficient to guarantee that the complement of the verb that 'stays behind' is not identical to the proposed VP – and violates the binding requirements for that very reason. The relevant examples follow:

(6) a. dat Jan zulke gedichten niet *schrijven zal/* zal schrijven
        that Jan such poems not write will will write

   that Jan will not write such poems

   b. dat Jan zulke gedichten niet *geschreven heeft/* heeft geschreven
       that Jan such poems not written has has written

   that Jan hasn't written such poems

(7) a. dat Jan nooit mooie gedichten ** te schrijven schijnt/* schijnt
        that Jan never nice poems to write seems seems

   te   schrijven
   to   write

   that Jan never seems to write nice poems

   b. dat Jan Cecilia niet zulke gedichten ** uit (te) geven helpt/* helpt
       that Jan Cecilia not such poems to publish helps helps

   uit (te) geven
   to publish

   that John doesn't help Cecilia publish such poems.

   c. dat Jan Cecilia nooit zulke liederen ** zingen hoort/* hoort zingen
       that Jan Cecilia never such songs sing hears hears sing

   that Jan never hears Cecilia sing such songs.

The relevant features shared by the base structures of the examples in (7) are repeated in (8). (As before, V ʃ INFL simply indicates that V and INFL must combine.)

(8) $[\overline{S} \text{ dat} \ldots [_S \text{ NP } [_{VP} \ldots V\ʃ \text{ INFL}] \text{ V/INFL}].$

In all of these cases the V ʃ INFL of the complement clause has to move to the right of the matrix verb by V-raising, as in (7). The reasoning, we have argued in Section 3, is that otherwise the subject of the complement will be governed in some way violating the binding theory. This is enough to guarantee that the structure of (7) is such that VP cannot be preposed: either preposing applies before the verb is moved out of the VP, in which case the NP has no grammatical value, or VP preposing applies after the verb has moved out of it, in which case it contains a trace of the moved verb, and this is not properly bound, i.e. not c-commanded by its antecedent. Whenever a VP is in a tenseless complement, this situation will arise.

This amounts to the requirement that in order for VP-preposing to be possible the 'resulting' structure must be essentially as in (9) – whether this is base generated or results from a preposing of $VP_i^{\#}$.

(9) $[_E \, VP^{\#}_i \, [_{\overline{S}} \, (dat) \, [_S \ldots [_{VP*} \, e]_i \ldots]]]$.

(Here, following Koster (1978), I assume that the structure containing both the preposed VP and the clausal remnant is a category sui generis, bearing the label E of Expression.) Structure (9) expresses the condition that a preposed VP, $VP^{\#}_i$, must be able to bind a VP, VP*, within the clausal remnant. This can only be accomplished if the $\overline{S}$/S does not contain any material 'originating from' $VP^{\#}$. Suppose that $\overline{S}$ contained such material; since E contains only two possible sources for VP-material (preposed $VP^{\#}$, and the 'original' VP*), material inside $\overline{S}$, but outside any of those VPs must have been moved out of one of them. If this material has been moved out of $VP^{\#}$, it does not c-command its trace. Hence, the structure is out. The other possible source is VP*. But, if a constituent has been generated in VP*, and moved out of it, it must have left a trace. This trace as such can be bound by the moved constituent. However, the resulting structure does not meet the conditions summarized in (9). Instead, it has the form of (10).

(10) $[_E \, VP^{\#}_i \, [_{\overline{S}} \ldots a_j \ldots [_{VP*} \, e \, [e] \, _j \, e] \, _i \ldots]]$.

Here, $[e]_j$ is some part of VP* which is not bound by $VP^{\#}$, but by some other constituent, a_j, which could in fact have been on either side of VP*. Now, in (10) $VP^{\#}$ simply does not bind all of VP*, but only some subpart of it, and this is illegitimate under any reasonable way of construing binding of an empty position by an antecedent.

Under our analysis, therefore, the requirement that an embedded verb be moved out of the VP in the complement of the verbs of (5), which is demonstrated by the ungrammatical forms in (7), yields a violation of the binding conditions in VP-preposing structures. Contrast this with the auxiliaries of (4). These we will analyse as base generated with a VP* which is *identical* to the preposed $VP^{\#}$. The auxiliary will be generated under INFL. The structure corresponding to (4) might therefore, if we abstract from the final placement of the auxiliary in second position, look something like (11):

(11) $[_E \, [_{VP^{\#}_i} \, zulke \, gedichten \, schrijven] \, [_{\overline{S}} \, (dat) \, [_S \, Jan \, [_{VP*} \, e]_i$
            $[_{INFL} \, wil]]]]$.

As represented here, the auxiliary wil was never in either $VP^{\#}$ nor VP*, and as evidenced by the alternations in (6), the verb in $VP^{\#}$ (= VP*) is not required to move from there. Thus given our analysis the contrast between (4) and (5) is predicted.

It remains only to deal with the possibilities that are open when the sentence contains only a single verb, not even an auxiliary. VP-preposing is then also ruled out — except for one option to be discussed below. Consider (12).

(12) $[_E \, VP^{\#} \, [_{\overline{S}} \, (dat) \, [_S \, Jan \, nooit \, [_{VP*} \quad gedichten \quad voor \quad geld$
                          that   Jan   never   poems   for   money

            schrijf-l $-[_{INFL} \, -t]]$
            write- $-s$

In a clause with only one verb, the inflection must be realized on this verb. This fact can be made to follow from some morphological principle to the effect that bound morphemes cannot be stranded, and from the reasonable stipulation that the value of INFL in (12) is a bound morpheme. So, the verb and the INFL have to merge.

Suppose this merger were in the syntax. Then, in fact it would have to be a movement raising schrijf- and associating it with INFL, since lowering INFL would leave Jan ungoverned. (To put it differently, having lowering of INFL in the syntax would represent Dutch as a PRO-drop language, which it isn't (cf. the discussion in Chomsky (1981b) of the PRO-drop parameter).) However, if this merger is effected by a raising rule, it must be assumed to leave a trace of the verb, to mediate government of the direct object NP, just as we assumed in the V-raising structures. But then we have the situation described above: Either the verb moves out of the preposed VP$^{\#}$, leaving an unbound verbal trace, which it is reasonable to assume, will neither mediate Case, nor transmit satisfaction of strict subcategorization requirements of the verb. Or else, under a base generation approach, i.e. with the preposed VP$^{\#}$ lacking a verb generated in situ, and the verb base-generated in the main VP*, and moved out in order to merge with INFL, we have the situation indicated in (10): The VP to be bound contains the trace of the verb, which is bound independently. Hence VP* cannot be bound. This accounts for the ungrammaticality of preposing an 'incomplete' VP, with the verb left behind. That is, it accounts for the ungrammaticality of structures such as (13).

(13)   *$[_E$ $[_{VP}^{\#}$ gedichten   voor   geld$]_i$ $[_{\overline{S}}$ dat $[_S$ [schrijf$_j$-t]   Jan
                       poems   for   money   that   writes   Jan

          nooit $[_{VP*} \ldots e_j]_i]$ $]$ $]$
          never

For sake of clarity, it is perhaps not superfluous to add, that this argument only needs to be given in case the merger of verb and inflection is indeed a rule in the syntax, raising the verb as indicated. If it is a rule in the phonology as in English, the assumption that INFL in these case cannot be stranded suffices. For reasons outside the scope of the present investigation, I think however, that the raising account is more promising. Hence consideration of this case has been included.

Somewhat earlier, I said that there is one option under which VP-preposing applying to clauses with one verb is not ruled out. This is the option under which the VP is preposed before the merger of the verb and the inflection, and in which the structure is saved by the same process we find in English to save structures with a stranded inflection, viz. by invoking *do*-support. Like English *do*, the Dutch verb **doen** 'do' can be inserted in order to prevent stranding of inflection. However, the cases in which it is necessary are very few. (Perhaps the case mentioned in Note 10 is one of them.) By **doen**-support the grammatical sentence in (14) can be derived as an alternative to (13).[16]

(14) $[_E$ $[_{VP}$ gedichten   voor   geld   schrijven$]_i$ $[_{\overline{S}}$ (dat) $[_S$ doet   Jan
                 poems   for   money   write   that   does   Jan

          niet $[_{VP}$ e$]_i]$ $]$ $]$
          not

          write poems for money Jan doesn't

Here, the sole purpose of **doet** is that of obviating the necessity for establishing an association between the inflection and **schrijven**. It is only the hypothesis that **schrijven** does, and inflection does not originate within the VP, that explains the insertion of **doet** in this case. All the restrictions on VP-preposing can now be explained on the basis of this insight: VP-preposing is possible whenever no constituent within the VP is syntactically associated with any position ·outside it. To put it differently, the phenomena of VP-preposing in Dutch are explained on the basis of the hypothesis that there is in Dutch a position for inflection outside the VP, and that *tensed auxiliaries*, but *not tensed main verbs* can be base inserted in a position directly associated with that inflection position. That is, the same hypothesis that was needed in order to account for the optionality of V-raising out of simplex complements of auxiliaries is needed to account for the possibility of preposing such complements. Hence, to the extent that any piece of nondemonstrative inference warrants a conclusion, the conclusion is warranted that the grammar of Dutch contains an Aux-like constituent outside the VP.[17]

NOTES

* Part of the research reported on in this article was carried out during a stay at MIT, supported by the Netherlands Organization for the Advancement of Pure Research. This support is hereby gratefully acknowledged. This study has greatly benefited from the discussions I had on this, or related subject matters with many people. I would like to express my special gratitude to Noam Chomsky, David Pesetsky, Ken Safir, Barry Schein and Tim Stowell. I am particularly indebted to Maria Luisa Zubizarreta for a suggestion as to the analysis of bare infinitivals in Dutch. Although not implemented in the present proposal, it convinced me that it would be worthwhile to look for a more principled approach than the one taken in my (1981c). I am also very grateful to Sue Steele for the comments on an earlier version of this article which she was so kind to send me. Finally, I would like to thank Frank Heny, and an anonymous reader for their valuable comments and helpful suggestions. None of these people is responsible for any of the opinions expressed, nor for any of the remaining mistakes and unclarities. A note for the record: the appendix of this article represents the final version of a paper I presented at the Salzburg Workshop on Auxiliaries, and which has been referred to and circulated under the titles 'Some Comments on the AUX in Dutch' and 'The Rule Move V revisited'. This workshop was organized in the summer of 1979 by Frank Heny, as part of the preparations for the Fourth Groningen Round Table in 1980.
[1] Cf. also their contributions to this volume.
[2] Sue Steele has drawn my attention to the fact that there is a difference in the appooach of ASW and that in SEA. SEA is most particularly concerned with the general methodological question as to how crosslinguistic identification of categories can be justified. The treatment of AUX is meant to exemplify how one can go about that question.
[3] Sue Steele has been so kind as to inform me, that personally, and currently, she would come down on the side of S-containment.
[4] In 1979 Tom Wasow (personal communication) expressed the view that the infinitival marker *to* cannot be analyzed as a realization of AUX. I have not assessed his current views, however.

5 According to Chomsky (1981b) cosuperscripting is a kind of coindexing without binding. Thus it can be used to express the closeness between a preposition and a verb, but also the requirement that some clitic (including AG) and a PRO in argument position be interpreted identically, or as part of a condition stating when government holds between AG and the subject (cf. also Rouveret and Vergnaud (1980)).

6 It should be noted in this connection, that one also finds absolute constructions with a subject in objective form instead of nominative. For the argument this is irrelevant, however, since these objective subjects behave identically in the relevant respects. In fact, presumably this is a remnant of the original dative Case. The point is that there must be some Case marking available, and in such a manner that the effects noted are derived. What happens is, that there is a rule like (14ii) for assignment of an elsewhere Case. This elsewhere Case may be realized as nominative, or objective (perhaps, rather oblique) depending on various factors which need not concern us here.

7 One possibility is to adopt a proposal by Youssef Aoun to the effect that the ECP effects in subject position are really violations of the binding theory. What is required is not government of the trace in subject position by the trace in COMP, but rather the subject trace should be c-commanded within its $\bar{S}$ by a binder, viz. this trace in COMP. Another possibility, advanced in Reuland (1980c), is that lexical government is the relevant factor. COMP is a lexical governor for AG. If AG is coindexed with COMP, which it is if COMP exhaustively dominates a trace coindexed with the subject position, we obtain a situation which is parallel with that of a preposition cosuperscripted with a verb. As in the case of the preposition, AG coindexed with a lexical governor is turned into a lexical governor, i.e. it governs like COMP does. Hence the subject trace is properly governed.

8 Of course, the analysis presupposes some version of Affix Hopping in order to have the relevant realization of INFL attached to the verb. The absence of *do*-support phenomena in tenseless clauses could be taken to follow from the analysis in ASW if the base generation of *do* is restricted to finite forms of *do*. That is, *do* in this construction simply has all the syntactic properties of modal auxiliaries.

9 The claim that there is reanalysis does not clash with the fact that the subject of the complement of *believe* can be extracted. There is no general problem with extracting from positions involved in reanalysis. Extraction is also possible in the following idiom, cf. *I gave John hell/John was given t hell*. Notice moreover that although in one sense *to* in the *believe* case is not adjacent to the matrix verb, in another sense it is: it is the head of a constituent adjacent to the matrix verb. In that sense, *John* does not intervene.

A reader of this article remarked that it seems unmotivated to analyse *to* (and te, zu) as a preposition. To that I would respond that such an proposal is as motivated as the account it enables one to give is explanatory. As far as such matters are concerned, there are no a priori insights that can be relied on. A different question is what this analysis entails in conjunction with $\bar{X}$ theory. Does it entail that infinitival clauses are PPs? I think it does not, since under this proposal the preposition is contained in INFL. Take the structure to be $[_{INFL} [_{p} to] \dots]$. Since S is a projection of INFL, not P, differences in the internal composition of INFL do not necessarily imply differences in categorial status of S. It remains $\overline{INFL}$.

10 Evers and Scholten (1980) argue that the conception of AUX as a VP-external constituent yields the wrong results for Dutch. The argument is based on the contention that gapping phenomena in Dutch (and German) are explained best on the basis of a

structure in which Auxiliaries (and verbs) are stacked in a V-cluster, whereas the multiple auxiliaries in English are due to stacking in VP-structures. Even if verbs in Dutch and German form a cluster of the kind argued for in Evers (1975) (but cf. Thiersch (1978)) the argument of Evers and Scholten does not establish what it is supposed to. In order to bear on the proposal in ASW it must crucially assume that the modal verb is within the VP to begin with. No argument is given for the contention that the verbal cluster as such is within the VP, and I have the impression that no such argument can be given. Briefly: the question whether there is a verbal cluster is distinct from the question what position is occupied by that cluster; it is the latter question which matters for their argument to carry weight. Despite this, one might contend that all the same, there is gapping of VP with stranding of the auxiliary in English, whereas there is not in Dutch. On the other hand it is suggestive that in Dutch there are two ways to obtain the same result as gapping of VP in English. One is by having an item such as dat 'that' in the gap, the other by having dat (te) doen 'that (to) do'. The first option, is open only if the remnant is an auxiliary. This is illustrated in (i)

(i) a.   Piet heeft geslapen en   Jan heeft *(dat) ook.
          Piet has   slept   and Jan has   that too

     b.   Piet schijnt een gedicht te schrijven en Jan schijnt * (dat) ook
          Piet seems   a   poem   to write   and Jan seems   that also

          * (te doen).
            to do

This suggests that the relation of an auxiliary to the remaining verb differs from the relation of a main verb to the verbs in its governing domain. See the appendix for a detailed analysis of the auxiliary-main verb relation; the conclusion to be reached there will be supported by the facts noted here.
11 In Reuland (1981c) I discussed a possible reason. I proposed that the conspiracy consists in the infinitival verb avoiding Case positions. The fact that tensed clauses too in principle have to extrapose was, I suggested, due to the complementizer dat having to avoid Case positions. As I noted there, there is a problem with this approach in that tensed complements can be retained in preverbal, i.e. Case, positions, with intonational help, but infinitival clauses cannot. This is unexpected if the same explanation is to hold for both cases. Especially te-infinitivals as in (34a) are beyond salvage. This is the more interesting, since Stowell (1981) using quite similar ideas, argues that finite clauses in English always avoid Case positions, but infinitives do not. If his account is correct the badness of preverbal infinitival clauses in Dutch is most in need of an explanation. This explanation will be given below.
12 The original analysis by Evers involved besides V-raising, a principle of S-pruning. After losing its verb the complement clause lost its status as a separate S. The arguments in Evers (1975) in favor of adopting an S-pruning convention are somewhat hard to evaluate; they are based on the fact that PPs are easily extracted from complements after V-raising, and e.g. quantifiers are easy to lower into such structures. However, the relevant contrasts all involve adverbial clauses, subject clauses, and extraposed clauses, all of which are known to be islands for any such operation, for quite independent

reasons. In Reuland (1980a) I showed that at least for the binding theory complements which have lost their verb by V-raising are opaque, in the sense that they are governing categories. Although there are some unclarities, I will assume then that the S boundaries remain unaffected.

Evers proposed that all V-raising resulted in the raised verb being adjoined to the matrix verb. Given our analysis of the clausal structure as containing a separate position for INFL, we have to assume something like adjunction to INFL. Evers argues that after raising the verbs will have to form one constituent because of the fact that they seem to behave like a unit under gapping. (Cf. Thiersch (1978) for discussion.) As we will see below, given my analysis of what happens in all those cases involving restructuring, the most natural assumption will be that the verbs do indeed end up as one constituent. At least in those cases, it is natural to assume that this constituent is INFL. It will be represented as such. As I noted in my (1981c), in general the rule of V-raising has the effect that a structure of the form (i) is converted into one of the form (ii), details omitted

(i) $V_1]_S V_2]_S \cdots V_{n-1}]_S V_n.$

(ii) $e_1]_S e_2]_S \cdots e_{n-1}]_S V_n V_{n-1} \cdots V_2 V_1.$

If V-raising is an instance of Move α, it is subject to subjacency, and the required result follows from this principle under straightforward assumptions.

[13] One way of explaining the fact that te, though a governor, is not a proper governor, is that te as a realization of INFL could never assign a θ-role. This uses a proposed link between proper government and θ-role assignment. Only those governors are proper governors that assign a θ-role or mediate in the assignment of θ-roles. (cf. e.g. Stowell (1981)). This approach has many ramifications which I will not discuss here.

[14] A reader of this article cites dat Anna ziek is gebleken te zijn 'that Anna ill is appeared to be = that Anna has appeared to be ill' as acceptable. To me it is not. In fact I am not sure it ought to be treated as grammatical. A ready explanation for its relative acceptability could be that it is very similar to the same sentence without te zijn, which has the same meaning and is grammatical, since it is a small clause. The reader observes that the fact that in this case the matrix auxiliary and the auxiliary in the complement are identical could be relevant. I agree, since we see that in (38), below, the only grammatical output is one in which the upstairs auxiliary is hebben 'have'. This is quite unexpected, since blijken requires a form of zijn 'be'. However, this is reminiscent of the case in Italian, where restructuring also has the effect of the upstairs verb taking the auxiliary required by the downstairs verb. So, the necessity of hebben is one more argument in favour of restructuring, as is the fact that the identity of auxiliary in the above Case favors acceptability.

Another unexplained example is het heeft even gedreigd te gaan regenen 'it has for a moment threatened to start raining'. To the extent in which it is acceptable, the problem posed by its acceptability is reducible to that posed by the acceptability of its variant het heeft even gedreigd *om* te gaan regenen, which has the same meaning, but where the presence of the complementizer/preposition om identifies the sentence as a control structure. Hence, the problem is not so much why there is no restructuring, but rather why it appears as a control structure. But this in fact is a quite different problem.

[15] The empirical differences concern the consequences for the theory of the fact that, subject to some idiosyncratic variation, IPP may optionally occur in control structures. I.e. with some verbs, e.g. **vragen** 'ask' IPP is totally impossible, with others, e.g. **proberen** 'try' it is fully acceptable. The simplest explanation is that the principle relaxing the rule by which **hebben** requires a participle, is spreading through the grammar. In forthcoming work I will however investigate alternative explanations. It is not clear to me why in the case of bare infinitivals IPP is always acceptable when necessary, whereas in constructions with **te-infinitivals** this is often not so, cf. the marginal status of IPP in the complement of **schijnen** 'seem'. It is also curious, that in the complement of **helpen** 'help' for some speakers IPP implies the disappearance of **te**. Possibly, the presence of **te** is in some sense an obstacle to restructuring, which is subject to overruling depending on idiosyncratic properties of the matrix verb.

[16] It should be noted that this use of **doen** is possible only in constructions with a preposed VP: * **Jan doet gedichten schrijven** 'Jan does write poems' is ungrammatical; even an emphatic interpretation is impossible. Insertion of **doen** might be executed in either of the following ways. (1) **doen** is subcategorized as taking an empty VP; given the assumption that inflection may not be stranded for some independent morphological reasons, it follows that **doen** will be inserted iff VP-preposing applied and the structure is to be grammatical. Insertion may be supposed to take place at S-structure (cf. Chomsky (1981b)). (2) One adopts a variant of the analysis of *do*-support in English proposed in ASW. I.e. a form of **doen** is inserted optionally, but freely, in the aux-position within INFL if this position is empty, and INFL tensed. If **doen** is not inserted, and no other auxiliary is present, the verb of the VP is associated with inflection. This process can also be taken to be optional, since the result if it does not apply (a stranded inflection) is ungrammatical for independent, morphological reasons. It seems quite plausible that the result of having both a verb in the VP and a form of *doen* associated with inflection could fall under some verbal counterpart of the avoid pronoun principle. Suppose *doen* is a pro-verb, one would expect that it shows up only where it cannot be avoided. In Dutch this is the case only when the VP has been preposed. Under both analyses our basic contention as to the structure of these constructions is supported.

[17] An anonymous reader of this article questioned whether Dutch contains VP-preposing at all. He suggested that the structures given might constitute a Dutch equivalent of gerunds, i.e. that they are basically NPs. The optional **dat** in Comp position might be construed as a resumptive pronoun bound by that NP. This would entail that the optional **dat** really is a direct object of the verb in the remnant. If so, then the verb in the remnant should always have to be transitive. Moreover, if **dat** is simply a pronoun, substitution of the 'gerund' for the pronoun should always be grammatical, and the presence of **dat** should always be explicable on the basis of some preposed gerund. None of these is true, however. Although some of the relevant auxiliaries can sometimes occur as transitive verbs with an NP object, at least one of them cannot, and in the case of others attempts at identification of the several uses are really implausible. So, although we do have **Jan moet dat** 'Jan must (do) that', and **Jan kan dat** 'Jan can (do) that', we don't have * **Jan zal dat** 'Jan will (do) that', instead of the latter we find either **Jan zal** 'Jan will', or **Jan zal het doen** 'Jan will do it'. **Jan heeft dat** 'Jan has that' is only possible with **hebben** 'have' construed as possessive, so identification seems very far-fetched. A similar observation can be made with respect to **zijn** 'be'. It seems far-fetched to relate the occurrence of **dat** in (4) to an NP as in **Jan is een soldaat** 'Jan is a soldier'. **Moeten**,

if transitive at all, is quite remarkable, since it can only take pronominal NPs as a direct object (*Jan moet veel werk 'Jan must a lot of work') in its core meaning. It only takes a direct object when it occurs with its secondary meaning 'need' as in Jan moet veel geld 'Jan needs a lot of money'. And this is not the force of auxiliary moeten. Finally, note that substitution of the gerund for dat and construing the result as an object of the auxiliary verb is impossible when the auxiliary is doen. Most interestingly, doen in its normal use, is an ordinary transitive verb, in fact it is ungrammatical when used without a direct object in its core meaning, as in Jan doet een hoop werk 'Jan does a lot of work', in contrast with *Jan doet 'Jan does'. However, although in all of the other cases the auxiliary does appear in the corresponding nonpreposed construction, i.e. with the supposed gerund as its direct object, doen cannot be used in this way. Compare Jan moet/zal [gedichten voor geld schrijven] 'Jan must/will write poems for money' with *Jan doet [gedichten voor geld schrijven] 'Jan does write poems for money'. Finally, even if some of the preposed constituents were 'gerunds', others cannot possibly be. So, in Ik denk dat zulke gedichten schrijven erg moeilijk is 'I think that writing such poems is very difficult' zulke gedichten schrijven might be a gerund-like construction. However, door Dries naar de ondergang gevoerd 'by Dries to ruin led' surely is not, yet here too we find the 'resumptive' dat in (4c). Hence, there really is no alternative to the account given in the text. Examples which might be adduced as violating condition (10), are all amenable to other parsings. This reader also remarks that it does not seem to constitute a problem that the trace (of a constituent left behind in the clausal remnant) would not be c-commanded by its antecedent. And he cites examples of anaphors that appear to be bound by non-c-commanding antecents. This is correct in the sense that it is a problem why trace requires a more strict adherence to the principle of c-command than ordinary anaphors (cf. Chomsky (1981b)). This appears to be a general difference. It is not clear, however, that Huybregts' antecedency binding condition should be invoked as suggested by the reader. Surely it would be better to reduce this fact to general properties of binding than to account for it on the basis of some different principle, which itself is in need of explanation.

It is perhaps useful to devote some space to a construction in Dutch that might seem to be related to VP-preposing: many ungrammatical sentences of the sort exemplified in (5) have grammatical counterparts containing an occurrence of doen. The examples are given in (i).

(i) a.   Mooie gedichten schrijven (dat) schijnt Jan nooit te doen.
          nice   poems   write   that   seems   Jan never to do

     Write nice poems, Jan seems never to do that.

     b. *Zulke gedichten uitgeven (dat) helpt Jan Cecilia niet (te) doen.
          such   poems   publish   that   help   Jan Cecilia not   to   do

     Publish such poems, Jan will not help Cecilia do that.

     c.   Zulke liederen zingen (dat) hoort Jan Cecilia nooit doen.
          such   songs   sing   that   hears Jan Cecilia never do

     Sing such songs, Jan never hears Cecilia do that.

However, this construction appears to be quite different. With VP-preposing in the sense discussed in the main text, inversion of the subject and the tensed verb is obligatory; the examples in (ii) are quite unacceptable.

(ii) a. ?* Zulke   gedichten   schrijven,   Jan zal   dat nooit.
           such   poems   write,   Jan will that never

      b. * Zulke   gedichten   geschreven,   Jan heeft   dat nooit.
           such   poems   written   Jan has   that never

In both examples of (ii) adding a form of doen 'do' after nooit, plus a clear comma intonation after the preposed constituent yields a quite acceptable construction. The second case is interesting, since heeft requires a past participle in its complement, hence doen appears as gedaan 'done'; however, now the past participle geschreven must be replaced by the infinitive schrijven, yielding zulke gedichten schrijven, Jan heeft dat nooit gedaan. Moreover, dat is obligatory now. The obvious conclusion is, that here dat is simply a pronoun with argument status in its own S, and is the direct object of doen. In fact, this construction does not require the verb doen; (ib) for instance is better with voor elkaar krijgen 'bring about' substituted for doen, suggesting that the link between the 'preposed' VP and the main predicate of the clause may be quite loose and nonsyntactic in nature. Anyhow, the effect of having doen in the clausal remnant is precisely that of circumventing the property of the main verbs in (i) such as schijnen and horen, that they have to be associated both with a position within the VP and with the inflection outside it. Again, this explains why VP-preposing is not blocked here.

BIBLIOGRAPHY

Akmajian, A., S. Steele, and T. Wasow: 1979, 'The Category "Aux" in Universal Gramar', *Linguistic Inquiry* 10, 1–64.

Besten, H. den: 1980, 'Verb Raising and Auxiliary-Main Verb Dependencies in Dutch', Paper presented at the Fourth Groningen Round Table, July 1980.

Besten, H. den and J. Edmondson: 1981, 'The Verbal Complex in Continental West Germanic', in W. Abraham (ed.), *Groninger Arbeiten zur Germanistischen Linguistik*, Nr. 19.

Bresnan, J.: 1970, 'On Complementizers: Towards a Syntactic Theory of Complement Types', *Foundations of Language* 6, 297–321.

Chomsky, N.: 1965, *Aspects of the Theory of Syntax*, MIT Press, Cambridge.

Chomsky, N.: 1973, 'Conditions on Transformations'. in S. Anderson and P. Kiparsky (eds.), *A Festschrift for Morris Halle*, Holt, Rinehart & Winston, New York.

Chomsky, N.: 1981a, 'Principles and Parameters in Syntactic Theory', in N. Hornstein and D. Lightfoot (eds.), *Explanation in Linguistics*, Longmans, London.

Chomsky, N.: 1981b, *Lectures on Government and Binding*, Foris, Dordrecht.

Evers, A.: 1975, *The Transformational Cycle in Dutch and German*, reproduced by the Indiana Linguistics Club.

Evers, A.: 1981, 'Two Functional Principles for the Rule Move V', in W. Abraham (ed.), *Groninger Arbeiten zur Germanistische Linguistik*, Nr. 19.

Evers, A. and T. Scholten: 1980, 'A Dutch Answer to the Luiseño Argument', *Utrecht Working Papers in Linguistics* 9.

George, L. and J. Kornfilt: 1981, 'Finiteness and Boundedness in Turkish', in F. Heny (ed.), *Binding and Filtering*, Croom Helm, London.

Horn, G.: 1975, 'On the Nonsentential Nature of the POSS-ING Construction', *Linguistic Analysis* 1, 333–388.

Jespersen, O.: 1940/1961, *A Modern English Grammar*, Allen & Unwin Ltd., London, Munksgaard, Copenhagen.

Kayne, R.: 1981a, 'ECP Extensions', *Linguistic Inquiry* 12, 93–133.

Kayne, R.: 1981b, 'On Certain Differences between French and English', *Linguistic Inquiry* 12, 349–371.

Koster, J.: 1975, 'Dutch as an SOV Language', *Linguistic Analysis* 1, 111–136.

Koster, J.: 1978, *Locality Principles in Syntax*, Foris, Dordrecht.

Kruisinga, E. and P. A. Erades: 1911/1953, *An English Grammar*, P. Noordhoff N.V., Groningen, Djakarta.

Lyons, J.: 1968, *Introduction to Theoretical Linguistics*, Cambridge University Press.

May, R.: 1978, *The Grammar of Quantification*, unpublished Ph.D. dissertation, MIT.

Pesetsky, D.: to appear, 'Complementizer-trace Phenomena and the Nominative Island Condition', to appear in *The Linguistic Review*.

Pullum, G. K.: 1981, 'Evidence against the "AUX" Node in Luiseno and English', *Linguistic Inquiry* 12.

Reinhart, T.: 1976, *The Syntactic Domain of Anaphora*, unpublished Ph.D. Dissertation, MIT.

Reuland, E.: 1979, *Principles of Subordination and Construal in the Grammar of Dutch*, Doctoral Dissertation Rijksuniversiteit Groningen.

Reuland, E.: 1980a, 'V-Raising in Dutch: Anomalies explained', in *Papers from the Sixteenth Regional Meeting Chicago Linguistic Society*.

Reuland, E.: 1980c, 'Governing "-ing"', mimeographed, MIT and Rijksuniversiteit Groningen, to appear in *Linguistic Inquiry* 14, No. 1.

Reuland, E.: 1981a, 'Domains of Governors versus Boundaries for Government', paper presented at GLOW 1981, Göttingen, mimeographed, MIT and Rijksuniversiteit Groningen.

Reuland, E.: 1981b, 'On the Governing Properties of Infinitival Markers', in L. Hellan and T. Fretheim (eds.), *Proceedings of the Sixth Scandinavian Conference of Linguistics*.

Reuland, E.: 1981c, 'On Extraposition of Complement Clauses', in V. Burke and Pustejovsky (eds.), *Proceedings of NELS XI*, University of Massachusetts, Amherst.

Riemsdijk, H. van: 1978, *A Case Study in Syntactic Markedness: The Binding Nature of Prepositional Phrases*, Foris, Dordrecht.

Reimsdijk, H. van: 1983, 'The Case of German Adjectives', this volume.

Rouveret, A.: 1979, 'Sur la notion de proposition finite', *Langages* 60.

Rouveret, A. and J.-R. Vergnaud: 1980, 'Specifying Reference to the Subject; French Causatives and Conditions on Representations', *Linguistic Inquiry* 11, 97–202.

Safir, K.: 1980, 'Inflection-Government and Inversion', mimeographed, MIT.

Safir, K. and D. Pesetsky: 1980, 'Inflection, Inversion and Subject Clitics', in V. Burke and Pustejovsky (eds.), *Proceedings of NELS XI*, University of Massachusetts, Amherst.

Steele, S., A. Akmajian, R. Demers, E. Jelinek, C. Kitagawa, R. Oehrle, and T. Wasow: 1981, *An Encyclopedia of AUX: A Study in Cross-Linguistic Equivalence*, MIT Press, Cambridge.

Stowell, T.: 1980, 'On the Independent Status of Case and Government', paper presented at GLOW 1980, Nijmegen.

Stowell, T.: 1981, *Origins of Phrase Structure*, unpublished Ph.D. dissertation, MIT.

Thiersch, C.: 1978, *Topics in German Syntax*, unpublished Ph.D. dissertation, MIT.

Weinberg A. and N. Hornstein: 1981, 'Preposition Stranding and Case Marking', *Linguistic Inquiry* 12, 55–91.

Zaenen, A.: 1979, 'Infinitival Complements in Dutch', in *Papers from the Fifteenth Regional Meeting Chicago Linguistic Society*.

Zubizarreta, M-L.: 1980, 'Remarks on Inflected Infinitives in Portuguese', mimeographed, MIT.

CRIT CREMERS

ON TWO TYPES OF INFINITIVAL COMPLEMENTATION

0. INTRODUCTION

Infinitival complements are considered to be *incomplete* by most of the modern linguists who account for them in their theories, in almost the same sense as atomic structures with fewer negative than positive elements are considered to be incomplete by chemists. Unlike these atomic structures, however, infinitival constructions containing less arguments than might be expected on the base of the infinitival's 'degree', are not necessarily unstable and seeking fulfilment from outside.

All current treatments of infinitival complements tend to *normalize* these predicate structures by postulating on some level of representation the argument that is felt to be missing. Linguistic theories differ considerably in the way they perform this normalization. In EST-type treatments the 'missing' argument shows up in the syntactic representation; strings like (1) and (2) are assigned structures like (1a) and (2a) respectively:

(1)   John tries to sell his Datsun.

(1) a.   [[John] [tries [[e] [to sell his Datsun]]]]

(2)   Mary seems to frighten you.

(2) a.   [[Mary] [seems [[e] [to frighten you]]]] [1]

In approaches to lexical grammar, the argument in question is stipulated in the logical or functional representation of lexical frames containing infinitival complements; for example, from Bresnan (1978):

(3)   *try*: V, [__$\overline{VP}$], NP_1 try ((NP_1) VP)

(4)   *compel*: V, [__ NP $\overline{VP}$], NP_1 compel NP_2 ((NP_2) VP)

In montegovian frameworks, the missing argument can be created as a semantic consequence of the interpretation, via the powerful device of meaning postulates. Thomason (1976), for example, presents some rules in

169

F. Heny and B. Richards (eds.), Linguistic Categories: Auxiliaries and Related Puzzles, Vol. One, 169–221.
Copyright © 1983 *by D. Reidel Publishing Company.*

which formulas that contain a predicate taking properties of individuals as arguments, are set equivalent to formulas that contain a predicate taking propositions as arguments.[2]

Great differences with respect to the nature and the theoretical role of the reconstructed argument follow from differences in the way of normalization.[3] All the accounts of infinitival complementation, however, agree in capturing *all* infinitival complements alike as to their category and interpretation.

In this paper it will be argued that at least Dutch provides evidence *against* the position that *all* infinitival complements must be represented as, or related to, zero place predicates (sentences, propositions). In Section 1, such a claim is introduced. In Section 2, the claim is confronted with some syntactic and semantic parameters for propositionality. Finally, I briefly discuss some practical and theoretical implications of the foregoing.

1. THE CLAIM

1.1. *Outline and Initial Motivation*

The main claim of this paper is:

(5)   some verbs in Dutch select as an argument infinitival complements of the category *S denoting propositions* (*infScomples*), other verbs select infinitival complements of the category *VP denoting properties* (*infVPcomples*)

This implies that in the grammar of Dutch two paradigms should be distinguished along the following lines:

(6)   V [$_{VP}$ ... infinitive ...]

(7)   V [$_S$ X ... infinitive ...]

(From now on, I'll refer to verbs that fit in frame (6) as *Vvp's* and to verbs that fit in (7) as *Vs's*). The X in (7) marks a position that functions or is to be interpreted as the subject argument of the infinitival construction. The presence/absence of a subject argument of whatever form on whatever level of representation is what I take to be the principal difference between the two types of infinitival complementation.

The particular way of representing the two paradigms (6) and (7) is not intended to reflect a choice of one descriptive theory rather than another.

In fact, my use of the terms 'VP denoting properties' and 'S denoting propositions' is more or less independent of any specific theory concerning the categorization and interpretation of natural language expressions. They are easy to transpose into established frameworks (cf. Sections 3.1. and 3.2.). But since we assume that for no linguistic theory, not even for a theory based on autonomy of syntax, can the relation between categorization and interpretation boil down to mere accident, the claim (5) reads more generally as:

(8)   some verbs in Dutch select infinitival constituents of the category A denoting things of type X, and some other verbs select infinitival constituents of the category B denoting things of type Y, and A is not equivalent to B with respect to syntactic operations and X is not equivalent to Y with respect to semantic operations.

Now claim (5) can be substantiated by partially listing the members of the *Vvp* and the *Vs* paradigms:

(9)   *Vvp:* **proberen** 'try', **durven** 'dare', **kunnen** 'be able',[4] ....

(10)   *Vs:* **zeggen** 'say', **denken** 'think', **beweren** 'claim', **beseffen** 'realize' ....

The following observations may illustrate the initial plausibility of a categorial and denotational bisection of the class of infinitival complements in Dutch, leaving aside the question how to realize this bisection in a grammar.

Examples (11a) and (11b) are correct sentences. So is (11c), with the 'pro-complement' anaphor **dat** interpreted as relating back to the preceding 'full' complement, as indicated graphically:

(11) a. Ik probeer dat.
         I try   that

     b. Jan durft 't niet.
         J.   dares it not

     c. Ik probeer *te springen* maar Jan durft *dat*   niet.
         I try   to jump   but J.   dares that not

Examples (12a) and (12b) are also correct:

(12) a. Jan beweert te springen.
     J.   claims   to jump

   b. Jan beweert dat.
     J.   claims   that

(13), however, is not correct when **dat** is interpreted relative to the preceding infinitival complement:

(13)   *Ik probeer *te springen* en Jan beweert *dat*   ook.
      I try   to jump   and J. claims   that too

A pro-complement in a **beweren** type predicate structure can not be linked anaphorically to a complement of a **proberen** type verb. This is unexplainable and unexpected when the infinitival complements of Vvp's and the infinitival complements of Vs's are taken to be equivalent in all relevant aspects, for there is no good reason why two infinitival positions can not be linked anaphorically if they can be filled by expressions of the same category and the same denotational type, and if the lexical strings of the complements are mutually exchangeable *salve* grammaticality. This topic is discussed more extensively in Section 3.3.

1.2. *Preliminary Remarks About the Nature of the Claim*

Before turning to some arguments in support of the claim made in the previous section, its relation to two other contributions to the syntax and semantics of complementation must be clarified.

The topic of this paper is only superficially comparable with the controversy provoked by Bresnan (1972), between EST oriented and Lexical Grammar oriented grammarians about the categorization of infinitival complements. Recently, this debate has been continued in a paper by Koster and May (1980), in which the authors once more reject VP categorization on various grounds. Both the defendants of the 'underlying S hypothesis' and the defendants of the 'underlying VP hypothesis', however, appear to generalize in their respective approaches over all *infcomples*; such a uniform treatment is exactly what I am arguing against in this paper. Furthermore, their debate concentrates on syntactic representation, for there is no disagreement amongst them as far as logical or functional representation is involved (cf. (1)–(4)). My claim extends to all levels of representation.

An important idiosyncracy of Dutch syntax is the phenomenon that in some cases several verbs that appear to originate at different levels of a sentence, cluster. In Evers (1975) this process is described in terms of a transformation of V-Raising: verbs that take infinitival complements either attract the infinitive, thus destroying the integrity of the complement by V-Raising, or trigger extraposition of the whole complement.[5] Reviewing Evers (1975), Nieuwenhuysen (1976) argues that complements undergoing V-Raising be categorized as VP's and complements that do not undergo this operation but are extraposed, as S's, while Evers assumes underlying S in both cases. Comparing the two verb classes *Vvp* and *Vs* as listed in (9) and (10) respectively, one could conjecture that the verbs listed as *Vvp*, all tend to trigger V-Raising and the verbs listed as *Vs*, all tend to trigger extraposition of their complements rather than V-Raising, and that the two classes therefore just parallel Nieuwenhuysen's distinction between verbs taking *infVPcomples* and verbs taking *infScomples*. I doubt, however, whether Nieuwenhuysen's approach and mine will turn out to characterize the same classes. There are *Vvp's* as well as *Vs's* that trigger either V-Raising or Extraposition; this double option is demonstrated in (14) with respect to a verb in the *Vvp* paradigm, and in (15) with respect to a verb in the *Vs* paradigm (the a-sentences illustrate V-Raising, the b-sentences Extraposition):

(14) a. ... omdat Harry een   vlammend pamflet [$_V$ probeert te
          because H.   a   blazing   lampoon   tries   to
          schrijven].
          write

b.   ... omdat Harry [$_V$ probeert] een vlammend pamflet te
     [$_V$ schrijven].

(15) a. ... omdat Harry de zaak [$_V$ zegt te winnen].
          because H.   the case   says to win

b.   ... omdat Harry [$_V$ zegt] de zaak te [$_V$ winnen]

In Nieuwenhuysen's approach, **proberen** and **zeggen** can therefore take *infVPcomples* as well as *infScomples*. According to the criteria presented in the next section, however, **proberen** is only in the *Vvp* class, and **zeggen** only in the *Vs* class. That the difference between these classes is not exhausted or even covered by reference to the V-Raising/Extraposition alternation, can be shown by exploration of an illuminating opposition between extraposed or dislocated *Vvp* complements and extraposed or dislocated *Vs* complements. This opposition has to do with the occurrence of the preposition **om** that optionally can be added to an extraposed or dislocated infinitival complement that is an object of a verb, without adding anything to the complement's meaning. In particular, it can occur in extraposed or dislocated *infVPcomples* (complements of *Vvp's*):

(16) a. Harry probeert om een vlammend pamflet   te schrijven.
         H.   tries   a   blazing   lampoon   to write

   b. Ik zou 't niet durven, om een vlammend pamflet te schrijven.
       I would it not dare, . . .

   c. Ik zou   dat   niet gekund hebben, om een vlammend pamflet te
       I would that not have-been-able-to, . . .
       schrijven.

The point is that **om** is absolutely ungrammatical in extraposed or dislocated *infScomples* (complements of *Vs's*):

(17) a.* Jan heeft beweerd om niet te komen.
        J.   has   claimed   not to come

   b.* Zij zal het niet toegeven om het pamflet geschreven te hebben.
       She will it   not admit   the lampoon written   to have

Why is **om** ungrammatical in an extraposed or dislocated *infScompl*, and grammatical in an extraposed or dislocated *infVpcompl*? The answer to this question can be derived from the well known observation that **om** blocks the linking of a position in its structural domain to a position outside its domain. This can be demonstrated in the case of Wh-Movement: (18a) is perfect, but (18b), which differs only from the first sentence in having **om** in the leftmost position of the extraposed complement, is bad:

(18) a. Wat   heeft zij geprobeerd Jan te sturen?
         What has   she tried   J. to send

   b.*? Wat heeft zij geprobeerd om Jan te sturen?

This observation, that **om** at the left boundary of an extraposed infinitival complement, blocks binding into its domain, provides an explanation for the ungrammaticality of (17) if we assume that *infScomples* contain an element that has to be bound from outside the complement. An occurrence of **om** would block this binding relation, and therefore leads to ungrammaticality and uninterpretability. *InfVpcomples*, on the other hand, are *closed* in the sense that they do not contain such an anaphor; therefore, **om** at the outset of an *infVPcompl* is harmless. Because it is clear that the anaphor that has to be bound from outside, can only be the (empty) subject of the *infScompl*, this explanation matches the structures (6) and (7) of *infVP*complementation and *infS*complementation, respectively. And because we arrived at this conclusion without any reference to the V-Raising/Extraposition alternation, but only looked at extraposed and dislocated complements, the distribution of **om** proves that the bisection between *Vvp/infVPcompl* on the one hand and *Vs/infScompl* on the other is independent of the V-Raising/Extraposition alternation (see also Section 2.5).

Finally: one could notice that the verbs listed in (10) as *Vs*, might have a common semantic feature which the verbs listed in (9) as *Vvp* do not have, and the other way around. I have no objections against noticing this, just as I have no objections against speculations upon the semantic impact of property denoting complements versus proposition denoting complements. I simply believe that making a distinction as to the type of complementation is the most systematic way of accounting for the differences between the *Vvp* paradigm and the *Vs* paradigm that are explored in the following sections.

2. InfVPcomples *VERSUS* infScomples

In this section, some reasons are given for not treating the infinitival complement of a *Vvp* on a par with the infinitival complement of a *Vs*. They deal with modality (2.1.), time (2.2.), ellipsis (2.4.) and extraposition/dislocation (2.5.). The argumentation may not be exhaustive but does indicate that the characteristics of *infVPcomples* and *infScomples* are incompatible within a grammar.

2.1. *Modality*

Modal auxiliaries in the verbal string of the complement of a Vvp can not be interpreted as epistemic, proposition level modalities; adverbial proposition level modalities can not take a scope restricted to the complement of a Vvp.

Let us define a proposition level modality as the interpretation of an element *M* in a structure *XMY* such that a paraphrase of the type *It (is) M (be) true that XY* makes sense and is equivalent to the proper interpretation of *XMY*. This criterion is an adaptation of a sufficient condition for qualifying as a sentential modifier discussed in Thomason and Stalnaker (1973). The criterion is rather informal but informative; for example, it disqualifies *to be able to*, one of the readings of the modal *can*/**kunnen**, as a preposition level modality (epistemic modal), for (19b) makes no sense and is not a possible paraphrase of (19a):

(19) a. Mary can walk on her hands.

     b. * It is able to be true that Mary walks on her hands.

The following Dutch sentences illustrate the first part of the statement at the outset of this subsection (in the word-for-word translation, CAN e.g. stands for the *can* that you can't use in English in positions in which you can use **kunnen** in Dutch):

(20) (?) Marie probeert binnen één jaar Arabisch te kunnen lezen.
         M.   tries   within one year Arabic   to CAN   read

(21) (?) Zij durfde niet invoerrechten te moeten betalen.
         She dared not import duty to MUST pay

Although these sentences seem to neglect some sort of selectional restrictions between the matrix verb and its complement, they are acceptable and interpretable according to the following paraphrases:

(20) a. Mary tries to be able to read Arabic within one year.

(21) a. She did not dare to be obligated to pay import duty.

In these paraphrases a non-epistemic interpretation of the modals **kunnen en moeten** is involved. Under this reading (20) and (21) are acceptable. But an epistemic interpretation of the modals is certainly *not* available. (20b) and (21b) are intended to reflect such an epistemic interpretation; in order to avoid clumsiness, the infinitival complements minus the auxiliary are represented as X and Y:

(20) b. Mary is going to try to let X be possible.

(21) b. She did not dare to let Y be conclusively true.

These paraphrases do not cover any possible reading of (20) and (21).

Now it is in every respect reasonable to assume, first, that the scope of modal auxiliaries is restricted to the predicate structure of the verbal complex they are attached to and, secondly, that the main difference between epistemic and non-epistemic readings of modal verbs is related to the logical structures that the readings impose upon the strings that are interpreted. If we assign the category **VP** to the complements of **proberen** en **durven**, the apparent impossibility of epistemic readings for modal verbs occurring in these complements can be explained neatly. For this categorization, by definition, gives rise to no suitable propositional domain for an epistemic reading.

Modal verbs occurring in *Vs* complements, on the contrary, allow for the full range of possible interpretations.

(22) a. Elke   deelnemer dacht   zijn lezing te kunnen publiceren.
Every participant thought his lecture to CAN   publish

b. Zij beseft niet jou op weg hierheen te moeten zijn gepasserd.
She realizes not you on way down here to MUST   have passed

(23) a. Jig   beweerde de wedstrijd te moeten winnen.
You claimed   the game   to MUST win

b. Gisteren   beweerde Agnes door Wim te   kunnen zijn
Yesterday claimed A.   by W. to CAN   be
beschuldigd.
accused

The a-sentences permit both an epistemic and a non-epistemic reading of the modal auxiliaries; this means that (22a) is ambiguous as to whether **kunnen** expresses an ability − the non-epistemic reading − or a possibility − the epistemic reading − and that (23a) is ambiguous as to whether **moeten** expresses an obligation (non-epistemic) or a necessity (epistemic). In fact, they are ambiguous in the same way as the following 'simple' sentences:

(24) a. Hij kan zijn lezing   publiceren.
He can his lecture publish

b. Jij   moet de wedstrijd winnen.
You must the game   win

When the internal structure of the verbal cluster forces an epistemic reading of a modal verb attached to it, as is the case in (22b) and (23b), this reading can be obtained. We can account for the ambiguity of (22a), (23a), and the epistemic reading of (22b), (23b) if the complement is 'governed' by a *Vs*. Therefore, by the same reasoning as above, the *Vs* complement has to be looked upon as a proposition.

The absence of a propositional domain in a *Vvp* complement would also explain why modal adverbs that qualify as sentential modifiers according to the criterion mentioned before, cannot be associated semantically with such a complement, while these adverbs exclusively take complement scope whenever they occur in an *infScompl*. This can be demonstrated by comparing two superficially identical structures like:

> (25)   Hij probeert haar waarschijnlijk te ontslaan.
>   He   tries   her   probably   to fire

> (26)   Hij zei   haar waarschijnlijk te ontslaan.
>   He   said her   probably   to fire

Although under the syntax of V-Raising (25) and (26) might represent different syntactic configurations,[6] the opposition as to the possible scope of **waarschijnlijk** is nevertheless striking. In (25) it can only be assigned matrix scope, but in (26) it only takes complement scope; (25a) is the sole reading of (25) and (26) has no interpretation but the one in (26a) (again, *X* stands for the 'core' of the complement):

> (25) a.   (It is) probably (true that) he tries X.

> (25) a.   (It is true that) he said that probably X.

This fact is also used in Nieuwenhuysen (1976) as an argument in favor of a VP analysis of 'V-Raised' complements. The phenomenon, however, is more general than is suggested by linking it to V-Raising; when a *infVPcompl* is extraposed, it must not contain a sentence modifier, on penalty of unwell-formedness: (27) is fine, but (28) is ungrammatical because its structural position blocks matrix scope assignment to the adverb, while in both sentences Extraposition rather than V-Raising is involved:

> (27)   Hij heeft geprobeerd (om) haar te ontslaan.
>   He has   tried   her   to fire

> (28)   *Hij heeft geprobeerd (om) haar waarschijnlijk te ontslaan

Obviously, then the best way to avoid unwellformedness and/or semantic anomaly, is to categorize a *Vvp* complement in such a way that no ad hoc restrictions on the occurrence and interpretation of proposition level modalities are needed.

2.2. *Tempus*

A Vvp and its infinitival complement form a temporal unit; an infScompl has an independent temporal denotation.

This statement amounts to the claim that the number of possibilities of specifying a string *Vvp + complement* with respect to tempus, equals the number of possibilities of specifying a 'one verb' string in this respect, whereas a string *Vs + complement* allows twice as many temporal specifications as a one verb string does. I count each single occurrence of a time adverbial or a time auxiliary and each co-occurrence of a time adverbial or time auxiliary and a tense marker as one temporal specification. For obvious reasons, I do not take tense as such to count as a distinct temporal specification, though doing so would require only a minor arithmetic change in the formulation of the claim.

In yet another form the statement reads as follows: every grammatical temporal specification of an *infVPcompl* is equivalent to the same specification of the *Vvp + infVPcompl* string as a whole; this slightly weaker version is expressed informally in (29), where T_i stands for any temporal specification and *Int* for some interpretation function:

$$(29) \quad \text{Int}(\ldots Vvp \ldots [\ldots T_m \ldots \text{inf} \ldots T_n \ldots]) \leftrightarrow$$
$$\text{Int}(\ldots T_m \ldots Vvp \ldots T_n \ldots [\ldots \text{inf} \ldots])$$

(29), however, will turn out to be formulated too strongly to hold without further conditions and specifications of the nature of *T*. In particular, the right-to-left implication is restricted by the fact that some time auxiliaries and adverbs compatible with a *Vvp*, are not compatible with a *infVPcompl*. But this restrictedness only indicates that an *infVPcompl* is not a temporal unit on its own, for it does not allow all kinds of temporal modification.

Even if only the left-to-right implication holds unrestrictedly in (29), no such implication could be valid in the *Vs* paradigm; for (30a) does not imply (30b) nor does (31a) imply (31b):

(30) a. Jan dacht   de wedstrijd overtuigend gewonnen te hebben.
     J. thought the game   convincingly won   to have

    b. Jan had gedacht de   wedstrijd overtuigend te winnen.
       J. had thought the game   convincingly to win

(31) a. Jan beweert ooit   een brilliante redenaar te zijn geweest.
       J. claims at some time a   brilliant orator   to have been

    b. Jan heeft ooit   beweerd een brilliante redenaar te zijn.
      J. has at some time claimed a   brilliant orator to be

On the contrary, the left-to-right implication holds within the Vvp paradigm; (32a) implies (32b) and (33a) implies (33b):

(32) a. Menno heeft geprobeerd mij gisteren   op te bellen.
      M.   has   tried   me yesterday to call

    b. Menno heeft gisteren geprobeerd mij op te bellen.
      M.   has   yesterday tried   me up to call

(33) a. Iedereen kan dit vóór de vergadering lezen.
      Everybody can this before the meeting   read

    b. Vóór de vergadering kan iedereen dit lezen.
      Before the meeting   can everybody this read

Note that the observation that a sentence implies another semantically, does not mean that they have the same conditions of use; word order mostly reflect different information structures in a discourse. Formula (29) only means that two sentences have similar truth conditions in that one can not consistently be denied and the other affirmed. With this reservation, the observations with regard to (30)–(33) show that Vvp predicate structures and Vs predicate structures differ in their capacity to exhibit independent temporal specification of infinitival complements. In the following sections, a more detailed examination of this important difference is presented.

2.2.1. In this subsection I will discuss a clear difference between *infVP-comples* and *infScomples* in regard to tense. The examples (34)–(36), in which a Vvp occurs, are both ungrammatical and hard to interpret, whereas (37)–(39), which differ from the foregoing only in having a Vs instead of a Vvp, are slightly redundant, perhaps, but fully grammatical and easy to interpret:

(34) *Jacoba probeert jou te zullen bezoeken.
      J.   tries   you to WILL visit

(35) *De postbode durfde de brief niet open te zullen maken.
      The postman dared the letter not open to WILL make

(36) *Geen atleet kon   de marathon binnen twee uur   zullen lopen.
      No   athlete could the marathon within two hours WILL run

(37) Jacoba *zegt* jou te zullen bezoeken.

(38) De postbode *beweerde* de brief niet open te zullen maken.

(39) Geen atleet *dacht* de marathon binnen twee uur te zullen lopen.

Note that the awkwardness of the *Vvp* sentences (34)–(36) is not due to ungrammaticality of the infinitival substrings as such. Therefore one could argue that it is a semantic feature of *Vvp's* to place their complements in the future, which would render an occurrence of **zullen** in the complement pleonastic and ungrammatical. Such an argument cannot be upheld in general. Pleonastic redundancy does not cause ungrammaticality, let alone uninterpretability, of the kind observed in (34)–(36). Compare these sentences with the following, which suffer from pleonastic redundancy in much the same way as could be argued for (34)–(36) but which are both grammatical and interpretable:

(40) Ik voorspel dat jij   zult winnen.
      I predict   that you wil   win

(41) Farah had beloofd dat ze met mij mee zou   gaan.
      F.   had promised that she with me along would go

(42) Morgen   zal hij zich   bij de voorzitter verontschuldigen.
      Tomorrow will he himself to the chairman   excuse

(Pleonasms as in (42) are even standard in English, though in Dutch simple present tense is sufficient when the future is otherwise marked). Because of this it is inadequate to ascribe the ungrammaticality of (34)–(36) to mere redundancy, and I will consider these sentences as evidence in support of the claim that there is no way to localize an *infVPcompl* on a time axis in its own right (cf. 2.2.3.).

2.2.2. The claim that a *Vvp* and its infinitival complement form a temporal
unit, is endorsed by the ungrammaticality of constructions like

(43)   *Vandaag   probeert   hij   je morgen   te bellen.
        Today   try   he   you tomorrow   to call

(44)   *Een week geleden   durfde zij   volgend jaar   de   reis te maken.
        A   week ago   dared she next   year   the   trip to make

(45)   *Frits kon   zoujuist nog   morgen   aanwezig zijn.
        F.   could   just-a-moment-ago   tomorrow   present   he

These constructions are ungrammatical whenever the leftmost time indicator
is interpreted in such a way that this would give rise to inferences like,
respectively, *today I try something, a week ago she dared something* and
just a moment ago Frits was able to do something. Let me call this excluded
reading of the leftmost time indicator the *transparent* one. One or more of
the sentences may be acceptable under a particular interpretation of the
leftmost time indicator that can be circumscribed as the *opaque* one; under
such an interpretation (43) for example would mean something like *today he
says/one can notice/it is told that he will try to call you tomorrow*. Simplex
predicates also admit an opaque time indicator in addition to a 'normal'
transparent one, even if the two indicators as such are incompatible:

(46)   Gisteren   kreeg ik mijn loon   vandaag.
        Yesterday   got   I my   salary today

(47)   Vandaag komt   ze   morgen   en overmorgen
        Today   comes she tomorrow   and the-day-after-tomorrow

        komt   ze   volgende   week
        comes she next   week

From (46) we may not infer that I got my salary yesterday and from (47)
we may not infer that she comes today and the day after tomorrow. So
the asterisks in (43)–(45) indicate that it is impossible to get the normal,
transparent reading of the leftmost time indicator.

    This reading, the one permitting the leftmost time indicator to interact
with the main predicate is clearly available in the following constructions
with a *Vs* as main verb:

(48) Vandaag deelt hij mee jou morgen te bellen.
    Today announces he you tomorrow to call

(49) Een week geleden zei ze volgend jaar de reis te
    A week ago said she next year the trip to
    (zullen) maken.
    (WILL) make

(50) Frits beweerde zojuist nog   morgen aanwezig te
    F. claimed just-a-moment-ago tomorrow present to
    (zullen) zijn.
    (WILL) be

There is no doubt that these sentences, unlike (43)–(47), have a transparent reading, on the basis of which inferences like *today he announces something, a week ago she said something* and *just a moment ago Frits claimed something* can be drawn. Consequently, three time indicators in a single sentence produce interpretable strings if the main verb is a *Vs* and strong ungrammaticality of uninterpretable strings if the main predicate is a *Vvp*:

(51) Gisteren deelde hij vandaag mee morgen niet te
    Yesterday announced he today   tomorrow not to
    (zullen) komen.
    (WILL) come

(52) Straks vertelt ze jou morgen vorig jaar te zijn gezakt.
    By and by tells she you tomorrow last year to have failed

(53) *Vandaag probeert hij morgen jou overmorgen
    Today tries he tomorrow you the-day-after-tomorrow
    op te bellen.
    up to call

(54) *Zojuist   durfde zij vandaag mij morgen te bezoeken.
    A-moment-ago dared she today me tomorrow to visit

(51), for example, can be used to express something like: yesterday it was the case that he would announce today that he would come tomorrow. No such reading is available for the *Vvp* cases (53) and (54). The ungrammaticality of these two sentences, having no reading at all, parallels, as was claimed before, the ungrammaticality caused by the occurrence of three different time indicators in a sentence with a simplex predicate:

(55)   *Gisteren   kreeg ik vandaag mijn salaris morgen.
        Yesterday   got I   today   my   salary   tomorrow

This sentence too has no reading at all.

These observations concerning multiple time indication support the claim that *Vvp* predicate structures behave like temporal units.

2.2.3. Suppose that the position of a time indicator in a *Vvp* predicate structure correlates with its semantic scope. Consider, then, the semantics of the following pairs. The only difference between the members of each pair is the position of the italicized time indicator; the brackets are meant to represent a scope option for this time indicator correlated with its position in the sentence: in the a-sentences, its scope is assumed to be restricted to the complement, while in the b-sentences its scope extends to the sentence as a whole:

(56) a. Iedereen   kan [*vóór   tien uur*   aanwezig zijn].
          Everybody can before ten o'clock   present   be

     b. [*Vóór tien uur* kan iedereen aanwezig zijn]

(57) a. Enkele studenten hebben geprobeerd [*de volgende dag* de
          A few students   have   tried   the next   day the

          colleges te verstoren].
          lectures to disturb

     b. [*De volgende dag* hebben enkele studenten geprobeerd de colleges
          te verstoren]

(58) a. De afgevaardigde durfde niet [zich   *tijdens de vergadering*
          The delegate   dared not [(himself) during the meeting

          over het voorstel uit te spreken.]
          upon the proposal out to speak

     b. [*Tijdens de vergadering* durfde de afgevaardigde zich niet over het
          voorstel uit te spreken.]

According to (29) – the formula expressing the semantic equivalency of all possible orderings of time indicators in the *Vvp* paradigm – the scope option represented by an a-sentence is equivalent to the scope option represented by the corresponding b-sentence. But this is a fairly weak interpretation of (29). The stronger and more interesting interpretation is that the ordering of time indicators within a *Vvp* structure is irrelevant because there is only one scope option for these time indicators whatever their position might be, as in 'one verb' sentences. Under this interpretation of (29), there is only one level of temporal scope in the *Vvp* paradigm. This level must correspond to the matrix, for there is at least one time indicator that can only occur at the matrix level: tense flexion. Therefore, all time indicators in a *Vvp* structure can be said to take matrix scope. As a consequence, the scope options represented by the a-sentence above can be said to be semantically inadequate.

Now suppose that (29) were not valid, i.e. that the a-sentences do represent an adequate scope assignment not equivalent to the scope assignment in the b-sentences, and that thus the ordering of a time indicator in a *Vvp* paradigm had some semantic impact. Then we would not expect a *contradictio-in-terminis* to arise from the conjunction of, e.g., the negation of an a-sentence and the affirmation of the corresponding b-sentence of one of the pairs (56)–(58). Yet such a conjunction is a *contradictio-in-terminis*, as can be seen in the following sentences; (59) is the conjunction of the negation of (56a) and the affirmation of (56b), (60) is the conjunction of the affirmation of (57a) and the negation of (57b).

(59) Niet iedereen   kan vóór   tien uur   aanwezig zijn maar
      Not   everybody can before ten o'clock present be   but

      vóór   tien uur   kan iedereen   aanwezig zijn.
      before ten   o'clock can everybody   present be

(60) Enkele studenten hebben geprobeerd de volgende dag   de
      A few   students   have   tried   the next   day   the

      colleges te verstoren maar de volgende dag   heeft geen
      lectures to disturb   but the next   day   has   no

      enkele student geprobeerd de   colleges te verstoren.
      single student tried   the lectures to disturb

Because such conjunctions are mere contradictions, the conclusion must

be that the a-sentences of (56)–(58) are equivalent to the b-sentences and
that (29) is valid for these sentences, with the implications as given above.

This means that no ordering of temporal indicators in the Vvp paradigm
leads to an independent temporal interpretation of an *inf VPcompl* or one
detached from the temporal interpretation of the matrix. By consequence,
the temporal reference of an expression of the form (61) as a whole depends
also on the interpretation of the time indicator T relative to the point of
evaluation of the expression, although T is embedded in the complement:

(61)   [NP Vvp [$_{VP}$ X T Y infinitive Z]]

For example, if T denotes future, relative to the point of evaluation of (61),
the expression as a whole denotes future relative to the point of evaluation.
Thus, if the time indicator **tijdens de vergadering** in (62a) denotes a future
interval relative to the moment of speech, the whole expression refers to the
future; its canonical meaning can be paraphrased as (62b):

(62) a. De afgevaardigde durft zich niet tijdens de vergadering tegen het
         voorstel uit te spreken. (= (58a))

     b. De   afgevaardigde *zal* zich   niet tijdens de   vergadering
         The delegate   *will* (himself) not   during the meeting

         tegen   het voorstel durven   uitspreken.
         against the proposal dare   speak-out

No matter how deep a time indicator is embedded in a Vvp structure, its
interpretation affects the interpretation of the whole structure. Sentence
(62a) is grammatical because the present tense of the Vvp is compatible
with an occurrence of a time indicator referring to the future. Whenever the
tense of the Vvp is incompatible with the interpretation of a time indicator
occurring to its left or to its right, the result is ungrammaticality and uninterpretability; in (63) the present tense of the Vvp is incompatible with the past
time indicator **gisteren**; in (64) the past tense of the Vvp is incompatible with
the future time indicator **morgen**:

(63) *Marie probeert haar boek gisteren   af te krijgen.
        M.   tries   her   book yesterday off to finish

(64) *Marie probeerde haar boek morgen   af te krijgen.
        M.   tried   her   book tomorrow off to finish

Recall that (29) implies that the ordering of time indicators in a *Vvp* predicate structure has no semantic consequences and that all time indicators take matrix scope. In fact, this means that (63) and (64) suffer from the same incongruity of time indicators as the 'one verb' sentences (65) and (66):

(65)   *Gisteren   schrijft Jan z'n brief.
         Yesterday writes   J.   his letter

(66)   *Jan schreef z'n brief   morgen.
         J.   wrote   his letter tomorrow

Again it can be seen that a *Vvp* + *infVPcompl* structure behaves like a simplex sentence, i.e. like a temporal unit. This is in sharp contrast to the interference of two or more time indicators in a *Vs* + *infScompl* structure; (67) differs from (63) in that the *Vvp* **proberen** is replaced by the *Vs* **denken**; and (67) is grammatical because the scope of **morgen** is restricted to the *infScompl* and therefore does not conflict with the matrix scope of the past tense of the *Vs*:

(67)   Marie dacht   haar boek morgen   af te krijgen.
         M.   thought her   book tomorrow off to finish

So we can see that the equivalence expressed in (29) marks an important difference between the semantic structure of a *Vvp* construction and the semantic structure of a *Vs* construction with respect to temporal interpretation.

2.2.4. The opposition in temporal behavior between *infScomples* and *infVPcomples* may be illustrated by reference to a simple model for the interpretation of natural languages.

Suppose we adopt a model consisting of a set of moments of time, a set of possible worlds and a set of truth values, and let propositions denote functions from pairs of worlds and moments (indices) to truth values. Assume that moments are identifiable and traceable across worlds and vice versa. Such a construction offers a fair possibility for analyzing the semantics of embedded propositions.

(68)   De   man denkt dat Marie hem wil   ontslaan.
         The man thinks that M.   him wants (to) fire

In this sentence at least two propositions are involved: the one corresponding to the **dat**-phrase, say *mhwo*, and the one corresponding to the whole expression, *the man thinks mhwo*. If we want to evaluate the latter proposition with respect to a world-time index (w, t), it can be observed that the value of *mhwo* at that index is completely irrelevant. So *mhwo* expressing truth at (w, t) is compatible both with truth and with falsehood of *the man thinks mhwo* at that index. The matrix proposition is extensionally independent of the embedded one. They can be related intensionally by the statement that (68) is truth at (w, t) if and only if *mhwo* is true at t in the world of the man's thoughts. Similarly, (69) can be said to express truth at (w, t) iff the embedded proposition was true at some t' before t in the world of the man's (actual) thoughts:

(69)   De   man   denkt   dat   Marie   hem   wou   ontslaan.
        The man   thinks that M.   him   wanted (to) fire

The same line of reasoning would hold for *infScomples* from which we would arrive at an embedded proposition if we claimed there to be an empty subject in the complement, that was anaphorically related to an NP in the matrix:

(70)   Piet$_i$ beweert ___$_i$ de beste rattenvanger van Malakka te zijn
        P.   claims   the best rat-catcher   in Malakka to have

        geweest.
        been

Then we could say that (70) is true at (w, t) iff the proposition constructed on the basis of this assumption, *Piet was the best rat-catcher in Malakka*, is true in the past relative to t in the world of Piet's actual claims, whether that proposition expresses truth at (w, t) or not. An analysis along these lines seems plausible for *infScomples*.

Two things are important thus far: the embedding proposition and the embedded one are extensionally independent and in the intensional connection the temporal reference of the embedded proposition follows rather straightforwardly from the temporal structure of the expression under consideration. What happens if, contrary to the main claim of this paper, we try to handle *infVPcomples* as if they denote (embedded) propositions? Again, we would arrive at an embedded proposition by spelling out a control relation between the subject of the *Vvp* phrase and the infinitival complement.

(71)   Jan$_i$ probeert ___$_i$ over het hek   te springen.
           J.   tries   over the gate to jump.

Let us, then, say that (71) is true at (w, t) iff the proposition *John jumps over the gate* expresses truth at t or some moment later than t in the world of John's (actual) attempts. This amounts to the claim that the value of the embedded proposition at (w, t) has no relevance for the evaluation of (71) at (w, t) and that the embedded proposition and the embedding one are, therefore, extensionally independent of each other. But they are not, as can be seen by comparision of the two following conjunctions; (72), with the *Vs* **geloven**, is easy to make sense of, while it is hard to discover any sense in (73), a *Vvp* case:

(72)   Marie wil   Kees   ontslaan,   maar Kees gelooft niet dat
           M.   wants K. (to) fire   but K.   believes not that

           Marie hem wil   ontslaan.
           M.   him   wants (to) fire

(73)   Jan springt over het hek, maar Jan probeert niet over het
           J. jumps   over the gate but J.   tries   not over the

           hek   te springen.[7]
           gate to jump

(74) and (75) are as contradictory as (73) appears to be:

(74)   Jan beklimt de   Mount Everest, maar Jan durft niet de
           J.   climbs (the) Mount Everest but J.   dares not (the)

           Mount Everest te beklimmen.
           Mount Everest to climb

(75)   Marie valt   Jaap aan, maar Marie kan Jaap niet aanvallen.
           M.   attacks J.   but M.   can J.   not attack

The affirmation of a proposition derived from an *infVPcompl* seems hardly reconcilable with a denial of an attempt, the '**durf**' or the ability to bring about the event that the proposition ought to describe as we see from (73)–(75). Now we could simply conclude that propositions derived from *infVPcomples* are *not* extensionally independent of their matrices. But such a statement inevitably implies that whenever a proposition describing

someone's attempt, 'durf' or ability to do something, is true at an index
(w, t), then the embedded proposition is either true or false at that index.
None of the following expressions of semantical consequence has a chance,
however, of being an instance of a relevant, valid schema. Such a schema
would have to look like (79a) or like (79b):

(76) a. Jan probeert   te zwemmen, dus Jan zwemt.
      J.   tries   to swim   so J.   swims

    b. Jan probeert   te zwemmen, dus Jan zal niet zwemmen.
      J.   tries   to swim   so J.   will not swim

(77) a. Marie kan fietsen,   dus fietst   Marie   niet.
      M.   can ride-a-bike so rides-a-bike M.   not

    b. Marie kan fietsen, _ dus zal Marie   fietsen.
      M.   can ride-a-bike so will M.   ride-a-bike

(78) a. Iedereen   durft   te komen, dus komt   iedereen.
      Everybody dares   to come   so comes everybody

    b. Iedereen   durft   te komen, dus zal iedereen   kommen.
      Everybody dares   to come   so will   everybody come

(79) a. [NP *Vvp* [*infVPcompl*]] $\models$ [NP (tense) *infVPcompl*]

    b. [NP *Vvp* [*infVPcompl*]] $\models$ not [NP (tense) *infVPcompl*]

Neither (79a) nor (79b) is supported by our intuitions; there does not exist
a relation of semantical consequence between expressions of attempt, 'durf'
or ability and some expression of result. Therefore, we cannot say that a
proposition derived from an *infVPcompl* is extensionally dependent on
its matrix. Yet, as we saw from (73)–(75), if there *is* such a proposition
involved in an *infVPcompl*, it cannot be totally independent of the matrix
proposition.

    Now let us turn briefly to a related, but distinct problem. Suppose that,
notwithstanding the vagueness of the connection between a proposition
derived from *infVPcompl* and its matrix, we want to abide by the proposition
hypothesis for this type of complement. Do we have any starting point at all
for determining the temporal reference of such a proposition? I have serious
doubts about that. Although it was assumed, in case of (71), for the sake of

argument, that an embedded proposition in a *Vvp* construction might refer to a future moment relative to the matrix proposition, this assumption would leave completely unexplained the observation made in Section 2.2.1. that any occurrence of the future tense auxiliary in an *infVPcompl* leads to ungrammaticality and uninterpretability. So the best we can do is to claim simultaneity of the embedded and the embedding propositions. The truth condition of (71) then reads as follows: the embedding proposition is true at (w, t) iff the embedded proposition is true at t in the world of Jan's attempts. Consequently, (80) should express intrinsical falsehood here and now:

(80)   Ik kan zwemmen en ik kan fietsen,   maar ik kan niet
       I can swim   and I   can ride-a-bike but   I   can not

       tegelijkertijd zwemmen en   fietsen.
       at-once   swim   and ride-a-bike

Under most of the interpretations of ik, however, (80) expresses truth.

In order to maintain the propositional character of *infVPcomples*, we could change our interpretation of the domain of temporal indices and look at them as intervals rather than as moments. Under this approach, the truth condition of (71) might read: (71) is true at a world w and an interval T iff *Jan jumps over the gate* is true at some subinterval of T in the world of Jan's attempts. Thus the idea that the temporal reference of the embedded proposition is somehow simultaneous to that of the matrix can be saved, while the problem raised by (80) is solved by the stipulation that the subintervals selected by *I swim* and *I ride a bike* respectively, need not intersect. But this way of analyzing the semantic relation between the denotation of an *infVPcompl* and the denotation of its matrix is just another way of expressing what was claimed before: a proposition derived from an *infVPcompl*, is indistinguishable, indexically, from the matrix proposition.

The conclusion must be that no interesting form of referential disjointness in time can be obtained by reconstructing an *infVPcompl* as a proposition. Furthermore, we do not need such a reconstruction in order to explain any extensional independence between the matrix proposition and the propositional content, if any, of the *infVPcompl*; for no such independence can be observed or otherwise reasoned out. So it seems preferable to hold that no proposition is involved in the interpretation of an *infVPcompl*.

2.2.5. There is a special type of construction that seems to weaken the claim that *infVPcomples* do not independently refer to time. This is the construction in which the perfective auxiliary **hebben** (have) – or **zijn** (be) – occurs inside an *infVPcompl*, attached to the complement's head verb, as in:

(81)   Marie probeert het rapport gelezen te hebben $\left\{\begin{array}{l}\text{vóór}\\\text{als}\end{array}\right\}$ jij belt.

      M.   tries   the report   read   to have $\left\{\begin{array}{l}\text{before}\\\text{when}\end{array}\right\}$ you call

(82)   Alle gasten kunnen $\left\{\begin{array}{l}\text{vóór}\\\text{om}\end{array}\right\}$ tien uur   gegeten hebben.

      All   guests can $\left\{\begin{array}{l}\text{before}\\\text{at}\end{array}\right\}$ ten o'clock   eaten   have.

(83)   Ik durf Kees de waarheid gezegd te hebben $\left\{\begin{array}{l}\text{voordat}\\\text{wanneer}\end{array}\right\}$ u

      I   dare K.   the truth   told   to have $\left\{\begin{array}{l}\text{before}\\\text{when}\end{array}\right\}$ you

      bijeen komt.
      assemble

It can be shown, however, that these grammatical occurrences of a perfective auxiliary in an *infVPcompl* are rather harmless to the position taken in the previous sections, that *infVPcomples* are 'timeless'. This can be argued in two ways. First: the occurrences of a perfective auxiliary in an *infVPcompl* are grammatical because of the aspectual content rather than because of the temporal content of the auxiliary; this argument is explored in the appendix to this paper. Second: a well-formed construction with **hebben** in the *infVPcompl* is semantically equivalent to a well-formed construction with **hebben** attached to the *Vvp*, in accordance with the general equivalence formula (29); this argument is explored in this section. In so far as the argument is valid, it supports the view that a *Vvp* predicate structure is a temporal unit.

In order to make clear what is special about the interpretation of the sentences (81)–(83), it is useful to compare them to occurrences of a perfective auxiliary in an *infScompl*. There is no doubt that in these cases **hebben** can function as a past time indicator, with scope restricted to the complement; one of the readings of the *infScompl* containing **hebben** in (84a) is given in (84b), with past tense in a 'full' clause:

(84a)   Jan schrijft [vaak van jou   te hebben   gedroomd.]
         J.   writes   often of   you to have   dreamed

(84b)   Jan schrijft dat hij   vaak   van jou droomde.
         J.   writes   that he   often of   you dreamed

In the interpretation of (84a), the occurrence of **hebben** causes the complement to be antedated relative to the matrix. The occurrences of **hebben** in
(81)–(83), however, do not lead to an interpretation in which the complement's event antedates what is expressed by the matrix. Sentence (81), for
example, does not imply that the reading of the report is prior to the attempt
to read it expressed by the matrix.

   In fact, we can safely say that a **hebben** occurrence in an *inf VPcompl* is
grammatical if and only if the context provides a specification of a future
moment that is outside the temporal reference of the matrix. In (81)–(83)
this specification is given by the adverbial phrases at the end of the sentences.
When no such specification is available, the construction as a whole is ungrammatical. In (85) the past tense within the adverbial phrase blocks any
reference to the future, thus causing ungrammaticality:

(85)   *Marie probeert het rapport gelezen te hebben vóór   jij   belde.
          M.   tries   the report   read   to have before you called

In (86) the adverbial phrase cannot be interpreted as fixing a moment outside
the temporal reference of the matrix; again, the result is both ungrammatical
and uninterpretable:

(86)   *Marie probeert het rapport gelezen te hebben terwijl jij   belt.
          M.   tries   the raport   read   to have   while   you call

The requirement that the context must provide a specification of a future
moment outside the temporal reference of the matrix, reduces the contribution of **hebben** to the semantics of the construction to zero, because
its perfective content is already covered by the context specification of a
moment posterior to and outside the temporal reference of the matrix. There
is no truth-conditional difference between (81)–(83) and the same sentences
without **hebben**, (87)–(89) respectively:

(87)   Marie probeert het rapport te lezen vóór   jij   belt.
        M.   tries   the raport to read   before you   call

(88)   Alle gasten kunnen vóór tien uur   eten.
      All   guests can   before ten o'clock eat

(89)   Ik durf Kees de waarheid te zeggen vóórdat u   bijeen komt.
      I dare K.   the truth   to tell   before you assemble

In accordance with the discussion in the previous sections and in particular with the equivalence statement (29), these sentences are in turn equivalent to, respectively

(90)   Vóór jij belt probeert Marie het rapport te lezen

(91)   Vóór tien uur kunnen alle gasten eten

(92)   Vóórdat u bijeen komt, durf ik Kees de waarheid te zeggen

which are merely ordering variants of (87)–(89). But if **hebben** does not contribute to the semantics of a sentence if the context provides a specification of a future moment outside the temporal reference of the sentence, we can add **hebben** to each of the *Vvp*'s in (90)–(92) without changing the truth conditions; (93)–(95) are equivalent to (90)–(91):

(93)   Vóór jij   belt heeft Marie geprobeerd het rapport te lezen.
      Before you call has   M.   tried   the report to read

(94)   Vóór tien uur   hebben alle gasten kunnen eten.
      Before ten o'clock have   all guests CAN   eat

(95)   Vóórdat u   bijeen komt, heb ik Kees de waarheid durven
      Before   you assemble   have I K.   the truth   dare

      zeggen.
      tell

So we have the rather surprising result that a construction with a perfective auxiliary in an *inf VPcompl* is equivalent to a construction with **hebben** attached to the *Vvp*, if only we keep constant the conditions under which **hebben** can occur grammatically in an *inf VPcompl*. This result, the pairwise equivalence of (81) and (93), (82) and (94), and (83) and (95), is strong support for the claim expressed in (29), that *inf VPcomples* are temporal units.

Clearly, no comparable equivalence holds with respect to the *Vs* paradigm.

Although **hebben** occurs grammatically in (84a), here repeated, this sentence is by no means equivalent to a construction with **hebben** attached to the *Vs*:

(84a)   Jan schrijft vaak van jou te hebben gedroomd.
         J.   writes   often of you to have   dreamed

(96)   Jan heeft vaak geschreven van jou te dromen. ≠
         J.   has   often written   of you to dream

Again, the *Vvp* paradigm and the *Vs* paradigm turn out to differ considerably with regard to temporal structure. Time indicators in a *Vvp* predicate structure are not 'bounded' by the infinitival complement, while time indicators in a *Vs* predicate structures are.

2.3. *From Tense and Mood to Gaps and Topics*

In Section 2.1. and 2.2. the line of reasoning has been that whenever it is possible to demonstrate that tense and modality do not fit into *infVPcomples*, the demonstration disqualifies this type of constituent as a candidate for propositionhood. Underlying this argument is the view that both being tensed and being modalized are prerogatives of propositions. Tense and modality, then, operate exclusively on the linking of a subject argument and a predicate, which is, semantically, a subcase of applying a property to an entity. It follows that whenever an expression lacks a subject (introducing an entity) or a predicate (introducing a property), neither tense nor modality is involved. In my opinion, nothing in a natural language forces us to assume that expressions of that language can refer to things like probable or future entities or like necessary or past properties. Even expressions that are not strictly extensional like (*the*) *former president* do not refer to properties or entities that became the victim of the flow of time. And elliptical phrases like *probably John, maybe a bookmaker, necessarily be identical to oneself* are hardly interpretable as referring to degrees of certainness or inevitability of entities or properties. Ultimately all expressions of this kind must be analyzed as tensed or modalized complexes of a property and an entity. Natural language does give rise to past or probable *state of affairs*, referred to by propositions, each of which is a tensed and modalized application of an expression denoting a property to an expression denoting entities.

As for *infVPcomples*, it is clear that they contain at least a property expression. *InfScomples*, of course, also contain a property expression, but because they can be shown to be affected by tense and modality, we must assume that they furthermore contain a nonlexical but semantically effective and 'visible' subject. If we go along with current linguistic theory in assuming that this semantically effective subject behaves like some kind of anaphor to be bound properly within the matrix, we would expect *inf VPcomples* and *infScomples* to behave differently from each other with respect to syntactic operations that affect the control configuration, where 'control' is the name of the type of binding operative between a matrix argument position and the nonlexical subject of an infinitival complement. In the following two subsections, it is argued that the expected difference between the subjectless *inf VPcomples* and the *infScomples* does show up in the context of at least two 'transformations', Gapping and Topicalization.

2.4. *Gaps and Remnants*

Neither infScomples nor parts thereof may serve as gapping remnants.

The main characteristic of a so called 'gapped' sentence is the occurrence of an ellipsis as the right member of a conjunction, the left member of which is a complete sentence itself. The precise nature of the Gapping operation as a rule of grammar (deletion or reconstruction) is not at issue here, neither is the fact that Gapping results are strongly dependent on stress assignment. But it must be noticed that the particular properties of Gapping constructions, e.g. the nonidentity of the remnants in the right conjunct and the stressed counterparts in the left conjunct, vanish as soon as we try to leave a finite verb as a remnant; whatever the reason may be, finite verbs do not occur grammatically as a remnant.[8] This is what makes it attractive to compare the effect of Gapping 'over' *Vs* with the effect of Gapping 'over' *Vvp*. In the following clusters, *a* and *a'* are conjunctions of full sentences; *b* is a gapped construction corresponding to *a*, and *c* is a gapped version of *a'*. The two gapping cases differ in that the first contains as a remnant a complete infinitival complement while in the second only a part of a complement remains. The zero symbol '$\emptyset$' marks a gap with respect to the corresponding conjunction of full sentences. Examples (97)–(99) illustrate the effect of Gapping on *Vs* predicate structures and (100)–(102) its effect on *Vvp* predicate structures.

(97) a. Jan denkt in Amsterdam te blijven en Karin *denkt* naar
     J.   thinks in Amsterdam to stay and K.   thinks to

     Utrecht te worden overgeplaatst.
     Utrecht to be   transferred

a'. Jan denkt in Amsterdam te blijven en Karin *denkt* in Utrecht *te blijven*.

b.* Jan denkt in Amsterdam te blijven en Karin Ø naar Utrecht te worden overgeplaatst

c.* Jan denkt in Amsterdam te blijven en Karin Ø in Utrecht Ø.

(98) a. Jij   beweerde Marie   te hebben gebeld en   zij   *beweerde*
         You   claimed M.   to have called and   she   claimed

         jou   te hebben geschreven.
         (to) you to have   written

a'. Jij beweerde Marie te hebben gebeld en zij *beweerde* jou *te hebben gebeld*.

b.* Jij beweerde Marie te hebben gebeld en zij Ø jou te hebben geschreven.

c.* Jij beweerde Marie te hebben gebeld en zij Ø jou Ø.

(99) a. Anna besefte   veel   geld   te kunnen verdienen in de
         A.   realized   a-lot-of money   to CAN   make in the

         wapenhandel en   Piet *besefte* van zijn kunst te kunnen leven.
         arms-trade   and P.   realized on his art   to CAN   live

a'. Anna besefte veel geld te kunnen verdienen in de wapenhandel en Piet *besefte veel geld te kunnen verdienen* in de kunst.

b.* Anna besefte veel geld te kunnen verdienen in de wapenhandel en Piet Ø van zijn kunst te kunnen leven.

c.* Anna besefte veel geld te kunnen verdienen in de wapenhandel en Piet Ø in de kunst.

(100) a. Jan durft in Amsterdam te blijven en   Karin *durft* naar
          J. dares in Amsterdam to stay   and K.   dares to

          Utrecht te gaan.
          Utrecht to go

a'. Jan durft in Amsterdam te blijven en Karin *durft* in Utrecht *te blijven*.

b. Jan durft in Amsterdam te blijven en Karin ∅ naar Utrecht te gaan.

c. Jan durft in Amsterdam te blijven en Karin ∅ in Utrecht ∅.

(101) a. Jij   probeerde Marie te bellen en zij *probeerde* jou
        You tried   M.   to call   and she tried   you

        te schrijven.
        to write

a'. Jij probeerde Marie te bellen en zij *probeerde* jou *te bellen*.

b. Jij probeerde Marie te bellen en zij ∅ jou te schrijven.

c. Jij probeerde Marie te bellen en zij ∅ jou ∅.

(102) a. Anna kon   veel   geld   verdienen in de wapenhandel
        A.   could a-lot-of money make   in the arms-trade

        en Piet *kon*   van zijn kunst leven.
        and P.   could   on his art   live

a'. Anna kon veel geld verdienen in de wapenhandel en Piet *kon veel geld verdienen* in de kunst.

b. Anna kon veel geld verdienen in de wapenhandel en Piet ∅ van zijn kunst leven.

c. Anna kon veel geld verdienen in de wapenhandel en Piet ∅ in de kunst.

Comparing (97)–(99) and (100)–(102), we learn that the ungrammaticality of the *b* and *c* sentences in the first sample is not due to the ungrammaticality of the terminal substrings forming the right conjunct as such, but must be ascribed to the failure to reconstruct the leftmost gap with respect to the *Vs* in the first conjunct.

The reason for the ungrammaticality of the *b* sentences in question does not have to be the same as the reason for the ungrammaticality of the *c* sentences. For both types of ungrammatical Gapping, however, explanations are available that are in full accordance with the hypothesis adopted and advocated here. The c-cases of (97)–(99) can be explained by reference to what appears to be one of the major conditions on remnants, namely that they must be clause mates (where S boundaries count as the critical boundaries for clause mate-ship). The remnants in the c sentences are not clause mates when Gapping operates on *Vs* predicate structure. However, they *are*, according to the *infS/infVP* complement distinction, when Gapping operates on *Vvp* predicate structures, which is the case in (100)–(102).

This line of explanation cannot be extended to the b cases, for no matter which type of verb is involved, the infinitival complement as a whole is a clause mate of the other remnant. The judgements (97b)–(99b) may gain in clarity if confronted with interactions of WH-Movement and Gapping.

Consider:

(103) Wie heb je in Parijs ontmoet en wie ∅ in Brussel ∅?
       Who have you in Paris met and who in Brussels

(104) Wie denk je dat gaat winnen?
       Who think you that is-going-to win

(105) *Wie denk je dat gaat winnen en wie ∅ dat
       Who think you that is-going-to win and who that

       tweede wordt?
       second becomes

(103) shows that subjects (i.e. je) may gap. (104) is an example of a peculiar kind of WH-Extraction: some verbs like **denken** allow extraction out of an embedded tensed S under quite restrictive conditions (which do not matter here).[9] The crucial sentence is (105): although **denken** is a so called 'bridge' for WH-Extraction as is shown in (104), an extracted WH-constituent and the 'disfigured' S do not constitute possible remnants in a Gapping context. The ungrammaticality of (105) must be a consequence of the fact that WH-Extraction needs a bridge in order to affect a tensed S; for (105) as well as for (104) there is an alternative WH-question based on a combination of a resumptive pronoun and explicit Case marking of the WH element; in this case no bridge is required for grammaticality. These two possibilities for questioning an element in an embedded tensed S may have slight differences pragmatically, as to whether or not the class of possible answers is restricted,

but semantically (106) and (107) are equal to (104) and (105), and (107) is
nevertheless grammatical:

(106)	Van	wie	denk	je	dat	ie	gaat	winnen?
	Of	whom	think	you	that	he	is-going-to	win

(107)	Van	wie	denk	je	dat	ie	gaat	winnen	en
	Of	whom	think	you	that	he	is-going-to	win	and

van wie ∅ dat   ie   tweede wordt?
of whom that   he   second becomes

The main difference between the WH-binding in (105) and the one in
(107) is that the type of binding involved in the first construction is dependent on a particular property of a lexical item, namely on the property of
a bridge verb. If there is no bridge (anymore), e.g. if the bridge is gapped,
the binding relation is cut off, which results in ungrammaticality. Suppose
that we generalize this observation by assuming that (108) holds for all
lexically governed relations:

(108)   If a relation R between two positions A and B in a string X A Y B Z
         depends on specific properties of a lexical item C, then R is not
         reconstructable whenever C is not *terminally present* in the string.

Condition (108) predicts ungrammaticality in those cases where one of A
and B is an anaphor of some type and is assigned no antecedent if R can not
be reconstructed. Because the trace left by WH-Extraction is some kind of
anaphor, (108) accounts for the ungrammaticality of (105).[10]
    This condition also accounts for the ungrammaticality of (97b)–(99b), i.e.
for the ungrammaticality of gapping a *Vs*, if we assume that an *infScompl*
contains an anaphor that is controlled by some NP argument of the *Vs* and
that this relation of control is lexically governed in that the specification of
the controller is an idiosyncrasy of the *Vs*. Then, if the *Vs* is not terminally
present because it is gapped, the relation of control can not be reconstructed;
this leaves the anaphor in the *infScompl* without antecedent and therefore
leads to an ungrammatical string. Clearly, the anaphor involved must be an
empty subject.
    Apparently, the absence of a *Vvp* under the standard Gapping conditions
has no particular consequences with regard to the reconstruction of the right
conjunct in (100b)–(102b); these sentences are grammatical. Therefore, if

(108) or some more formal, general version of it holds, we should conclude that in a *Vvp* predicate structure no additional relation is imposed upon the arguments of the *Vvp*, the reconstruction of which would be blocked when the verb is absent. Thus one may expect *Vvp* predicate structures to behave under Gapping as 'ordinary' transitive predicate structures; (102b)–(102b) show that they do.

We may conclude that the opposition between the grammaticality of Gapping applying in the *Vvp* paradigm and the ungrammaticality of Gapping applying in the *Vs* paradigm can be explained in a fairly general and consistent way if we assume *infScomples* but not *infVPcomples* to be clauses containing an anaphoric subject.

2.5. Topicalization

InfScomples Cannot Be Topicalized

The relevant judgements are fairly clear, I believe, because they concern simple string ungrammaticality:

(109) * De *Nachtwacht* te zullen kopiëren beweerde zij helemaal niet.
         The *Nightwatch* to WILL copy   claimed she not-at-all

(110) * Ooit   met Anna te trouwen heeft Jan lang   gedacht.
         Sometime (with) A.   to marry   has Jan a-long-time thought

(111) * Jan gezien te hebben vertelde zij me niet.
         Jan seen   to have   told   she me not

(It is well known that as a stylistic condition on Topicalization, the un-affected string must be somehow — semantically and/or syntactically — 'heavy', but this is not at issue here.)

InfVPcomples, on the other hand, can be topicalized easily in Dutch:

(112)   De *Nachtwacht* (te) kopiëren heeft ze niet eens geprobeerd.[11]
        The *Nightwatch* (to) copy   has she not even tried

(113)   Met Anna op vakantie (te) gaan durft Jan niet.
        With A. on holiday (to) go   dares J. not

(114)   Jou vergeten kan ze   niet.
        You forget   can she not

Thráinsson (1979, Section 2.4.) refers to a version of the Backwards Anaphora Constraint in order to account for restrictions on topicalization of infinitival complements in Icelandic. If we take his lead in this matter, the opposition between *infScomples* and *infVPcomples* with respect to movement to COMP suggests that *infVPcomples* do not contain an anaphor in need of an antecedent while the presence of such an anaphor (an empty subject of course) in *infScomples* leads to destruction of the required binding structure when the complement is moved to the left. There is a strong argument in favor of this way of explaining the ungrammaticality of (109)–(111): tensed S complements of *Vs* verbs are perfect in the leftmost position of a sentence, and of course they contain a pronoun or full NP subject – never an anaphor.

(115) Dat ze de *Nachtwacht* zou   kopiëren beweerde ze
       That she the *Nightwatch* would copy   claimed she
       helemaal niet.
       not-at-all

(116) Dat hij ooit met Anna zou   trouwen heeft Jan
       That he ever with A.   would marry   has J.
       lang   gedacht.
       a-long-time thought

(117) Dat ze Jan gezien had vertelde zij me niet.
       That she J. seen   had told   she me not

The undeniable divergence in acceptability between (109)–(111) and (115)–(117) is the more striking as these sentences are pairwise equivalent under a coreferential reading of the subjects.

Thus, both the Gapping and the Topicalization phenomena can be analyzed in a way that illustrate aspects of the relation of Control which appears to be exclusively operative in *Vs* predicate structures.

Following the course taken by EST, one would expect *infVPcomples* and *infScomples*, if analyzed in the way advocated here, to behave differently from each other with respect to extraction 'out of' or binding 'into' the complement. The crucial postulates are those that refer to S's as cyclic or as governing categories, and adaptions or generalizations thereof (e.g. Freidin (1978) and all the recent work of Chomsky). This expectation turns out to be warranted, as we have seen: but there is yet more evidence for our analysis.

It is much more difficult to arrange discontinuity of the complement such that one constituent 'belonging' to the complement occurs in the leftmost (i.e. COMP) position if the complement is sentential than it is if the complement is verb phrasal; compare (118)–(119) and (120)–(121):

(118) *? Vanuit Amsterdam beweerde ze   iedereen   kaarten   te
       From   Amsterdam claimed   she everybody postcards to

       zullen sturen.
       WILL   send

(119) *? Naar Piet heeft Jan gezegd geen kaart   te zullen sturen.
       To   P. has J. said   no   postcard to WILL send

(120)   Het eindverslag probeerde ze   alle docenten te laten lezen.
         The final-report tried   she all teachers to let   read

(121)   Vanuit Amsterdam durft ze Piet geen kaart   te sturen.
         From   Amsterdam dares she P.   no   postcard to send

Nothwithstanding the complexity of the syntax of these constructions, I believe these examples support my analysis. I restrict myself to two remarks about them.

First: in an EST framework the operation causing discontinuity in these cases is movement to COMP or, equivalently, nonargument binding. Consequently, a strong similarity between the acceptability of Topicalization and the acceptability of WH-movement in comparable constructions can be expected. In particular, the easier it is to get a WH-constituent binding into a complement, the easier it should be to get any constituent binding into that complement from COMP, and vice versa. It is noteworthy, furthermore, that there is a parallelism between the possibility of binding into a tensed complement and the possibility of binding into an infinitival complement in case a verb (a *Vs*) selects both types of complements. For example, **zeggen** (say) is a bridge for binding from COMP into tensed S, while **vermoeden** (presume) seems to resist this type of binding. And binding into an infinitival complement of **zeggen** is in proportion easier than binding into an infinitival complement of **vermoeden**:

(122a) Waar zegt hij dat hij zal gaan   wonen?
        Where says he   that he   will be-going-to live

(122b)   Waar zegt hij te zullen gaan   wonen?
          Where says he   to WILL be-going-to live

(123a) *? Waar vermoedt hij dat hij gaat wonen?

(123b) *? Waar vermoedt hij te zullen gaan wonen?

Equally, if a bridge is destroyed by, e.g., intervention of some lexical item between the *Vs* and the tensed complement, the corresponding sentence with binding into an infinitival complement is bad too:

(122c) *? Waar zegt hij tegen Marie dat hij zal gaan   wonen?
          Where says he to   M.   that he   will be-going-to live

(122d) *? Waar zegt hij tegen Marie te zullen gaan wonen?

These obsevations, that tensed complements and infinitival complements in a certain context affect nonargument binding with equal force, are favorable to the claim that in that context the two complements are of the same syntactic category, which is, of course, not disputed by linguists who level all infinitival complements upto S. Now, as was pointed out above, binding from COMP into complements does not meet any problems in *Vvp* predicate structures. So we could argue that the verbs listed here as *Vvp* are in fact *Vs's* having the property of being a bridge for 'binding into'. Such a statement, however, seems incompatible with the fact that being a bridge, whatever it amounts to is exceptional rather than regular, in the present grammar of binding. As we may expect the class of these verbs to be quite large and because it is hard to find any independent motivation for turning the grammar of binding upside down to the effect that binding into S is regular rather than exceptional, a categorization of *Vvp's* as V's exhibiting the bridge property is an improper explanation of the acceptability of binding into the complements of these verbs. Moreover, the possibility of binding into an *infVPcompl* is not, as was the case with **zeggen** (cf. (122c, d)), affected by the intervention of lexical material:

(124)   Wie probeert Anna voortdurend te bereiken?
         Who tries   A.   continuously to reach

The second remark about (118)–(119) concerns the syntax of V-Raising. One might argue that the acceptability of the COMP being filled with an element originating in the infinitival complement of a *Vvp*, is due to the tendency of *Vvp's* to trigger V-Raising which is an operation that affects constituent structure and 'prunes' clausal boundaries for binding. This argument would amount to the claim that movement to COMP giving (121), for example, operates on a structure like (125) rather than on a structure like (126), the latter being the relevant D-structure under the assumption that Dutch is basically SOV:

(125) $[_S [_{COMP} -WH] [_S [_{NP} ze] [_{VP} [_{NP} Piet] [_{PP} vanuit$ Amsterdam] $[_{NP} geen kaart] [_V durft te sturen]]]]$

(126) $[_S [_{COMP} -WH] [_S [_{NP} ze] [_{VP} [_{\bar{V}} [_{NP} Piet] [_{\bar{V}} [_{PP} vanuit$ Amsterdam] $[_{NP} geen kaart] [_V sturen]]] [_V durft]]]]$

(125) represents the configuration resulting from V-Raising on either an embedded S or an embedded VP.

However, aside from the fact that V-Raising is not limited to *Vvp's* (see Section 1.2.), the structure (125) is so far from what ought to be the corresponding Logical Form that it should only be derivable in a subdivision of the grammar that either follows or is completely irrelevant to any application of Move α. In an EST framework it would be rather inconsistent to accept (125) as a D-structure, because doing so would force major adaptions, if not worse, of essential subtheories like those concerning Government and thematic relations. It seems very hard to incorporate V-Raising in any well motivated grammatical framework at all. Hoeksema (1980) for example shows that V-Raising structures might be dealt with in a Gazdar type accepting grammar, but only at the high price – in that framework – of loosening compositional semantics. Thus, while there is no doubt about the central role of the operation giving (121) in whatever grammar we choose to represent natural language, it will be very problematic to elevate V-Raising to the same level in the grammar. Therefore I fail to see any gain in claiming that (121) is derived from (125).[12]

Summarizing, the observation that *infScomples* cannot be topicalized and the observation that parts of *infScomples* cannot be topicalized, are explained differently. In EST terms, the topicalization of the complement as a whole offends binding conditions, while topicalization of parts, i.e. extraction out of the complement, offends bounding conditions. Neither binding nor bounding is problematic when Move α is applicated to *infVPcomples*. Therefore, the two types of infinitival complementation should be distinguished in a radical manner by the categorial component of a grammar.

3. SOME CONSEQUENCES AND COROLLARIES OF THE DISTINCTION

At it stands, the claim is that the foregoing observations and reflections justify the statement that Dutch has — at least — two different kinds of infinitival complements, distinguishable by their syntactic and semantic properties. A functional mapping from syntactic categories into denotational types is assumed, a weak form of compositionality.

3.1. *Syntax*

3.1.1. Syntax is involved to the extent that the arguments of Section 2 are taken to be compelling evidence for the need to categorize the two types of complements differently. If so, it can be shown that in what I see as the most sophisticated syntactic theory at the moment, the Government-Binding framework (GB) as synthesized in Chomsky (1981), exactly one categorial opposition is available.

In GB there are three categories that can cover a string consisting of an infinitive, some object phrases and adverbial modifiers: $\bar{S}$, S and VP. So in principle we can get three binary categorial oppositions: $\bar{S}$ vs S, $\bar{S}$ vs VP, and S vs VP. Now $\bar{S}$ expands to COMP + S, S expands to NP + INFL + VP; in languages like Dutch and English, a subject is obligatory in clausal structures. If the subject position has no phonological content in a certain structure, the empty category $[_{NP} e]$ is either a variable or an NP-trace or PRO. $[_{NP} e]$ is a variable iff it is properly governed, bears Case, is locally bound by an NP in a non-argument position and has independent thematic content (this and subsequent definitions are not minimal ones, but slightly redundant). $[_{NP} e]$ is an NP-trace iff it is properly governed, without Case and bound by an argument with no independent thematic role. $[_{NP} e]$ is PRO iff it is ungoverned and free or bound by an argument with an independent thematic role.

Now suppose that one or both of the complement types to be distinguished, is clausal, i.e. $\bar{S}$ or S. Then it follows that the empty subject cannot be a variable, for because of its properties a variable can only be bound from COMP or — equivalently — is a WH trace.

This does not reduce the number of possibilities for categorizing the two complements differently. It does imply that if the category $\bar{S}$ is assigned to one of the complements, the empty subject must be PRO, and if the category S is assigned, the empty subject must be NP-trace, because of the government pattern. If a complement is of the category S, the subject is NP-trace and the complement would be of the *seem*-type where we have an instance of Move α. Clearly, in both types of infinitival complementation discussed above, the 'binding argument' in the matrix predicate structure bears thematic content independent from the binding relation. Therefore the complement subject cannot be NP-trace. So in order to maintain the possibility of assigning one complement or the other to the category S, we would have to create a new type of realization of the empty category [$_{NP}$ e] with the properties of being governed and bound by an argument bearing an independent thematic role. We could think of this realization of the empty category as the result of deletion-under-identity (as opposed to free deletion). Such a move certainly would not be unattractive for the **beweren**-type complements (the *infScomples* of the foregoing sections), for they have, as a rule, full tensed counterparts with lexical subjects. Suppose we were to enrich the grammar with a rule *Delete* α operating between D-structure and S-structure and mapping, e.g., (127) to (128):

(127)   Jan beweert [$_{\bar{S}}$ dat   hij   komt.]
         J.   claims   that   he   comes/will come

(128)   Jan beweert [$_S$ [$_{NP}$ e]   te   komen.]
         J.   claims   to   come

This rule looks very much like Move α in its Move NP instantiation, with one notorious exception: it has to check anaphoric relations (identity) for it should only operate in case the deleted subject is anaphorically related to some other NP. But no such check could take place 'between' D- and S-structure for construal is a process on the level of Logical Form. Therefore, Delete α is not a possible rule. So (128) would have to be base generated and **beweren** would have to be subcategorized both for $\bar{S}$ and S complements. But then we would have to make sure that whenever $\bar{S}$ is selected, this category expands to a [+ Tense] INFL, for otherwise we would get two superficially indistinguishable complements belonging to different categories.

Both the Delete α approach and the subcategorizational alternative with conditions on expansion seem, if not 'out' by independent principles, quite contrary to the spirit of GB. Thus it is fair to say that S is not a suitable category for either of the two complement types within GB. For similar reasons, a 'small clause' analysis for either of the two complement types is untenable: 'small clauses', lacking INFL, are not maximal projections, so their subject is governed and must be trace, and so on.

As a result, the only categorial opposition left within GB, is $\overline{S}$ vs VP. All four arguments of Section 2 appear to require that the **proberen**-type complement, the *infVPcompl*, is the 'smaller' one, lacking both a subject and INFL, the location of tense and mood. So in GB, *infVPcomples* must be of the category VP and *infScomples*, the *beweren*-type, of the category $\overline{S}$. Because both categories look elementary for natural languages, it may be expected that this distinction is somehow reflected in any syntactic theory.

3.1.2. Yet there is a problem in categorizing an infinitival complement as VP, i.e. in assuming it to be a constituent without INFL and thus without subject. The problem is how to account for the observation that the features like person, gender and number of an *infVPcompl* must match the features of an NP in its context in order to get a grammatical string; (129) is un-. grammatical, because the feature *plural* of the complement does not match the feature *singular* of the NP *Jan*:

(129)   * Jan probeert   [echte   boeren   te worden].
        J.   tries   real   farmers   to become

One way of accounting for the requirement that the features of an infinitival complement match the features of an NP in its context, is assuming there to be a PRO subject in the infinitival complement that agrees, like subjects do, with the complement VP, which contains all the lexical material of the complement, and that this PRO subject is co-indexed with the NP whose features are to match. The co-indexing relation that keeps track of the features, between the PRO subject and the NP is generally referred to as *control*. This account, however, is of course not available to explain the required feature match in a *Vvp* predicate structure, for under the present analysis *infVPcomples* do not contain a non-lexical anaphor, or indeed anything, in subject position involved in a control relation.

Fortunately, it is possible to adopt an alternative account from Williams (1980). He presents indexical patterns like

(130)   John$_k$ tries [PRO$_i$ [to become a real farmer]$_i$]$_k$

in which it is the complement as a whole rather than the PRO subject that is co-indexed with the NP whose features are to match. Williams takes this co-indexation to be an instance of a very general process of *predication*. Predicative constituents that do not contain anaphoric subjects, like AP's and expressions of the type *as NP* that are also sensitive to feature matching can also be involved in the relation of predication. It is thus for reasons of generality that in (130) the agreement of PRO and the complement VP is formally detached from the relation between *John* and the complement as a whole; the latter is an instance of predication.

Now it can be seen that if the general relation of predication can account for the required feature match of an infinitival complement and an NP, it is not necessary to assume there to be an empty subject in the complement, unless we have independent reasons to postulate that. The subject plays no role in the account of the required concord in terms of predication.

In the previous sections it was argued, on grounds independent of the feature matching, that *infVPcomples* do not have (anaphoric) subjects. If we take predication rather than control to be responsible for the required concord of infinitival complement and NP, this analysis of *infVPcomples* can be maintained.

Furthermore it was argued, also on independent grounds, that *infScomples* do have anaphoric subjects. The relation of control therefore holds in a *Vs* predicate structure. This relation is lexical in that it is a lexical property of a *Vs* to specify which of its argument NP's is the controller. Predication, on the contrary, is a general and therefore structure based relation. Predication and control therefore are not depending on each other, though they may interact in a *Vs* predicate structure.

Under these assumptions, we can come to an interesting prediction as to the categorization of complement taking verbs and of the complements themselves. As Koster (1978) shows, there are good reasons for considering all structural relations to be conditioned by some form of locality. Very roughly, this means that structural relations hold between constituents as close to each other in the structure as possible. If so, then predication will also be sensitive to locality. Now suppose that we have a structure of the form

(131) NP_1 V NP_2 $[_X \ldots$ infinitive $\ldots]$

and that we can observe that it is NP_1 rather than NP_2 that must match the infinitival complement. This would be the case, for example, if we fill in **beloven** (promise) for the V in (131). Then it cannot be the relation of predication alone that is involved, for predication when not interfering with other relations, would obey locality principles and thus incorrectly select NP_2 rather than NP_1 to be related to the infinitival complement of **beloven**. Therefore, we must assume that a lexcial relation, not conditioned by locality, interferes with predication and 'overrules' it. This relation must be control. But then the verb must be a *Vs* and the complement an *infScompl* containing an anaphoric subject that is *controlled by* NP$_1$ on the basis of *lexical specification*. Therefore, it is predicated correctly, that **beloven** is a *Vs*. On the other hand, if we fill in a suitable *Vvp*, e.g. **dwingen** (force), predication must be the only relation linking an NP to the complement. Because predication obeys locality, it will select NP$_2$ rather than NP$_1$ to match the complement. So it is predicted that in a *Vvp* predicate structure of type (131), it is the object NP that will match the *infVPcompl*. This appears to be the case.

So we have two predictions with respect to a structure like (131). First, if in such a structure the infinitival complement is matched by NP$_1$, the structure is in the *Vs* paradigm as defined in the previous sections; second, if we take the structure to be in the *Vvp* paradigm according to the criteria in Section 2, only NP$_2$ can match the complement.

Similar predictions can be made with respect to the binding of lexical anaphors in the complement of a structure like (131). Anaphora, too, is a structural relation submitted to locality principles. Now suppose that we observe in a sentence that only NP$_1$ can match a lexical anaphor in the complement, e.g. a reflexive. Then the complement must be an *infScompl* containing a PRO subject that takes care of local binding of the anaphor and that is controlled by NP$_1$ because of a lexical property of the *Vs*. If the complement were an *infVPcompl*, and thus without subject, the relation of anaphora would select NP$_2$ as antecedent of the anaphor because of locality.

It is easy to see that the predictions based on the interaction of predication and control and the predictions based on the locality of the relation of anaphora, are consistent with each other in that they subsume a particular realization of (131) under the same paradigm, either the *Vvp* or the *Vs* paradigm. I am not aware of any counterexamples to these predictions, i.e. I do not know a verb in Dutch fitting (131) in such a way that its category and the category of its complement according to the criteria of Section 2, are contrary to the categories they should have because of the locality of predication and anaphora.

3.2. *Semantics*

The assumption that there is a functional mapping from syntactic categories to denotational types and that *infScomples* and *infVPcomples* are in different categories is, as such, not sufficient to guarantee that the two sorts of complementation are also of a different kind from the semantic point of view; yet this was claimed in Chapter 1.

Clearly, the interpretation of expressions of the category S is relative to the domain of truth values. On the other hand, the interpretation of expressions of the category VP is relative to the domain of individuals. For our present purposes it is not necessary to determine for each of the categories under which circumstances they denote which kind of function relative to the respective domains: intensional, extensional, first order or second order. The distinction between the domain of truth values and the domain of individuals is so fundamental in the interpretation of natural language, that any overlap in the denotations of $\overline{S}$-expressions and VP-expressions is excluded.

It follows from the nature of the arguments of Section 2 that the semantic distinction thus established, may not be 'overruled' by other grammatical operations giving structures in which both $\overline{S}$ and VP may be exhaustively dominated by one other category, for example NP. Such a 'supercategorization' resulting in structures like $[_{NP} [\overline{s} \ldots]]$ and $[_{NP} [_{VP} \ldots]]$ would destroy any distinction of the sort advocated here.[13] But it seems quite fair to exclude syntactic zero-operations that do not affect the terminal string, with a possible exception for operations dealing with quantification.

A second type of operation that must be rejected as contrary to the spirit of the proposed distinction, can be illustrated by the following fictitious fragment of a Montague type grammar:

(132)   If A is an expression of the category VP/t and B an expression of the category VP, then AB is an expression of the category VP. If A translates as A' and B translates as B', then AB translates as $\lambda x [A' (B' (x)) (x)]$.

In this combined rule the 'verbal' status of the *inf VPcompl* is conserved, but control is spelled out by propositional means. This move can be excluded by requiring all syntactic rules to be strictly categorial, again with a possible exception for rules dealing with quantification. Then verbs like **proberen** are categorized as VP/VP and therefore 'control' can not be spelled out by propositional means.

A third way of dealing with infinitival complements that I consider to be incompatible with the proposal here, is what Thomason (1976) does; he stipulates for every class of verbs that take VP's as arguments, a meaning postulate in which the type of relation, corresponding to the class, between individuals and properties (VP denotations) is set equivalent to some relation between individuals and propositions. I believe that the arguments of Section 2, especially those concerning mood and tense, make it very unlikely that the equivalence of properties and propositions as complements, postulated by Thomason, could hold generally. In fact, there are no simple or complex verb phrases in Dutch that correspond to the 'propositional' counterparts of *Vvp's*. Though meaning postulates are not translations, lack of correspondence between postulated relations and natural language expressions reduces the former to mere metaphysical obejcts, with little or no relevance for the interpretation of natural language.

3.3. Pro-complements

3.3.1. The perfect grammaticality of constructions like (133) shows that Dutch has lexical proVP's:

(133) a. Ik zal 't proberen.
          I   will it try

b. Wat kan Kees?
    What can K.

c. Dat durf ik niet.
    That dare I not

Like all lexical pro-forms, proVP's are constituents. Therefore VP is an autonomous category in the syntax of Dutch. This may not look very surprising, but there is little further motivation for assuming a category VP in Dutch. From the 'VP point of view' Dutch allows too much discontinuity in its word order to postulate VP as a basic category without extended theoretical motivation: VP is hardly identifiable as an immediate constituent of Dutch strings. This type of discontinuity can be described as resulting from rather complex interaction of reordering operations like V-Second, V-Raising, PP-over-V and the like, but the nature of these rules is imperfectly understood. Because it is by no means certain that every language has a syntactic VP (cf. McClosky (1979)), the discontinuity and the mainly descriptive character of the reordering rules meant to lead an underlying VP to the surface, may also serve as arguments for the lack of VP in Dutch syntax. Moreover, Dutch has no rule of VP Deletion of the type analyzed and argued for with respect to English in Sag (1976). So the occurrence of proVP's is important for the grammar of Dutch.

Furthermore, it follows from (133) that VP is a maximal category in the sense of the X-bar system. Pro-elements only occur in positions open to maximal categories (English *one* being a possible exception).[14] Thus S and S̄ cannot be V expansions, as is sometimes suggested, for if they were, VP would not be maximal, which is in turn incompatible with the occurrence of pro-elements in VP positions.

3.3.2. Let us say that a pro-element P is *linked to* a constituent A of the category C in its context iff P occupies a position open to contituents of the category C and P denotes whatever A denotes.

A proVP can be linked to any VP in its context (in the following examples, linking is represented by italicization of the P and the A in question):

(134)   Kees *vist   op   het   IJsselmeer, wat*   ik nooit heb gedurfd.
         K.   fishes on   the   IJsselmeer, which I   never have dared

(135)   Marie *zwom over   Het   Kanaal,*   maar Jan probeerde *'t*
         M.   swam   across the   Channel, but   J.   tried   it

         niet   eens.
         not   once

According to what is said in Section 2.2., a proVP can only be linked to a bare VP, i.e. without time indicators. So the proVP in (134) is linked to the VP *op het IJsselmeer vissen* 'on the IJsselmeer fish', and the proVP in (135) is linked to the VP *over Het Kanaal zwemmen* 'across the Channel swim'. In particular, a proVP can be linked to any *infVPcompl* in its context and to any VP properly contained by an *infScompl*, even if this VP happens to be equal to the terminal string of the *infScompl* containing it:

(136)   Marie probeerde *over Het Kanaal te zwemmen* maar Jan durfde
         dat niet.

(137)   Marie beweerde *over   Het   Kanaal   te* (zullen) *zwemmen,*
         M.   claimed   across the   Channel to   (WILL)   swim

         maar Jan zei *dat* niet te durven.
         but   J.   said that not to dare

On the other hand, a proS cannot be linked to an *infVPcompl* nor to any other VP, not even when we take the time indicators to 'go along' in this case (the asterisk marks failure of linking between the italized constituents):

(138) *Marie probeerde *over Het Kanaal te zwemmen* en Jan
       M.   tried   across the Channel to swim   and J.

       beweerde *dat* ook.
       claimed   that too

(139) *Marie *zwom over Het Kanaal* en Jan zei *dat* ook.
       M.   swam across the Channel and J. said that too

The proS in these sentences cannot be interpreted as *to swim across the Channel* by linking them to a VP that has this meaning, although the terminal string of such a VP could be the same as the terminal string of an *infScompl* replacing the proS grammatically, because a VP cannot denote a proposition; a proS can only be 'resolved' by linking it to a proposition.

What about (140)?

(140) ?Jan beweert *over   het Kanaal te zullen zwemmen*, maar ik
       J. claims   across the channel to WILL swim   but I

       heb *dat* nooit verteld.
       have that never told

At it stands, this linking between a proS and an *infScompl* is — at least — highly infelicitous, in that it is ambiguous as to whether it states that I have never said that Jan would swim across the Channel or that I have never said that I would swim across the Channel. Suppose that the structure of the *infScompl* is [$_S$ PRO **over** ... **zwemmen**]. The first of the two readings would mean that the proS is linked to that structure while PRO is somehow marked for being controlled by **Jan**. The second reading involves the linking of proS and *infScompl* while control has not (yet?) been stipulated. But notice that this ambiguity is rather surprising. The linking of proS to the *infScompl* must take place at some level of interpretation. Though this level may be far away from the grammatical 'hard ware', it is hard to see how we would have at that level or any other the choice between — say — a coindexed PRO subject and an un(co)indexed PRO subject. Therefore, I prefer to say that the linking of (140) is ungrammatical rather than infelicitous or vague because of ambiguity.[15] If it is ungrammatical, it is on a par with the following failures to link a pro-element to a constituent:

(141)   * Who did the police arrest *the girlfriend of t* and did *she* cry?

(142)   * Who do you want *to marry t* and does your sister want *it* too?

Observations of this sort have inspired Daly (1975, p. 146) to an 'Antecedent Condition' that prohibits the linking of a pro-element to a constituent that contains a trace but not the antecedent of that trace. Following a suggestion of Guéron,[16] we could rephrase this condition as follows (the words are mine): a pro-element can only be linked to names; names are constituents that are semantically independent; a constituent is semantically independent iff it contains no empty category free within that constituent; an empty category is free in A if it is not coindexed within A. This formulation generalizes over PRO and traces of Move α. It excludes the linking in (140) on the same grounds as the linkings in (141)–(142): a free occurrence of an empty category in the constituent linked to a pro-element. I take it to be a nice result that *infVPcomples* behave like names, i.e. semantically independent constituents, while *infScomples* appear to be semantically dependent.

3.4. *Summary*

> *A property is a proposition*   AUTOMATICALLY FALSE
> (theorem in PTQ-B, Parsons (1979, p. 142)).

APPENDIX

In Section 2.2.1. it was observed that **zullen** (WILL) can not occur grammatically in *infVPcomples*, while in Section 2.2.5. it was argued that an occurrence of **hebben** (have) – or **zijn** (be) – as an auxiliary may be grammatical but does not oppose the claim that a *Vvp + infVPcompl* construction is a temporal unit. Because both **hebben** and **zullen** are time auxiliaries, it is an interesting question with respect to the main topic of this paper why **hebben** but not **zullen** is acceptable in an *infVPcompl*, the more so because one would – superficially – expect this to be the other way around: **zullen** OK, but **hebben** no, because of the semantics of the verb.

This asymmetry can be explained if we assume that semantically **hebben** is a complex operator, that incorporates an aspectual operation on predicates and a temporal operation on propositions. There are good reasons for making such an assumption. Consider a sentence like

(i)   Elke   student heeft enige artikelen gelezen.
         Every student has   some   articles   read

Two things should be noticed. First, (i) does not imply that all students were reading at one and the same moment or interval in the past. In this respect (i) differs considerably from

(ii)   Elke   student las   enige artikelen
            Every student read some   articles

which places all the reading in one interval in the past. The temporal operation associated with **hebben**, tends to take narrow scope with respect to the universal quantifier.

Secondly, whatever the scope of the temporal operator, no reading of (i) gives rise to an implication that all the individuals that have read some articles, *have been* students or that the things they read, *have been* articles (though it may be easier to grasp what it means to have been a student than to realize what a have-been article looks like). The aspectual (perfective) operation of **hebben** appears to be restricted to the verbal predicate. It does not act upon the interpretation of the nominal predicates. In this respect, (i) and (ii) also behave differently, for to the extent to which past tense combines aspectual and temporal elements, (ii) places in the past not only the 'being reading' and the 'being read' but also the 'being student' and the 'being article' of the individuals involved.[17]

Suppose we analyzed the semantic contribution of **hebben** as one single operation — say: H —, to be interpreted for any formula A in the scope of H as, roughly: there is a moment in the past such that A is the case at that moment and actually A is not the case (any more). Then, if we take (iii)–(vii) to represent the logically possible transcriptions of (i) in the nonspecific reading of **enige artikelen**, only (vii) is compatible with the intuitions expressed above:

(iii) $H \forall x \, [\text{stud}\,(x) \longrightarrow \exists y \, [\text{art}\,(y) \,\&\, \text{read}\,(x,\,y)]]$.

(iv) $\forall x \, H \, [\text{stud}\,(x) \longrightarrow \exists y \, [\text{art}\,(y) \,\&\, \text{read}\,(x,\,y)]]$.

(v) $\forall x \, [\text{stud}\,(x) \longrightarrow H \, \exists y \, [\text{art}\,(y) \,\&\, \text{read}\,(x,\,y)]]$

(vi) $\forall x \, [\text{stud}\,(x) \longrightarrow \exists y \, H \, [\text{art}\,(y) \,\&\, \text{read}\,(x,\,y)]]$.

(vii) $\forall x \, [\text{stud}\,(x) \longrightarrow \exists y \, [\text{art}\,(y) \,\&\, H \, \text{read}\,(x,\,y)]]$.

(I have omitted those transcriptions into some predicate language in which the scope of H would be restricted to *stud* or *art*, for they would be very unnatural; for the specific reading of the object, a comparable list of options can be constructed, but this does not add anything to the point I want to make about the logic of **hebben**).

If we want to avoid postulating *having-been-students* and *having-been-articles* by an interpretation of (i) because (i) does not appear to call into existence those kinds of individuals, (iii)–(vi) should be rejected for in these transcriptions one or both nominal predicates are in the scope of H, the perfective operator. (iii) also is out because of the first intuition, that (i) does not evoke one interval for all the readings, which would conflict with widest scope for the tense operator.

So if we opted for interpreting **hebben** as a simplex operation, we would end up with hebben as an operator on the smallest proposition in a predicate logical representation of a sentence, which amounts to saying that the hebben operation merely affects the denotation of the verb to which the auxiliary is attached. This situation is represented by (vii). One could, however, argue that (i) is ambiguous as to whether or not the reading individuals were students at the time of their reading and whether or not the things read were articles at the time of their being read. In order to resolve that particular type of ambiguity, we need an additional operator that links, in the case of (i), moments of being a student, moments of being an article and moments of reading. Whatever properties are to be assigned to this operator, it may not be identified with the aspectual (perfective) one, for even if we allow, in the interpretation of (i), the readers to be students when reading, it should not follow that they aren't students any more – 'having been students' – whereas the act of reading still is to be considered as brought to an end, in every possible interpretation of (i).

Therefore we have the following situation: either hebben is interpreted as a simplex operation on the denotation of the verb it is attached to, or it is interpreted as a complex operation such that one of the suboperations (the aspectual one) is restricted to the denotation of the verb. In both options, we are left with the possibility that hebben is a verbal modifier. Of course I want to claim that hebben is acceptable and interpretable in inf VPcomples because of the possibility that (one of) the operation(s) associated with it is the aspectual one with domain restricted to the verbal predicate. If it is the aspectual (sub)operation that warrants the occurrence of hebben in an inf VPcompl, this nicely explains why hebben can so easily be dispensed with in just this context (see the discussion in 2.2.5., especially (75a)–(77a): the aspectual operation, in contrast to a temporal one, does not contribute anything essential to the meaning of the inf VPcompl.

Unlike hebben, zullen contributes only to the temporal (and – maybe – modal) frame of a sentence. The operation to be associated with zullen, can take the full range of possible scopes. It even tends to take wider scope than the temporal suboperation, if any, induced by hebben; compare:

(viii)   *? Marie heeft een roman zullen   schrijven.
          Marie has   a novel   WILL   write

(ix)   Marie zou   een roman schrijven.
          Marie would a   novel write

The intended meaning of (vii) is expressed grammatically by (ix). (viii) seems to be out because the linear ordering forces zullen to be in the scope of the perfective auxiliary. The suboperation associated with hebben which could take scope over zullen must be the temporal one, for reasons given before. But (viii) hardly ranks as grammatical. Thus it is hard to consider the meaning of zullen as 'governed' by the meaning of hebben. This suggests that even if we analyze hebben as evoking a tense operation, it is a small scope operation, as stated before for other reasons. In any case, hebben and, on similar grounds, zijn (the other perfective auxiliary Dutch) turn out to be rather harmless to the claim that the infinitival complements of Vvp's do not constitute propositional domains.

Groningen University

NOTES

* Many colleagues of mine at Groningen State University listened patiently and made valuable comments while I was working on this paper. In particular I am grateful to Frank Heny for his critical encouragement. Remarks made by an anonymous reader of the first draft led me to a broader approach. None of them can be blamed for what I have written down.

1 Although the 'derivational history' of the empty arguments in (1a) and (2a) diverge in some essential respects under the assumptions of EST (cf. Section 3.1., but see Koster (1978) for an argument in favor of generalization), both types of complements are taken to be clausal on every level of representation.

2 The use of a meaning postulate may have the advantage of avoiding problems with regard to compositionality; it seems to me that this is the reason why Thomason introduces a meaning postulate rather than a translation rule to express the propositional nature of infinitival complements (see also Section 3.2.).

3 Syntactically, it is a 'hole' (Gazdar, 1979) or an abstract element of an indexical chain (Chomsky, 1981), semantically it can be a free variable (Thomason, 1976) or a context expression (Groenendijk and Stokhof, 1979).

4 Kunnen has also another interpretation as an epistemic modality (cf. Section 2.1.). Under that interpretation, it is on a par with verbs like schijnen (seem), the complements of which are surely of the propositional variety. These verbs are not discussed here.

5 V-Raising is only one of the possible options for dealing with verb clustering; see e.g. Hoeksema (1980) for an alternative approach. The phenomenon as such, however, is a major topic in Dutch syntax.

6 It is conceivable that (25) is derived from a 'V-Raised structure' by Verb Second, while (26) is derived by Extraposition and Verb Second.

7 NP + Proberen is not a characteristic function of VP denotations. It is not the case that every VP denotation is either an attempt of every NP denotation or not. Therefore, niet proberen te (not try to) is not equivalent to proberen niet te (try not to). It is the second configuration that is involved in (73).

8 See for an extended discussion of this and other aspects of Gapping Neyt-Kappen (1979).

9 See Erteschik (1973).

10 Suppose Zwarts (1978) is right in taking the remnants rather than the zero strings to be the target predicates of the rule of Gapping. Suppose furthermore that a constituent is *open* iff it contains an empty category but not the antecedent of that category, and *closed* otherwise. Then (100) is simply an instance of the following general condition: *a constituent can be the target of a rule of grammar iff it is closed*. The idea is that both constituents disfigured by WH Extraction and *infScomples* (containing an empty subject) are open and thus not possible targets for the rule of Gapping. Cognate conditions can be found in Huybrechts (1976, p. 346), Daly (1975) (with respect to coreferentiality) and Guéron (1981). See also Section 3.3.2.

11 The infinitive marker te is optional in these cases; I am not aware of interesting implications of this optionality.

12 These doubts as to whether it makes sense to manoeuvre V Raising into a central part of the grammar of Dutch, does not have to lead to the conclusion that there could not be any relation between verb clustering and Move α on some level. It is widely

noticed among students of Dutch that, although V Raising and Extraposition are the only alternatives for deriving grammatical strings from underlying SOV order, binding within a V raised structure gives better results than binding into an extraposed infinitival complement. Especially, binding into an extraposed complement tends to be ungrammatical as soon as the extraposition marker om shows up at the beginning of the complement:

(i)   ?? Aan wie   heb je   geprobeerd om een brief te schrijven?
       T   whom have you tried   a   letter to write

Are we able to decide whether it is Extraposition as such or the interference of the preposition om that makes (i) so bad? If it is due to Extraposition, a couple of sound conditions prohibiting an operation to break into a constituent that was target to another operation (cf., Huybrechts (1976)) is available, on the basis of which one could conclude that it is not the structure of an *infScompl* that is responsible for the failure of 'binding into' but the fact that *infScomples* tend to be extraposed. Native speakers, however, generally find the extraposition structure (ii) that differs from (i) merely in the absence of om, far better if not fully acceptable:

(ii)   Aan wie heb je geprobeerd een brief te schrijven?

In Section 1 it was noticed that om cannot occur with *infScomples*. Because of the opposition between (i) and (ii), it cannot be upheld that Extraposition as such is responsible for the ungrammaticality of binding into these complements. In fact it is questionable whether om in (118) and comparable constructions is an extraposition marker at all; it is conceivable that its occurrence in some cases of Extraposition originates in an analogy with final adverbial phrases that are introduced by prepositional, meaningful om. The analogy of the 'extraposition marker' om with this clearly prepositional use gives a fair explanation why it creates opacity for binding into: it is a misplaced, but semantically 'traceable' use of a preposition.

   Dutch prepositions tend to block extraction out of their domains; Dutch has no regular form of preposition stranding but only a WH escape mechanism (cf. Van Riemsdijk (1978)).

[13] See Klein (ms.) for several good arguments against this kind of supercategorization.

[14] In particular, the pro-forms that can occur as proVP's, are certainly maximal constituents whenever they occur as pronouns: * de groene dat (the green that) etc.

[15] Suppose that we describe the problem with (140) as an ambiguity between a sloppy and a strict reading of dat. Note that pro-forms in *infVPcompl* position never would give rise to a reading other than the sloppy one. See also Partee and Bach (1981, p. 459 ff) for interesting comments on this phenomenon.

   Instead of trying to deal with the possible denotations of pronouns, I prefer the line expressed by the statement *we can share properties, but we can not share propositions.*

[16] See Guéron (1981).

[17] Cf. Cremers (1980).

BIBLIOGRAPHY

Bresnan, Joan W.: 1972, *Theory of Complementation in English Syntax*. Ph.D. dissertation MIT, Garland, New York, 1979.
Bresnan, Joan W.: 1978, 'A Realistic Transformational Grammar', in M. Halle, J. Bresnan and G. A. Miller (eds.), *Linguistic Theory and Psychological Reality*, MIT Press, Cambridge Massachusetts, pp. 1–59.
Chomsky, Noam: 1981, *Lectures on Government and Binding*, Foris Publ., Dordrecht.
Cremers, Crit: 1980, 'Over Nominale en Verbale Tijd', *Tabu* 11, 32–49.
Daly, David Michael: 1975, *Anaphora and Coreference in English*, unpublished Ph.D. dissertation, University of Texas.
Erteschik, Nomi: 1973, *On the Nature of Island Constraints*, unpublished Ph.D. dissertation MIT.
Evers, Arnold: 1975, *The Transformational Cycle in Dutch and German*, University of Utrecht dissertation, Indiana University Linguistics Club mimeo.
Freidin, Robert: 1978, 'Cyclicity and the Theory of Grammar', *Linguistic Inquiry* 9, 519–550.
Gazdar, Gerald: 1979, English As a Context-free Language, unpublished paper, University of Sussex.
Groenendijk, Jeroen and Martin Stokhof: 1979, 'Infinitives and Context in Montague Grammar', in S. Davis and M. Mithun (eds.), *Linguistics, Philosophy and Montague Grammar*, University of Texas Press, Austin, pp. 287–310.
Guéron, Jaqueline: 1981, 'Logical Operators, Complete Constituents and Extraction Transformations', in R. May and J. Koster (eds.), *Levels of Syntactic Representation*, Foris Publications, Dordrecht, pp. 65–142.
Hoeksema, Jack: 1980, 'Verbale Verstrengeling Ontstrengeld', *Spektator* 10, No. 3.
Huybrechts, M. A. C.: 1976, 'Vragende (r)wijs: Progressieve Taalkunde', in G. Koefoed and A. Evers (eds.), *Lijnen van Taaltheoretisch Onderzoek*, Tjeenk Willink, Groningen, pp. 303–367.
Klein, Ewan: ? 'VP and Sentence Pro-forms in Montague Grammar', unpublished paper.
Koster, Jan: 1978, *Locality Principles in Syntax*, Foris Publications, Dordrecht.
Koster, Jan and Robert May: 1980, 'On the Sentential Status of Infinitives and Gerunds', unpublished paper, read at the 1980 GLOW Conference.
McCloskey, James: 1979, *Transformational Syntax and Model Theoretical Semantics*, Reidel Publishing Company, Dordrecht.
Nieuwenhuijsen, Peter: 1976, 'Evers' V-Raising', *Spektator* 5, 589–602.
Neyt-Kappen, Anneke: 1979, *Gapping; a Contribution to Sentence Grammar*, Foris Publications, Dordrecht.
Partee, Barbara and Emmon Bach: 1981, 'Quantification, Pronouns and VP Anaphora', in J. Groenendijk, Th. Janssen and M. Stokhof (eds.), *Formal Methods in the Study of Language*, Mathematical Centre, Amsterdam, Part Two, pp. 445–482.
Parsons, Terence: 1979, 'Type Theory and Ordinary Language', in S. Davis and M. Mithun (eds.), *Linguistics, Philosophy and Montague Grammar*, University of Texas Press, Austin, pp. 127–152.
Thomason, Richmond H.: 1976, *On the Semantic Interpretation of the Thomason 1972 Fragment*, Indiana University Linguistics Club mimeo.

Thomason, Richmond H. and Robert Stalnaker: 1973, 'A Semantic Theory of Adverbs', *Linguistic Inquiry* 4, 195–220.

Thráinsson, Höskuldur: 1979, *On Complementation in Icelandic*, Ph.D. dissertation, Harvard University. Garland, New York, 1979.

Williams, Edwin: 1980, 'Predication', *Linguistic Inquiry* 11, 203–239.

Zwarts, Frans: 1978, 'Extractie uit Prepositionele Woordgroepen', in A. van Berkel e.a. (eds.), *Proeven van Neerlandistiek*, Nederlands Instituut, Groningen University, pp. 303–399.

HENK VAN RIEMSDIJK

THE CASE OF GERMAN ADJECTIVES *

1. ON THE NEUTRALIZATION OF SYNTACTIC CATEGORIES AND CASE THEORY

In this paper I wish to address certain questions relating to the fact that adjectives in Modern High German have the property of being able to assign case to their complement NP. In particular, I wish to raise three questions: (1) why is it that adjectives in German have this property at all?, (2) why are the cases that are assigned to the complements of adjectives dative and genitive, but not accusative and nominative?, and (3) why does there appear to be a correlation between the existence in a language of a morphological case system and the possibility for adjectives to assign case?

I will offer an analysis of the German phrase structure system, and of the structure of adjective phrases in particular, which accounts for question (1). This is the main subject of Section 1. A partial answer to question (2) will be offered in Section 2. Question (3), finally, will remain largely unanswered. All I can do here is offer a number of highly speculative remarks in the conclusion.

Before embarking upon this enterprise, I wish to make a few preambulary remarks about case theory. The theory of abstract case, as developed by Vergnaud (1979) and Chomsky (1980, 1981), makes a very precise claim. This is that verbs and prepositions can assign case to a noun phrase in their complement, but that nouns and adjectives cannot. It is this prediction which gives rise to question 1. In other words, in the absence of any theory about case assignment, there is nothing surprising about the facts of German. What is interesting about German is that, while the facts appear to refute abstract case theory, they confirm this theory at a more abstract level of analysis. To be a little more precise, it would be counter productive for German to simply reject the theory of abstract case. A theory which made no distinction between adjectives and nouns on the one hand and verbs and prepositions on the other would raise at least as many questions with respect to German. Instead, I will argue that a slight relaxation of abstract case theory produces desirable results for the grammar of German. Interestingly, the relaxation itself is not parametric, but it is such that it will accommodate certain cross-

223

F. Heny and B. Richards (eds.), Linguistic Categories: Auxiliaries and Related Puzzles, Vol. One, 223–252.

linguistic distinctions, such as those between English and German, at the level of phrase structure. This approach to language typology is one which I have explored in some detail for another domain of syntax in van Riemsdijk (1978, cf. in particular Chapter 7). I am aware that other languages may raise different, and more severe, problems for the theory of abstract case (cf. e.g. Platzack (1980)). However, I will basically disregard these problems which arise in languages of which I have little or no knowledge. All I can say about them is that if they turn out to refute the theory of abstract case more radically, German will still have to be accounted for.

A second general remark concerns the relationship between the theory of so-called abstract case and morphological (or surface-) case systems. The theory of abstract case, as elaborated in the references cited above, is by and large a partial theory about the distribution of noun phrases, as opposed for example to prepositional phrases. In this sense this theory says very little about what cases these noun phrases may have. The fact that subjects of tensed clauses behave in a special way led to the incorporation into case theory of a nominative case. Preposition stranding phenomena appeared to require a distinction between objective and oblique cases (cf. Hornstein and Weinberg (1981); Kayne (1981)). Finally, a special provision was included for genitive case. Nevertheless, the relationship between these abstract case distinctions and actual morphological cases in those languages that exhibit them has been left largely unspecified. Attempts to elaborate specific proposals as to this relationship have been extremely scarce. See Franks (1981) for an interesting discussion of many relevant questions. By and large this reticence on the part of the linguistic community is not unexpected given the extreme complexity of the problem. Note that despite the quite model-bound nature of abstract case theory, questions regarding the analysis of morphological case systems are, for the time being, hardly theory-bound at all. In this sense, I see little or no difference in principle between the pioneering work of Jakobson (1936) the interesting discussions in recent work by Silverstein (1980), and my own sketchy contributions in Section 2 of this article. In essence, what I propose there is a partial theory of surface case which incorporates the basic distinctions drawn by the theory of abstract case.

Let us turn now to the problem of case assignment in German adjectives.

1.1. *Some Facts*

The following are partial lists of adjectives which assign the genitive and the dative case (cf., for example, Behaghel (1923) and Paul (1919)):

(1) *Genitive*: bedürftig (needy), eingedenk (mindful), (un-)mächtig
((not) in command of), überdrüssig (weary), habhaft
(in possession of), gewiss (certain), (un-)teilhaftig ((not
partaking), ledig (single, free of), bar (devoid of), beflissen
(studious), bewusst (conscious), fähig (capable), geständig
(confessing), gewärtig (expectant, conscious), verdächtig
(suspected)

(2) *Dative*:   befreundet (friendly), beschwerlich (troublesome), (un-)er-
träglich ((in-)tolerable), geheuer (kosher), gleichgültig
(indifferent), verhasst (hated), widerlich (disgusting), be-
kannt (known), vertraut (familiar), dienlich (convenient),
bewusst (conscious), deutlich (clear), geläufig (familiar,
fluent), klar (clear), verständlich (comprehensible),
verwandt (related), streitig (controversial), beschieden
(given), geneigt (well disposed), ergeben (devoted),
gewogen (well disposed), verbunden (solidary), verfallen
(addicted), verpflichtet (indebted), zugetan (attached),
abträglich (detrimental), (un-)zugänglich ((in-)accessible),
abhold (averse), angeboren(innate), gleich (equal), eben-
bürtig (of equal match), egal (indifferent), fremd (foreign),
gelegen (opportune), übrig (left), willkommen (welcome),
beschoren (given)

(1) and (2) give an approximation of those adjectives that are still productively construed with case in the present day language. It should be obvious
from the examples that no straightforward semantic classes can be established,
although, of course, some subregularities exist. The sets are large enough not
to be dismissed as completely idiosyncratic. Below are some examples of how
these adjectives and their NP-complements are used in sentences:

(3)   Dieser Mann muss des Französischen **mächtig**   sein.
       this   man   must of French   in command of be

This man must speak French.

(4)   Der Hans ist seiner Freundin **überdrüssig** geworden.
       Hans has of his girl-friend   weary   become

Hans has grown tired of his girl friend.

(5)   Das Französische ist ihm   **ungeläufig**.
        French   is to him not-fluent

He is not fluent in French.

(6)   Die Universalgrammatik soll   dem Menschen **angeboren** sein.
        universal grammar   is-said to   man   innate   be

Universal grammar is said to be innate to man.

Let us first dispense with some simple theories which are probably wrong. For example, one might suppose that case is really assigned by the copula in these cases. For one thing, the NP that appears to receive case from the adjective may not be part of the adjective phrase at all. And the copula might function like a verb in assigning case. But it seems implausible that the copula should function this way since normally a noun phrase in the domain of the copula receives case not from the copula, but via agreement. Correspondingly the case on that NP is generally a nominative or an accusative, but never a genitive or a dative. Furthermore, as was noted above, the choice of case is largely an idiosyncratic property of the adjective — it would seem excessively redundant to distinguish as many different copulas as there are adjectives assigning case.

A somewhat more refined proposal would be to say that the adjective and the copula are reanalyzed into a complex verb, an extension of a suggestion in Kayne (1979). The complex verb would then pick up the idiosyncratic properties of the adjective. But the question would still remain why the adjective has those properties in the first place, and why the complex verb does not inherit the crucial property of the copula, which is not to assign case. Finally, such a proposal also appears inadequate in the case of prenominal adjectives, which we will turn to below.

It would appear then that none of these attempts at reconciling German with the general tenets of the theory of abstract case (cf. Vergnaud (1979), Chomsky (1980, 1981)), viz. that V and P are case-assigners and that A and N are not, will work. Consequently we will explore possibilities of minimally relaxing case theory in order to accommodate the German facts.

Note first that the NP to which case is assigned is not always external to the adjective phrase. For example, NP — A structures may occur prenominally, i.e. attributively.

(7)   Ein [ihm **ungeläufiges**] Wort.
      a to him unfamiliar   word

      a word (which is) unfamiliar to him.

(8)   Die [dem Illyrischen **verwandten**] Sprachen.
      the to   Illyrian   cognate   languages

      the languages related to Illyrian.

(9)   Der [seiner Freundin **überdrüssige**] Student.
      The of his girl-friend weary   student

      the student (who is) tired of his girl friend.

The derivation of such constructions from participial ones, where the copula
would have the participial form and where that participle would then be
deleted, does not seem to be a viable one in view of the fact that (a) the
non-deleted variants are at best very highly stylistically marked, and (b) that
there are many idiosyncratic restrictions on which adjectives can occur in
the attributive position and which cannot. We will not argue this in detail,
here, but will simply assume without further discussion that these brief
observations provide prima facie evidence that the bracketed constituent in
(7–9) must be an adjective phrase, and hence that the NP-complement is
internal to that phrase. A similar conclusion can be drawn from an unrelated
constituency test. It is a well-known fact that the finite verb in German root
sentences can be preceded by at most one constituent. By this criterion, the
following sentences show NP-complements internal to the adjective phrase.

(10)   [Ihm   ungeläufig] scheint diese Sprache   nicht zu sein.
      To him   not-fluent seems   this   language not   to be

      This language does not seem to be unfamiliar to him.

(11)   [Dem Illyrischen verwandt] sind ferner die folgenden Sprachen.
      To   Illyrian   related   are further the following languages

      In addition the following languages are related to Illyrian.

(12)   [Dieser Tatsache eingedenk] , haben wir uns entschlossen, . . .
      Of this fact   mindful   have we (us) decided

      Bearing this fact in mind, we have decided . . .

This does not mean that the NP which receives its case from the adjective is always internal to the AP. The following examples demonstrate several ways in which the NP and the adjective can be separated by material which cannot be part of the AP.

(13)a. Er wird **des Französischen** niemals **mächtig**   werden.
       he will of French   never   in-command-of become

b.?* Ein des Französischen niemals mächtiger Mann.

(14) **Dieser Oper** könnte ich nie **überdrüssig** werden.
      Of this opera could I never weary   become

(15) **Wem**   ist dieses Wort **geläufig?**
      To whom is this word familiar

(16) **So geläufig** kann **ihm** dieses Wort unmöglich sein.
      so familiar can to him this word impossibly be

(17) **Wie vertraut** ist **dir** diese Umgebung?
      How familiar is to you this area

In view of these facts it seems reasonable to propose that this type of adjective phrase is generated with the NP-complement internal to it, that case is assigned to that NP in its base position in the usual structural configuration of (minimal) c-command, and that the separation of the adjective and the NP occurs at a later stage of the derivation.

1.2. *A Problem for the $\bar{X}$-theory*

It appears from the examples discussed so far that the NP-complement always precedes the adjective. We may thus assume that these constructions are generated, following the principles of the $\bar{X}$-theory, as $[\bar{A}$ NP A$]\,\bar{A}$. The next question to ask, of course, is: what about the specifiers? Here, we would expect the specifier to either precede or follow the $\bar{A}$. But now we run into trouble because the specifier actually intervenes between the adjective and the NP. The specifier cannot even be external to the $\bar{A}$ as we would expect under normal interpretations of the $\bar{X}$-system. The following examples, which illustrate this fact, are again given in the contexts that are diagnostic for AP-constituency.

(18) a. Ein [mir $\left\{\begin{array}{l}\text{völlig} \\ \text{seit langem} \\ \text{so}_i\end{array}\right\}$ ungeläufiges] Wort ([dass . . .]$_i$).

   A   to me $\left\{\begin{array}{l}\text{completely} \\ \text{since long ago} \\ \text{so}\end{array}\right\}$ unfamiliar word that

   b.* Ein [$\left\{\begin{array}{l}\text{völlig} \\ \text{seit langem} \\ \text{so}_i\end{array}\right\}$ mir ungeläufiges] Wort ([dass . . .]$_i$).

(19) a. Ein [seines Studiums $\left\{\begin{array}{l}\text{geradezu} \\ \text{im Wesentlichen} \\ \text{mehr als}\end{array}\right\}$ überdrüssiger] Student.

   An of   studies $\left\{\begin{array}{l}\text{downright} \\ \text{essentially} \\ \text{more than}\end{array}\right\}$ weary   student

   b.* Ein [$\left\{\begin{array}{l}\text{geradezu} \\ \text{im Wesentlichen} \\ \text{mehr als}\end{array}\right\}$ seines Studiums überdrüssiger] Student.

(20) a. [Des Französischen   ganz   unmächtig]   scheint
      Of   French   completely   not-in-command-of seems

      er nicht zu   sein.
      he not   to   be.

      Totally unable to speak French he does not seem to be.

   b?? [Ganz des Französischen unmächtig] scheint er nicht zu sein

(21) a. [Ihm   100% geläufig] ist dieses Wort anscheinend nicht.
      To him 100% familiar is   this   word apparently   not

      This word is apparently not 100% familiar to him.

   b. * [100% ihm geläufig] ist dieses Wort anscheinend nicht.

Note that these facts constitute a problem not only for the $\overline{X}$-theory, but also for the assumption that the NP, in order to receive case, must not only be governed by the case-assigning head but also be adjacent to it. The latter observation is interesting in that it carries over to VP, a fact that is obvious when we consider case-marking in the VP in German. As is well known, the verb is last in the VP. The NPs that receive their case from the verb, however, tend to appear in the initial positions in the VP. Strictly sub-categorized PPs, predicative constituents, etc. intervene between the V and the NP. Furthermore, NP-subjects of infinitivals that are subject to exceptional case-marking are separated from the matrix verb by the complement VP. Thus, the adjacency condition cannot be maintained in German in any straightforward way.

What emerges from the preceding discussion is that there is at least one interesting parallelism between AP and VP in German. Pursuing this idea, note that what we have called specifiers above occur in exactly the same form and in exactly the same position within the VP:

(22)   Weil   dieses Buch mir $\left\{ \begin{array}{l} \text{völlig} \\ \text{seit langem} \\ \text{so}_i \end{array} \right\}$ gefällt ($[\,$dass$\ldots\,]_i$)

     because this   book to me $\left\{ \begin{array}{l} \text{completely} \\ \text{since long ago} \\ \text{so} \end{array} \right\}$ pleases   that

(23)   dass   er   sein   Studium $\left\{ \begin{array}{l} \text{geradezu} \\ \text{im Wesentlichen} \\ \text{mehr als} \end{array} \right\}$ hasst

     that   he   his   studies $\left\{ \begin{array}{l} \text{downright} \\ \text{essentially} \\ \text{more than} \end{array} \right\}$ hates

On this parallelism we may base our first tentative hypothesis. While the fact that German adjectives function as case-assigners constitutes a problem for case theory, the fact that the contexts in which they assign case are isomorphic to VP, a typical case-assignment environment, is reassuring. In the next subsection we will present an analysis of the isomorphism which is designed to capture the idea that case theory should not be relaxed to such an extent that adjectives can assign case whenever they govern an NP but only when certain more restrictive conditions hold.

1.3. *The Neutralization of Syntactic Features*

Whenever certain syntactic constructions share the properties of two syntactic categories, as for example in the case of gerunds, the question arises as to how these constructions-in-between can be accounted for without introducing excessively powerful mechanisms of relaxing the $\overline{X}$-theory to near-vacuity. For a discussion of the border line between the categories A and P, for example, see Maling (1983).

The same problem arises in connection with the isomorphism between VP and AP in German. The heads of these APs are true adjectives in the sense that they have their own morphological characteristics, quite distinct from those of verbs. Nevertheless the syntactic structure in which they occur is like a VP. A fairly restrictive solution to this problem can be obtained by making use of the feature system that is already part of the $\overline{X}$-theory, and which is in part designed to capture cross-categorial phenomena.

Let us assume, in fact, that phrase structure rules may be cross-categorial in a specific way. The cross-categorial formulations of base rules in Chomsky (1970) or Jackendoff (1977) are to be interpreted as abbreviatory conventions which are part of the evaluation measure. But the rules yield fully specified d-structures. What I wish to suggest here is that certain feature distinctions in the phrase structure rules can be neutralized so as to derive d-structures in which the distinction is equally neutralized. We may then say that German does not have constituents of the type [+V, +N], i.e. adjectives, but only degenerate constituents of the type [+V], which are generated, with the appropriate number of bars, in the relevant attributive and predicative positions. We may further assume that constituents of the type [+V] [i] have all the characteristics of [+V, −N], the only type of constituent in the language from which they are nondistinct. Below we will sketch a system of phrase structure that will give this effect, but for now we will leave it at the assumption. Another assumption that needs to be made is one concerning lexical insertion. Recall that, lexically speaking, adjectives are distinct from verbs, so let us suppose that they are entered in the lexicon as [+V, +N]. We can now stipulate that the necessary and sufficient condition for lexical insertion is not identity of features but non-distinctness of features, a natural corollary of the neutralization hypothesis.

This neutralization hypothesis, in fact, is quite in line with some proposals made by Aoun (1982). Aoun shows that the distinction between adjectives, participles, and verbs is neutralized in varying degrees in different Arabic dialects and proposes to account for these facts in terms of feature neutralization, linked to a markedness convention for syntactic features. It may indeed be the case that neutralization is a step on the way to the total disappearance of a category. Extending the markedness considerations invoked in Aoun's paper, we may impose a restriction on possible neutralizations. In fact, it appears that minimal categorial systems would consist only of nouns and verbs, which need not, of course, be fully specified. Such a categorial system would only have the categories [+V] and [+N]. We may then assume that neutralization may only be to one of these, a desirable restriction, a further application of which will be discussed below.

What, then, are the structures resulting from these assumptions? For ease of exposition we take the maximal projection of [+V] to have one bar, but nothing hinges on this.

(24) predicative adjectives:

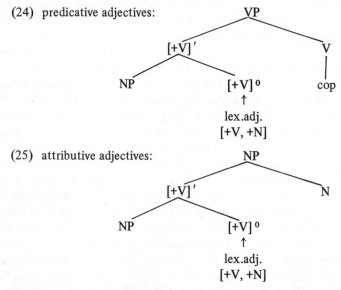

(25) attributive adjectives:

We are now in a position to make some further assumptions regarding case assignment. Let us say that abstract case is assigned by the structural head of a phrase, but that inherent case is assigned, trivially, by the lexical head which is inserted into such a position. In the lexicon heads of any feature composition may carry inherent case assignment features, since abstract case decides whether an NP which is to receive such an inherent case is permissible. The principle for abstract case assignment may now be formulated as follows:

(26)   Abstract case is assigned by structural heads that are nondistinct from [−N].

In Section 2 we will offer a feature analysis of this rule. For the present purposes, it suffices to point out that the introduction of the notion of nondistinctness is the only modification we have made to the standard version of case theory. Note that it is not necessary to assume that this addition is an option of a parameter along which the principle of abstract case marking may be relaxed, since the parameter is already present in the theory of neutralized categories. In languages that do not neutralize, such as English, only P and V will be non-distinct from $[-N]$, as before.

Observe that in view of the separation phenomena noted in (13) through (17) the interaction of (26) with the binding theory of Chomsky (1981) is problematic. If the separation is the result of NP-movement in examples like (13) and (14), then these examples should be ungrammatical by the binding theory, because the trace would receive case by (26) and would thus have to be a variable, which it cannot be. Hence it appears that the complementary distribution of case-marked trace and non-case-marked trace is also neutralized in the domain of $[+V]$.

One way in which this fact could be accounted for would be to specify the canonical case markers in the statement of the binding theory, but not in (26). This would amount to replacing principle B of the binding theory by B′ as shown below:

B   If a non-pronominal NP is case-marked, then

    (i) it is a lexical anaphor; or

    (ii) it is free in every governing category

B′   If a non-pronominal NP is governed by $[-N]$, then

    (i) it is a lexical anaphor; or

    (ii) it is free in every governing category

Detailed discussion of this issue would take us too far afield in the present context, however.

Before going on to elaborate on a theory of case into which (26) may be incorporated, let us consider some further evidence for the neutralization analysis for German adjectives.

1.4. *The Distribution of* $[+V]$′

The neutralization analysis as developed so far is designed to account for the internal ismorphism of VP and what we originally believed was AP. But the analysis also makes a straightforward prediction with respect to the external distribution of such neutralized constituents. Given the fact that lexical verbs can be freely inserted into positions specified as $[+V]^0$, we expect to find verbal constructions wherever we find adjectival ones. We do. In the attributive position, the context imposes restrictions on the morphology: the head of the prenominal phrase is inflected for gender, number, and case. Since verbs cannot be inflected in this way they must be inserted in their participial forms (**-end-**) which have the property of being able to carry such inflections. Observe that the verb keeps the infinitive marker (**zu**) in these cases. In the predicative position, on the other hand, no such inflection is required.

(27)   Ein [sein   Studium   seit   langem   *Participle*.
        a   his   studies   since   long

        hassend**er**]   Student
        hating   student

        A student hating (who has hated) his
        studies for a long time.

(28) a. Ein [nicht **zu** verkennend**es**] Zeichen   *Participial.*
         a   not   to   mistake   sign   *form*. (Attributive)

         An unmistakable sign.

     b. Das Zeichen wird [nicht **zu** verkennen] sein. *Infinitival*
         the sign   will   not   to mistake   be   *form*. (Predicative)

         The sign will be unmistakable.

(29)   Französisch ist [ohne Weiteres **zu** lernen]. *Infinitival*
         French   is   offhandedly   to learn   *form*. (Predicative)

         French is easily learnable.

Hence the neutralization analysis accounts for the fact that English, which has no neutralization, does not possess these participial possibilities. The prenominal participles of English exist only as reanalyzed lexical items (such as *a pipe-smoking man* etc.). In the predicative position we now have an explanation for the fact that *tough*-movement-type clauses must always be headed by an adjective (or some other *tough*-type head) in English, but not in German. See van Riemsdijk (1981b) for an analysis of the corresponding infinitival construction in Dutch.

Making the usual assumption that constituent coordination requires categorial identity, we further predict that adjectives and infinitivals (or participles) can be conjoined in these positions. This is indeed possible:

(30) a. Das sind **interessante** und in jeder Weise **zu**
These are interesting and in every way to

empfehlende Bücher.
recommend books

These are interesting and in every way recommendable books.

b. Er ist ein sehr **intelligenter** aber nicht leicht **zu**
He is a very intelligent but not easy to

überzeugender Junge.
convince boy

The order participle – adjective is generally excluded in such cases, but, hedging, we may hope to attribute this to general principles governing prenominal adjective order.

1.5. *An Extension of the Neutralization Analysis to Predicate Nominals*

The analysis, as we have presented it thus far, encounters a problem when we consider cases like the following.

(31) a. Er ist [auf Musik erpicht]
he is on music keen

b. Er ist [erpicht auf Musik]

Evidently there are adjectives whose complements can follow them. The question then arises as to whether this is a property that is shared by verbal structures. Note that in (31) it is a PP which can both precede and follow the adjective. NP-complements of the type that we have studied so far do not have this property:

(32) a. Er ist [dieses Problems gewärtig]
he is of this problem conscious

b.* Er ist [gewärtig dieses Problems]

We may assume, for example, that there is a rule which extraposes PPs, but not NPs, rightward over $[+V]^0$. It is, in fact, a very general property of German that the (VP-final) verb position can only be followed by PP or $\bar{S}$, but not by NP or AP (cf. also Groos and Van Riemsdijk (1982)). We may now extend this property to adjectives by formulating, for example, the filter in (33).

(33) $* [+V]^0 [+N]^{max}$ (where $\bar{S} = V^{max}$).

(We may note, incidentally, that (33) is a cross-categorial filter which will apply correctly, regardless of whether we have neutralization of [+V] at the level of phrase-structure. All that (33) does is provide evidence for the naturalness of the class composed of verbs and adjectives.)

There is, however, another way of looking at the phenomena in (31) and (32). Consider the positions in the phrase structure of German that are affected by the neutralization. These are the attributive and the predicative positions. As for the former, this position can be filled either by an adjective phrase or by a participial phrase. Thus these two are properly characterized by the notation $[+V]^n$. But take the predicative position. Here, in addition to $[+V]^n$ we also have NPs. (We will assume that PPs like those in *He is of superior intelligence* or *He is in the know*, are ordinary PPs like locative PPs, as in *He is in Athens*). Predicate NPs, like the other predicative constituents, immediately precede the verb, and consequently they follow other NPs and all PPs within the VP. As a result the predicative position will be characterized as $[+V]^n$ or $[-V, +N]^n$. But notice that we may now also neutralize the predicative NP to $[+N]^n$, because under the non-distinctness clause for lexical insertion the only other type of constituent that can be inserted is adjectives, which are permitted anyway. In other words, what we can say is that the predicative position is categorially reduced to the absolute minimum that is permitted under the markedness interpretation of the system of categorial features.

Recall that we interpreted the neutralization in such a way that a neutralized constituent has all the relevant properties of those categories of the language that it is non-distinct from. Consequently we expect items appearing under [+N] to have the properties of [−V, +N], which (modulo certain genitive NPs) is essentially that they subcategorize PPs on their right. Thus our extension permits us to add to the verb-like properties which we predict adjectives will acquire when inserted under [+V], certain noun-like properties which they derive from insertion under [+N], and this extension of neutralization to all of the predicative constituents correctly predicts the paradigm of (31) and (32). (The one exception to this is the fact that nouns do permit genitive NPs to occur on their right, but here we may say that this type of genitive assignment is structural rather than lexical, and that it is assigned in or from the determiner of $[-V, +N]$. This will account for the fact that, by and large, it is not possible to have more than one genitive assigned within an NP.) In other words genitives aside the correct predictions are made.

Observe now that the approach we have been taking makes an interesting prediction for the attributive position. Attributive NPs do not exist, hence this position is uniquely characterized by the statement $[+V]^n$. Consequently we would expect adjective phrases that occur in this position to exhibit solely the verbal (left subcategorizing) but not the nominal (right subcategorizing) behavior. This prediction is borne out. Prenominal adjectives cannot have a PP-complement on their right.

(34) a.   Ein [auf Musik erpichter] Student.

    b.*Ein [erpicht(er)   auf Musik]   Student.
       a   keen   on music   student

This may well be a redundant prediction, since structures like (34b) might also be excluded by some principle that excludes rightward recursion in specifiers. Formulations of such a principle may be along the lines of Emonds' (1976) surface recursion filter or via an adjacency requirement on the assignment of inflection from the nominal head onto the adjective (or participle) as suggested in Reuland (1979).

We will leave these matters here. While the extension of the neutralization to $[+N]$ may be redundant, it is in itself interesting to explore the consequences of the maximization of our hypothesis. Under a natural interpretation of Aoun's (1982) proposals for the markedness of categorial systems, the maximally neutralized analysis may in fact be forced by the theory. Be that as it may, it is interesting to note that the extension of neutralization appears to make only correct and no incorrect predictions.

At this point, recall again the first of the questions that we asked about German adjectives and case at the beginning of this article: Why can German adjectives assign case at all? The answer has now been provided by the conjunction of the neutralization analysis and a slight reformulation of the principle under which abstract case is assigned.

2. DATIVE AS THE UNMARKED OBLIQUE CASE IN GERMAN

Let us now turn to the second question: Why do adjectives in German usually assign a dative, sometimes a genitive, and hardly ever an accusative? I will suggest that this is because the dative case is the unmarked case in oblique contexts. First, I will outline a theory of case from which this follows, and second I will present evidence from a variety of constructions in German which supports this theory.

Before elaborating on the theory of case, one premise must be made. This is that cases should be represented in a feature system. I will not argue for this premise in detail here. Considerations have to do with phenomena of syncretism, both language-internal and cross-linguistic, and synchronic as well as diachronic. Other considerations relate to the fact that it is inconsistent to combine categories which are analysed in terms of features with cases which are not. Finally, such notions as unmarked case are best characterized in terms of features.

The system which I will sketch here consists of several parts: four features, feature assignment rules, morphological correspondence conventions, an agreement theory, and a case filter. The system as a whole leaves much to be desired and should be regarded as a first step in what hopefully is a good direction. Since so little is known about feature representations for case systems, for example, many arbitrary decisions had to be made. The system is also quite powerful, and here too it is hoped that improvement will turn out to be possible. Finally, parts of the system are highly redundant. This is an aspect that I believe is an artefact due to the matching of this case system onto a quite structured X-bar-system, and one that I believe it will be possible to remedy.

2.1. *Four Features*

I will assume that the German case system is characterized in terms of the following features: $[\pm S]$, $[\pm CA]$, $[\pm ACC]$, $[\pm GEN]$. The first two, which stand for the mnemonic categories 'subject' and 'closest argument' respectively, are, I believe, well-motivated, but the other two are arbitrarily chosen, because there appears, at present, to be no non-arbitrary way to cross-classify the cases dative, genitive, and (oblique) accusative. Ultimately, however, these features must be assumed to be part of a universal set of cases features.

The main characteristic of the features $[\pm S]$, $[\pm CA]$ is that the nominative-accusative distinction and the absolutive-ergative distinction are co-represented in the same syntactic structure. Another important consequence is that there is a straightforward characterization of the notions grammatical vs oblique case.

The features are specifically designed to generalize over nominative-accusative and absolutive-ergative systems in a straightforward way. This is a particularly important property given the fact that the two systems often coexist in one and the same language. In other words, a given type of NP may be spelled out according to one system if it is a (certain type of) pronoun and according to the other system if it is another type of noun phrase. Thus we have the following situation.

(35) *NP classes*: [+S, +CA] = intransitive subjects
              [+S, −CA] = transitive subjects
              [−S, +CA] = direct object
              [−S, −CA] = oblique

(36) *Spelling-out systems*:

   (a) nominative-accusative:

          [+S]   = nominative
          [−S, +CA] = accusative

   (b) absolutive-ergative:

          [+CA]   = absolutive
          [+S, −CA] = ergative

   (c) three way systems:

          [+S, +CA] = nominative
          [+S, −CA] = ergative
          [−S, +CA] = accusative

Note that this proposal reflects a Praguian type of morphological markedness in that nominative and absolutive have the simplest feature representation in the spelling-out component. Three way systems are correctly predicted to be marked. Very few languages have this as a major option and those that do apply it only to a small subclass of noun-types. See Silverstein (1976) for a wealth of information about such 'split' ergative systems.

2.2. *Feature Assignment Rules*

We will assume that these features and their values are assigned to syntactic categories. Thus a matrix of the type [+N, −V] is gradually built up to a full morphosyntactic matrix. In the following rules, the arrow is to be interpreted as 'is assigned to'.

(I)   a.   [+S] $\Rightarrow$ AG of S

       b.   [−S] $\Rightarrow$ AG of NP

       c.   [−S] $\Rightarrow$ NP_i iff NP_i is governed by a head H, H non-distinct from [−N]

(II)   a.   [+CA] $\Rightarrow$ NP_i iff NP_i is governed by a (transitive) verb [+V, −N]

       b.   [αCA] $\Rightarrow$ AG /____ [−αCA] $_{VP}$

       c.   [−CA] $\Rightarrow$ AG of NP

       d.   [−CA] $\Rightarrow$ NP_i iff NP_i is governed by a head H, H non-distinct from [−N]

(III)   a.   [+GEN] $\Rightarrow$ AG of NP

       b.   [+GEN] $\Rightarrow$ NP 'inherently' by a head H

       c.   [−GEN] $\Rightarrow$ NP elsewhere

(IV)   a.   [+ACC] $\Rightarrow$ NP 'inherently' by a head H

       b.   [−ACC] $\Rightarrow$ NP elsewhere

Some remarks on these rules. First AG stands for 'agreement marker', a kind of generalized position containing the main morpho-syntactic features of a sentence (verb) or a noun phrase (noun). See Chomsky (1981) for details. It is assumed that features are assigned to AG rather than to the (subject) NP adjacent to AG for reasons that have to do with doubling phenomena (see below). (Correspondingly a similar solution might be envisaged for the feature assignment to clitics instead of NPs, but this has not been attempted here because it is irrelevant to the German situation.) The transfer from AG to NP will be discussed below. Second, several of the rules can presumably be collapsed, for example IIb and IIc (for IIb it is assumed that the transitivity feature, i.e. [±CA] is automatically a feature of the VP-node by percolation; alternatively, the structural description of the rule would have to refer to the internal structure of the VP) and Ia and Ib, depending on what the categorial features of S are. No attempts in this direction have been undertaken here to avoid loss of perspicuousness. Third, the way that genitive is assigned in NPs by rule IIIa implies that there is only one structural genitive in an NP; hence the only way an NP could have a second genitive NP in it is by having the head noun inherently assign genitive to its complement NP by rule IIIb. For German this appears to be by and large correct, though nothing much hinges on the issue. Fourth, the principle for assigning abstract case (26) as modified in Section I, is now incorporated into the rules Ic and IId.

Note that every NP now gets feature specifications for the features [ACC] and [GEN] via the elsewhere condition, but that not every NP automatically gets a specification for [S] and [CA]. In other words, when the rules for [S] and [CA] fail to apply to a given NP, for whatever reason, that NP will end up with an incomplete or defective case feature matrix. This characteristic is, of course, instrumental in preserving the effect of the case filter which we can now formulate as follows:

(37)   CASE FILTER: *defective matrix

The rules, as formulated, constitute essentially a translation from a categorial notation into a morphological notation. In this sense the subcomponent of the grammar in which these rules apply can be regarded as a kind of readjustment component. This fact explains why the notation introduced by the rules is quite redundant in some ways. Subjecthood, for example, is encoded primarily as [NP, S] in this system, but redundantly as [+S]. In non-configurational languages however, the feature notation may well be taken to be primary. In fact, it may be argued that the configurational character of some languages, superficially expressed by the X-bar-theory, is just one specific type of expression of the feature system and its projections (cf. van Riemsdijk (1981a)).

2.3. Morphological Correspondence Conventions

One of the properties, in fact one of the advantages, of the system is that it only mediates between syntactic structures and case-forms but does not give any one-to-one correspondence. These correspondences are in fact quite idiosyncratic across languages, obeying principles that have to do with noun-classes and the like. The present features system attempts to abstract away from such factors. Let us assume then that the correspondence rules for German are the following:

(38)   [+GEN]   ⇒ genitive case

        [+ACC]   ⇒ (oblique) accusative case

        [−S, +CA]   ⇒ (direct object) accusative case

        [−S, −CA]   ⇒ dative case

        [+S]   ⇒ nominative case

It should be considered a problem of this analysis that there are two correspondence rules for the accusative case. While the distinction between direct
accusative and oblique accusative is syntactically real (see below), it has
no morphological correlate. Hence this is probably a defect of the feature
system, specifically of the features [ACC] and [GEN]. Improvement must,
however, be deferred to future research.

Another point to be considered is the following. The correspondence
conventions in (38) work with minimal feature specification. This implies
that there might be ambiguities. For example, [−S, −CA, −ACC, +GEN]
corresponds to both genitive and dative case. This may be remedied by
assuming that the features [+GEN] and [+ACC] take precedence over the
others. Alternatively, the correspondence rules may be formulated with fully
specified feature matrices.

2.4. *Illustration of Case Assignment by Adjectives*

In order to see how the system works, let us see how case assignment works
for the adjective cases discussed in Section 1. Take, for example, **ihm
ungeläufig** (5) and **des Französischen mächtig** (3). The rules will work in the
following way:

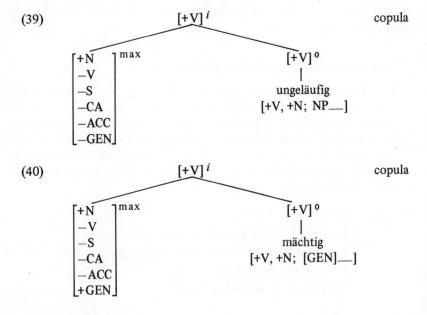

In (39) the NP corresponds to a morphological dative, in (40) to a genitive. The few accusatives that are assigned by adjectives will get their case in the same way as (40).

This then is basically what can be said about question two: the unmarked 'transitive' adjective takes a dative, but it can inherently assign a genitive (or, rarely, an accusative) to its NP.

2.5. Agreement and Transfer

Certain types of NPs receive their case via *agreement*. These include at least predicate nominals and appositive NPs. We will assume that agreement can apply freely, copying case features and their values from some NP to another NP, and that independently motivated structural conditions will characterize possible pairs of agreeing NPs. Furthermore, we will assume that agreement applies to features individually, not to a feature matrix as a whole. Agreement is always optional. It results in the normal course of events in two NPs which share certain features.

Regarding the transfer of case features from AG (of NP or S) to the adjacent NP, we will assume a somewhat different idea which is borrowed from the theories of clitic doubling of Jaeggli (1980) and Aoun (1980). A case which is quite parallel to those they discuss and can thus serve as an illustration of doubling is discussed in the next subsection. The difference between agreement and doubling has to do with the notion of case-absorption. In essence, the feature [+GEN], when spelled out phonetically as an independent grammatical formative, cannot give rise to agreement. Conversely, when transfer applies, the features in question are copied and there is no spelling out. Thus the transfer of (a set of) features by doubling results in case-absorption and, unlike agreement, does not normally yield forms in which NPs share features. We will take such doubling to be a property of non-phrasal categories such as AG (and also CLITIC), and call this phenomenon *case transfer*.

2.6. Possessive Noun Phrases

Let us now consider the transfer of case from the AG of NP to the adjacent NP, which we will call the possessive NP. This we offer as a first piece of independent evidence that the dative is the unmarked oblique case. We may assume that the relevant structure is as in (41).

(41)

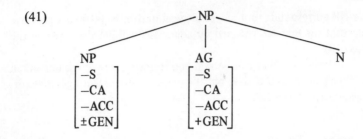

The AG has received its feature matrix by the operation of the assignment rules. Now the features must be transferred to the possessive NP. Agreement will assign the possessive NP the features [−S] and [−CA]. Notice that while agreement is optional, it must apply here, because otherwise the case filter takes effect and assigns * to the NP. The possessive NP will get the value [−ACC], either by agreement, or by the elsewhere condition in IVb. For the GEN feature, there are two possibilities. Either it gets spelled out in AG, in which case, by convention, it cannot serve for agreement and we get [−GEN] on the possessive NP via the elsewhere condition, or it does not get spelled out, in which case transfer must apply and we get [+GEN] on the possessive NP. The former possibility would correspond to the doubling situation which frequently arises with clitics. Doubling here refers to a situation where two coreferential nominal expressions have one and the same thematic role. The second possibility would be represented by a genitive possessor NP. Both structures occur, in fact.

(42) a. [Dem Mann] $_{NP_{dat}}$ [sein] $_{AG}$ Vater
     the man   his   father

   the man's father.

   b. [Des Mannes] $_{NP_{gen}}$ Vater
     that man's   father

   c. * Des Mannes sein Vater

   d. * Dem Mann Vater

What the system presented here predicts correctly is that when the genitive case is absorbed the dative case shows up on the possessive NP.

2.7. *Appositive Noun Phrases*

As a second piece of independent evidence for the treatment of dative as the unmarked oblique case, consider appositive NPs. I will assume that these have the structure given in (43), though little hinges on this choice.

(43)

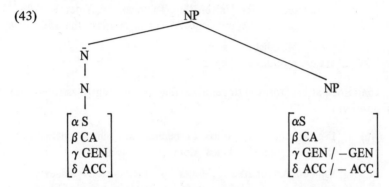

The appositive NP may receive a fully agreeing feature matrix by the application of the agreement convention. Recall that agreement is *de facto* obligatory for S and CA because of the case filter. For GEN and ACC, however, agreement may or may not apply, and when it doesn't the elsewhere condition gives rise to the minus values. For the grammatically assigned case forms this has no effect, for they are all [−GEN, −ACC] anyway, but for the oblique accusative and the genitive, we predict that the appositive NP either appears in the same case as the head ([+ACC] or [+GEN]), as a result of agreement, or in the unmarked (i.e. dative) case, where agreement has not applied. The interesting, dative, construction, which has been criticized and suppressed by normative grammar, has been studied by Leirbukt (1978) for the accusative − dative pairs, and by Winter (1966) for the genitive − dative pairs. We will restrict ourselves here to some illustrative examples from these articles. For more details the reader is referred to the two articles in question.

Take the genitive first:

(44) Sie war im Besitz   **zweier Kleidungsstücke**   der
      She was in possession of two pieces of clothing (gen) of the

      Ermordeten,   **einem** **Persianermantel** und **einem** **roten**
      murdered (f), a   fur coat (dat)   and a   red

      Kimono ...
      kimono (dat)

Here, the appositive NP, which is itself coordinated, modifies an adnominal genitive. Similarly in (45).

(45)　Nach Ansicht des Verfassers,　dem Ordinarius　für
　　　according to　the author (gen),　the　professor (dat)　for

　　　Soziologie an der Universität　Tübingen, muss der Soziologe
　　　sociology　at the university of Tübingen　must the sociologist

　　　stets　Moralist . . . sein.
　　　always moralist　　be

The same pattern arises with genitives that are inherently assigned from a preposition:

(46)　Die Hauptgestalt, Amos　Comenius, war schon　dem
　　　the main figure　Amos　Comenius　was already to the

　　　Knaben Kokoschka . . . teuer　gewesen wegen　seines
　　　boy　Kokoschka　dear　been　because of his

　　　'Orbis Pictus',　dem alten Lehrbuch　in Bildern.
　　　Orbis Pictus (gen) the　old　schoolbook in pictures (dat)

Finally, consider the following example of a dative appositive to a genitive object to a verb.

(47)　Endlich hat sich ein　kompetenter Mechaniker meines Wagens
　　　at last　has　a　competent　mechanic　my　car (gen)

　　　angenommen, einem hierzulande　seltenen russischen
　　　attended-to　a　in-this-country rare　russian

　　　Modell
　　　model (dat)

Regarding the accusative, inherent accusatives from verbs are rather too rare and frozen to base any conclusions on, but we get the non-agreement pattern again with accusatives from prepositions:

(48)　Der Verkauf des　Grundstücks an den Komponisten,　dem
　　　the sale　of the land (gen)　to the　composer (acc)　the

　　　späteren　Ehrenbürger　der　Stadt, . . .
　　　later　honorary citizen (dat) of the city

(49)   Der König kam aber   ohne   **Krone und Zepter,**   **den**
         the king   came however without crown and scepter (acc) the

         wichtigsten   **Symbolen**   seiner Macht und Würde.
         most important symbols (dat)   of his power and dignity

Note that these are cases of oblique accusatives. We correctly predict that
direct object accusatives do not exhibit non-agreement:

(50) a.* Ich besuchte dann **Herrn Müller,**   **unserem**
         I   visited   then mr.   Müller (acc) our

         Vertreter   in Pforzheim.
         representative (dat) in Pforzheim

   b. Ich besuchte dann Herrn Müller, **unseren** (acc) Vertreter in
       Pforzheim.

Similarly, a nominative can never give rise to a dative appositive NP.

(51) a.* Im   Haus   wohnte **ein alter Mann,**   **einem**   **der**
         in the house lived   an old man (nom), one   of the

         ältesten Bewohner   der   Stadt.
         oldest   inhabitants (dat) of the city

   b. Im Haus wohnte ein alter Mann, **einer der ältesten Bewohner** (nom)
       der Stadt.

In both cases, the reason is that the relevant feature specification, $[-S, +CA]$
in the case of (50), $[+S, \pm CA]$ in the case of (51), is obligatorily transferred
to the appositive NP by the agreement rule. For if agreement fails to apply,
the case filter (37) will block the derivation. The ensuing feature matrices
on the appositive NPs are both unambiguous in terms of the spelling-out rules
(38): accusative in the case of (50) and nominative in the case of (51).

   We may thus conclude that appositives provide another argument for the
contention that the dative is the unmarked oblique case.

2.8. *Intermezzo: An Example from Walbiri*

Walbiri has an agreement rule which applies in constructions involving body
parts. (These facts were pointed out to me by Ken Hale. Cf. also Van
Riemsdijk (1981a).) For example:

(52)   Kurdu   ka   wanti-mi   rdaka   ngulya-kurra
        child-abs pres. fall-nonpast hand-abs hole-allative

This sentence means something like 'the child's hand falls into the hole', that is, the child falls into the hole with his hand. The person and the body part agree obligatorily in case, here the absolutive case, since the child (or: the child's hand) is the subject of an intransitive verb; in other words it is [+S, +CA]. Similarly, when the sentence is transitive and the body part is the object, the 'possessor' of the body part agrees with it in absolutive case:

(53)   Maliki-rli ka   kurdu   yarlki-rni   rdaka
        dog-erg   pres. child-abs bite-nonpast hand-abs
        The dog bites the child in the hand.

Agreement occurs also with the ergative, that is with the subject of a transitive sentence:

(54)   Maliki-rli ka   kurdu   yarlki-rni   kartirdi-rli
        dog-erg   pres. child-abs bites-nonpast mouth-erg
        The dog bites the child with its mouth.

Some constructions have a dative object, which is also marked by a special dative marker on the auxiliary element. With such a dative, agreement also occurs.

(55)   Kurdu   ka-rla   maliki-ki yarnka-mi   ngirnti-ki
        child-abs pres-dat dog-dat   go-for-nonpast tail-dat

In the above cases agreement is obligatory, as in the non-oblique appositives in German, for example. With the possible exception of (55), which could be analysed either way, these cases are indeed those which, by virtue of our feature system, we have characterized as grammatical or non-oblique, and for which, as a consequence, agreement is in effect obligatory. However, Walbiri also has oblique cases, and here, as in German, agreement is optional with the dative case showing up when agreement does not apply.

(56) a. Yumangi ka   langa-**kurra** yuka-mi   maliki-**kurra**
         fly-abs   pres. ear-allative   enter-nonpast dog-allative

     b. Yumangi ka-**rla** langa-**kurra** yuka-mi   maliki-**ki**
         fly-abs   pres-dat   ear-allative   enter-nonpast dog-dative

These examples, while only suggestive, to be sure, appear to support our conception of the dative as the unmarked oblique case and of agreement as an essentially optional phenomenon.

3. CONCLUDING REMARKS

The preceding section has been dedicated to an analysis of the dative case in German. This analysis grew out of an attempt to answer the second question we asked at the beginning of Section 1 about adjectives. What we have established is that the dative is the unmarked case that we would expect an adjective to assign to an NP it subcategorizes, in much the same way that a transitive verb will assign an accusative to its object. What we have not answered is the question as to why the genitive should be practically the only other oblique case available to the adjective for marked subcategorization. In other words, why don't adjectives in a language like German make use of the oblique accusative (with the possible exception of a few cases such as **einen Deut wert** 'worth a nickel', which we will disregard)?

I will not attempt to answer this subsidiary question here. Ultimately, the answer may be rooted in an independent subtheory about the relationship between case-assigning categories and the case-system. The intuitive generalization appears to be that there are two hierarchies that are matched: one for the case-assigning heads, and one for the cases. The first is essentially as follows: $V - P - A - N$, and the second goes from least to most oblique. Consequently, we might expect prepositions to be capable of assigning oblique accusatives, but not adjectives. Similarly, we would expect nouns to assign only highly oblique cases in the quite marked situations where they can assign case at all. Locative cases might qualify, for example, while the dative might not. Although the main thrust of the question (viz. Why don't adectives assign objective case?) is accounted for in the system I have presented, I would be somewhat hesitant to say that I have explained why they cannot assign objective case. This is because in setting up the system a large number of stipulations had to be made, not all of which are firmly supported. Observe that the introduction of these stipulations is not a weakness *per se*, since the theory will ultimately have to incorporate a full-fledged sub-theory about morphological cases, case features, agreement, etc. Nevertheless, the explanatory force of my proposal is heavily dependent of the success of the sketch of such a theory that I have given.

In pursuing this question further, I have been exploring a somewhat different, though not necessarily incompatible, approach to the same question.

See Van Riemsdijk (1981b) for some preliminary results. Essentially, what I suggest there is that the $[+V]^{max}$ analysis is correct, and furthermore that $[+V]^{max}$ is a syntactic environment in which the absorption of objective case is obligatory (in the sense of Chomsky (1981)). If this is correct, then there may be an independent reason why the only cases available for adjectives are oblique cases.

What about the third question which we asked at the beginning? Here we can only speculate. A not too unreasonable story might be the following. When a language loses the morphological means of expressing the unmarked oblique case, i.e. the dative, it will only be able to maintain adjectives in the system at very high cost, because every adjective which takes an NP will now have to be marked for taking the case with which the dative has merged. If, for example, the dative and the accusative have merged into the accusative case, then every adjective will have to be marked for taking an (oblique) accusative. In such a situation the adjective can only revert to an unmarked subcategorization frame by starting to take a PP rather than an NP (cf. the appendix of the earlier version of this paper referred to in the *-note).

It should be obvious to the careful reader that the notion of markedness that we have been concerned with, in particular in the second part of this article, is a Praguian one rather than one which corresponds to the usage that prevails (or should prevail, at least, cf. Kean (1975)) in generative linguistics. Nevertheless I have tried to point out a number of ways in which the Praguian notion can be incorporated into a theory of core grammar and how it relates to our pretheoretical notions of what a theory of markedness incorporating core grammar will ultimately be like. In particular, it is my belief that primitive groundwork of the type illustrated here will be an indispensible cornerstone of such a theory of markedness because such a theory must eventually (cf. Van Riemsdijk (1978)) be construed as a theory about morpho-syntactic features.

Tilburg University

NOTE

* The research reported on here was greatly furthered by the hospitality of the MIT-Linguistics department, which suffered my presence during my sabbatical, in 1979/80, by the generosity of the Amherst Sloan grant program, which invited me to talk about my research, and by a grant from the Netherlands Organization for the Advancement of Pure Research under number R30-115. Some of the ideas presented in Section 2

originated in a seminar at the University of Amsterdam Linguistics Department, and I would like to thank the participants to that seminar, in particular Hans Bennis, for stimulating discussion. All the other helpful discussions I have had I will just mention collectively, because otherwise I am sure to forget someone.

The present article is a revised version of a paper which originally appeared in J. Pustejowsky and V. Burke (eds.), *Markedness and Learnability*, University of Massachusetts Occasional Papers in Linguistics, Vol. 6. An appendix on the relationship between oblique noun phrases and prepositional phrases contained in that version has been omitted here.

BIBLIOGRAPHY

Aoun, Y.: 1980, 'On Government, Case-Marking, and Clitic-placement', unpublished ms., MIT.

Aoun, Y.: 1982, 'Parts of Speech: A Case of Redistribution', in Belletti, Brandi, and Rizzi (eds.), *Theory of Markedness in Generative Grammar*, Proceedings of the GLOW conference, Scuola Normale Superiore, Pisa.

Behaghel, O.: 1923, *Deutsche Syntax*, Vol. I, Carl Winter, Heidelberg.

Chomsky, N.: 1970, 'Remarks on Nominalizations', in R. A. Jacobs and P. S. Rosenbaum (eds.), *Readings in English Transformational Grammar*, Ginn, Waltham, MA, pp. 184–221.

Chomsky, N.: 1980, 'On Binding', *Linguistic Inquiry* 11, 1–46; reprinted in F. Heny (ed.), *Binding and Filtering*, Croom Helm, London and MIT Press, Cambridge MA.

Chomsky, N.: 1981, *Lectures on Government and Binding*, Foris, Dordrecht.

Emonds, J.: 1976, *A Transformational Approach to English Syntax: Root, Structure-preserving, and Local Transformations*, Academic Press, New York.

Franks, S.: 1981, 'Deep and Surface Case', in Proceedings of NELS XI, University of Massachusetts, Amherst.

Groos, A. and H. van Riemsdijk: 1982, 'Matching Effects in Free Relatives', in Belletti, Brandi, and Rizzi (eds.), *Theory of Markedness in Generative Grammar*, Proceedings of the GLOW conference, Scuola Normale Superiore, Pisa.

Hornstein, N. and A. Weinberg: 1981, 'Case Theory and Preposition Stranding', *Linguistic Inquiry* 12, 55–91.

Jackendoff, R.: 1977, $\bar{X}$-Syntax: A Study of Phrase Structure, Linguistic Inquiry Monograph Two, MIT Press, Cambridge, MA.

Jaeggli, O.: 1980, 'On Some Phonologically-null Elements in Syntax', unpublished Ph.D. dissertation, MIT.

Jakobson, R.: 1936, 'Beitrag zur allgemeinen Kasuslehre, Gesamtbedeutungen der russischen Kasus', *Travaux du Cercle Linguistique de Prague* 6, 240–88. Reprinted in: *Selected Writings of Roman Jakobson* II, 23–71, Mouton, The Hague, 1971.

Kayne, R.: 1979, 'Extensions du liage et du marquage du cas', *Linguisticae Investigationes* III.

Kayne, R.: 1981, 'On Certain Differences between French and English', *Linguistic Inquiry* 12, 349–371.

Kean, M.-L.: 1975, 'The Theory of Markedness in Generative Grammar', Ph.D. dissertation, MIT, distributed by the Indiana University Linguistics Club.

Leirbukt, O.: 1978, 'Über dativische Appositionen bei akkusativischem Bezugswort im Deutschen', *Linguistische Berichte* 55, 1–17.

Maling, J.: 1983, 'Transitive Adjectives: A Case of Categorial Reanalysis', in this volume.

Paul, H.: 1919, *Deutsche Grammatik*, Vol. III, Max Niemeyer, Halle a.S.

Platzack, C.: 1980, 'Adjectives with Noun Phrase Complements in Swedish', unpublished ms., University of Lund.

Reuland, E.: 1979, *Principles of Subordination and Construal*, doctoral dissertation, Groningen University.

Riemsdijk, H. van: 1978, *A Case Study in Syntactic Markedness*, Foris, Dordrecht.

Riemsdijk, H. van: 1981a, 'On "Adjacency" in Phonology and Syntax', in Proceedings of NELS XI, University of Massachusetts, Amherst.

Riemsdijk, H. van: 1981b, 'A Note on Case Absorption', to appear in *Wiener Linguistische Gazette*.

Silverstein, M.: 1976, 'Hierarchy of Features and Ergativity', in R. M. W. Dixon (ed.), *Grammatical Categories in Australian Languages*, Linguistic Series nr. 22, Australian Institute of Aboriginal Studies, Canberra.

Silverstein, M.: 1980, 'Of Nominatives and Datives: Universal Grammar from the Bottom Up.' unpublished manuscript, Chicago/Nijmegen.

Vergnaud, J.-R.: 1979, 'Quelques éléments pour une théorie formelle des cas', chapter of forthcoming book, ms.

Winter, W.: 1966, 'Vom Genitiv im heutigen Deutsch', *Zeitschrift für Deutsche Sprache* 22, 21–35.

JOAN MALING

TRANSITIVE ADJECTIVES: A CASE OF CATEGORIAL REANALYSIS*

This paper is an investigation into the criteria for establishing syntacitc categories, and more specifically, into the problem of distinguishing between the categories of Adjective and Preposition. I will argue that in the history of English, at least two adjectives, *like* and *worth*, were reanalyzed as prepositions. Two questions come to mind: Why did the categorial reanalysis take place? What were the grammatical consequences of the reanalysis, i.e. what change(s) in the words' use followed as a result? The answers to these questions provide evidence as to the grammatical function of complements of different syntactic categories. They also show how very little of the evidence traditionally used by linguists to establish categories is strictly syntactic in nature.

The problem of distinguishing between the categories of Adjective and Preposition turns out not to be as trivial a problem as it may at first seem. Jackendoff (1973) noted that linguists had not taken prepositions seriously; that oversight has since been remedied in the work of Emonds, Jackendoff, van Riemsdijk, and Baltin, among others. The adjective, however, remains as the one major category which has not been seriously studied; not because no one takes it seriously as a category (at least for the familiar Indo-European languages), but rather because the internal syntax of adjective phrases has seemed less interesting.[1] With the recent development of abstract case theory, however, adjectives have taken on a new importance. We will look at one theoretical claim that has been made (e.g. in Chomsky (1981)), namely that the categories V and P can assign case (and therefore take NP-complements), while A and N do not.[2] The claim that adjectives cannot assign case figures in the analysis of passive: if all passive participles are adjectives, then their inability to assign case explains why NP-movement of the deep object is obligatory in the context of a passive participle.

It is clear that the claim could only be true at the level of abstract case, since it is not universally true that adjectives never assign morphological case. For example, as van Riemsdijk (1983) has amply documented, German has lots of what we might call 'transitive adjectives', i.e. adjectives which take case-marked NP-complements. So do Icelandic, Russian, Latin and many other case-marking languages. I use the term 'transitive adjective' advisedly, to

253

F. Heny and B. Richards (eds.), *Linguistic Categories: Auxiliaries and Related Puzzles,*
Vol. One, 253–289.

indicate only that the adjective is directly followed by a NP complement; in fact, the diachronic developments reported here suggest that the NP-complements to adjectives are usually not grammatical 'objects' but rather 'oblique objects' (cf. Bresnan (1981)).

The categorial reanalysis discussed in this paper suggests that there is something essentially correct about the idea that it is less natural for A and N to take NP-complements than for V and P to do so. The historical evidence suggests that NP-complements to adjectives are 'oblique' objects which can be realized in either of two ways: by prepositional phrases, or, in languages with surface morphological case, by case-marked NPs. The difference between case and a preposition would in this instance be a mere surface fact of a language. Once surface case is lost, then oblique NP-complements are typically replaced by PP-complements; e.g. dative case is typically replaced by *to*, genitive case by *of*. Within the Germanic family, the languages with transitive adjectives, e.g. German, Icelandic, Old English, Old High German, are those with productive case marking. The loss of transitive adjectives in English can be seen as a consequence of the almost complete loss of morphological inflection. Dutch and the Scandinavian languages other than Icelandic have also lost inflection to varying degrees, albeit more recently, and I would argue that they too, seem to be in the process of losing transitive adjectives.[3] The same development occurred in the Romance languages. In sum, there is a correlation between having transitive adjectives and having surface morphological casc, at least in the unmarked situation.

If this were the only possible change, there would not be much of interest to say. But in English (and some dialects of Dutch), just the right set of conditions existed for another solution to the problem of the surface realizations of oblique complements: namely the reanalysis of the head from A to P. Such a reanalysis took place for at least two words in English. In this paper, I will discuss the synchronic status of three lexical items, *like, worth* and *near*, which were all unambiguously adjectives in Old English. These have all been analyzed as prepositions in moden English by at least some grammarians, e.g., Quirk *et al.* (1972), but some or all of them have been considered adjectives by other linguists, e.g. Bresnan (1978, fn. 2) and Lightfoot (1980).

Apart from the categorial reanalysis itself, this change provides evidence bearing on the problem of what criteria the language learner uses to identify syntactic categories. And in turn, there are implications for the synchronic analysis of categories: among the criteria that linguists use to identify syntactic categories, which ones are really categorial and which are essentially semantic or functional? I will begin in Section 1 with the last question, because I can hardly argue for categorial reanalysis without first deciding what counts as evidence; I need to make clear what criteria can be used to decide the synchronic status of these words, and what cannot. In Section 2 I will discuss the categorial status of *like, worth* and *near* in modern English, and then in Section 3, briefly document the change for *like* from A to P. The diachronic evidence shows that neither the meaning of *like*, nor those properties which I argue to be essentially functional, changed. However, other properties, strictly categorial properties, did change as a result of the categorial reanalysis. These changes testify to the role of the phrase-structure rules in the identification of syntactic categories.

1. EVIDENCE FOR SYNTACTIC CATEGORIZATION

I will begin by looking at three of the diagnostic criteria often used to identify adjectives, namely, strict subcategorization, coordination, and co-occurrence with various degree modifiers.[4] The data show clearly that this kind of distributional criteria is actually semantic in nature, and hence it is not surprising that the facts cut across syntactic categories. The simplest statement of such distributional restrictions seems to be in terms of traditional grammatical functions such as 'locative' and 'predicate complement' rather than in terms of phrase structure categories such as AP or PP. (See Peterson (1981a, b), Grimshaw (in prep.) for arguments to the same effect.) As a result, such evidence cannot be used to argue for the syntactic category a given lexical item is assigned to.

1.1. *Subcategorization*

A classic test for adjectives is the ability to occur as predicate complements to 'linking' verbs such as *seem, become, look, act, turn, feel*, etc., which do not allow PPs (at least in the relevant sense of the verb). Another characteristic adjective position is as objective complement to transitive verbs like *consider*. Subcategorization frames have traditionally been stated in terms of syntactic categories, as shown in (1a), on the basis of contrasts like those shown in (1b).

(1) a.   seem, [__ AP]
         consider, [__ NP AP]

(1) b. Sandy seems $\left\{\begin{array}{l}\text{* out of town.}\\ \text{clever.}\end{array}\right\}$

We consider Sandy $\left\{\begin{array}{l}\text{* out of town.}\\ \text{clever.}\end{array}\right\}$

But it is simply not the case that only adjectives can occur in these contexts, as shown by the impeccable sentences under (2):

(2) a. Robin looks a bit under the weather today.

   b. Kim was acting out of character.

   c. That suggestion seemed completely off the wall.

   d. Everyone considers Kennedy out of the running.

   e. We found the patient in good spirits.

The internal structure of the complement phrases in (2) is obviously that of PP. Their ability to occur in what are considered adjective frames cannot be attributed to some idiosyncratic property of a particular preposition, e.g. *out of*, since the very same prepositions are sometimes good, and sometimes not, as illustrated by the contrasts in (3). (I will use the verb *seem* throughout because it does not have any irrelevant readings.)

(3) a. Lee sure seems $\left\{\begin{array}{l}\text{* out of town.}\\ \text{out of it.}\end{array}\right\}$

   b. Lee sure seems $\left\{\begin{array}{l}\text{* out of the house.}\\ \text{out of his mind.}\end{array}\right\}$

   c. Lee sure seems $\left\{\begin{array}{l}\text{* onto the roof.}\\ \text{onto something.}\end{array}\right\}$

   d. Lee sure seems $\left\{\begin{array}{l}\text{* under the old apple tree.}\\ \text{under the weather.}\end{array}\right\}$

Such contrasts show clearly that what is relevant is not the syntactic category of the complement, but rather the distinction between locative and directional PPs on the one hand, which are bad in these contexts, and what I will call 'metaphorical' PPs, which have nonliteral, nonlocative readings, and which are good in these contexts.

Note that if a particular PP is ambiguous between a locative and a metaphorical reading after the verb *be*, then only the metaphorical reading is available after *seem*.

(4) a.   The patient finally $\left\{ \begin{array}{l} \text{is} \\ \text{seems} \end{array} \right\}$ out of the woods.

      b.   Robin finally seems at home here, $\left\{ \begin{array}{l} \text{after years of living in this} \\ \text{country.} \\ \text{* after a long day's work.} \end{array} \right\}$

      c.   Lee seems over the hill as a sprinter.

      d.   A brook $\left\{ \begin{array}{l} \text{* seems} \\ \text{lies} \end{array} \right\}$ just over the hill.

Nor can the ability of such metaphorical PPs to occur as predicate complements be attributed to lexical reanalysis as complex adjectives, i.e. to category conversion (Quirk *et al.* (1972), Appendix I).[5] The usual test for lexicalization is the ability to occur prenominally. It is true that many of the metaphorical PPs which can occur in complement positions can also occur prenominally, as attributive modifiers:

(5) a.   Out-of-shape professors shouldn't attempt the marathon!

      b.   Chris made a completely off-the-wall suggestion.

But if we take the ability to occur in prenominal position as both necessary and sufficient evidence of lexicalization, then the question to ask is whether the class of complement PPs exemplified in (2)–(3) is the same set as the class of prenominal modifiers.[6] The answer seems to be that the two classes are distinct, and that neither is a proper subset of the other. Many locational PPs seem not to occur predicatively, even when they have clearly been lexicalized.

(6) a.   An off-Broadway show will be appearing on campus.

      b. * The show seems off-Broadway.

(7) a.   Yaz hit an inside-the-park home run.

      b.?* The winning home run $\left\{ \begin{array}{l} \text{was} \\ \text{seemed} \end{array} \right\}$ inside-the-park.

(8) a.   This is an over-the-counter drug.

     b. * This drug looks over-the-counter.

And many of the PPs which can occur predicatively cannot occur prenominally.

(9) a. * An out-of-it student walked into my office.

     b. * An onto-something reporter hounded the President.

     c. * Only in-good-spirits guests are welcome.

     d. * We will not consider your beside-the-point objection.

     e. * No out-of-the-running candidates will be given air time.

Individual speakers may vary considerably in their tolerance for such crea-
tions, as would be expected of a lexical process.[7] It is clear, however, that
lexicalization cannot account for the occurrence of metaphorical PPs in
adjectival subcategorization frames.

   Thus it appears that subcategorization frames should not be stated solely
in terms of syntactic category. One possible alternative is to use grammatical
functions, e.g. predicate complement. In Bresnan (1981), this function is
designated 'XCOMP', where XCOMP means a predicate complement of
category X.

(10)   seem, [___ XCOMP],
          consider, [___NP XCOMP] .

XCOMP's can be predicated of either the subject NP, e.g. of *seem* or the object
NP (e.g., of *consider*), depending on the given verb. Some additional feature
will be needed to exclude locative and directional PPs, which also involve
predication, as usually understood (see e.g., Williams (1980)). What is needed
is something like the semantic class of 'gradable predicates', where gradability
cuts across syntactic category.[8]

(11) a. Robin seems $\begin{Bmatrix} \text{a fool.} \\ \text{prime-minister.} \end{Bmatrix}$ (NP)

     b. The number three seems $\begin{Bmatrix} \text{odd.} \\ \text{* even.} \end{Bmatrix}$ (AP)

     c. $\begin{Bmatrix} \text{Lee} \\ \text{* The square root of two} \end{Bmatrix}$ seems irrational.   (AP)

Examples for PP are given above in (3). Note that in (11b), *odd* has only the gradable sense of 'unusual, unexpected', and not the mathematical binary opposition of odd/even. Adjectives are usually gradable, whereas locative and directional PPs are typically not; hence a semantic feature of gradability would correctly exclude them. Note, however, that just as there are non-gradable adjectives, so are there (a few) gradable locatives, as illustrated in (12).

(12) a. On a map, Rowley doesn't look terribly far from Boston.

b. * On a map, Rowley doesn't look by a river.

c. * On a map, Rowley looks on the wrong side of the tracks.

d. Now that there's train service, Rowley no longer seems so out in the sticks.

I will not pursue further just what property characterizes the set of possible predicate complements to verbs like *seem*, nor whether the correct characterization is in terms of semantic features and/or grammatical functions.[9] What is clear is that phrase structure categories alone are inadequate. It is obvious that although phrase structure categories may be associated with typical grammatical functions and vice versa, the mapping between them is not one-to-one. The sentences in (2)–(4) above show that in addition to predicate nominals and predicate adjectives, there are also (nonlocative) predicate PPs. Hence the fact that a phrase occurs as predicative complement to *seem* cannot be used as evidence that its head is an adjective.

1.2. *Coordination*

Another diagnostic often used to test syntactic category is coordination, based on the assumption that only phrases of the same syntactic category can be conjoined. Many linguists, e.g. Schachter (1977), have argued that category identity is not a sufficient condition: there must be semantic or functional identity in addition to syntactic identity for the coordination to be acceptable.

(13) a. * Pat is in the next room and over the hill.

b. * Pat is in love and in the next office.

A few linguists, e.g. Dik (1968) and Peterson (1981a), have argued that category identity is not even a necessary condition: as long as there is semantic and functional identity, coordination is possible even without category identity. This can easily be seen for adverbs, which conjoin freely with PPs of the same function. Thus a manner adverb can conjoin with a manner PP, as in (14).

(14)   The surgeon operated slowly and with great care.

In order to preserve the categorial identity condition, a higher syntactic node such as AdvP must be invoked, so that the identity condition can be met at that higher level.

(15)

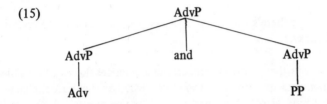

The same is true of predicate complements. It is possible to conjoin an AP with a PP, provided that both are XCOMPs, as illustrated in (16).

(16) a.   Doctors are always warning us of the dangers of being fat and out of shape.

     b.   The patient seemed cheerful and in good spirits.

Here too, the category condition cannot be maintained without invoking a new syntactic node or feature for the class of predicate complements.

   Thus, like subcategorization, coordination is a test that must be used with extreme caution. As long as the mapping between grammatical function and syntactic category is basically one-to-one, then it is impossible to determine what the correct generalization is. Whether the conditions on subcategoriza- or coordination are stated in terms of syntactic category, e.g. PP, or grammatical function, e.g. locative, the same predictions are obtained. Crucial evidence comes from those cases where the one-to-one mapping breaks down, as it does in the case of predicate complements and locatives, and in such cases, the evidence shows that the generalizations cannot be stated in terms of syntactic category.

1.3. *Specifiers*

Another difference between AP and PP lies in the range of specifiers that they take. The ability to take *very* as a premodifier has always been used as a test for adjectival status, especially in discussion of passive participles (cf. Wasow (1977, 1980)). The contrasts in (17) illustrate the fact that adjectives typically take *very* but not (*very*) *much* as a modifier, and that locative PPs take neither.

(17) a.   The birds were very $\begin{Bmatrix} \text{* in the tree.} \\ \text{noisy} \end{Bmatrix}$

   b.   The kids were very (*much) noisy.

   c. * The kids were very (much) in the tree.

Various accounts of these facts have been proposed in the literature. Bresnan (1973) generates *very much* as a specifier to A, and posits an obligatory rule of *much*-deletion. Jackendoff (1977) argues that APs take only simple degree words, whereas PPs take quantifier phrases (QPs) as specifiers, which in turn can optionally contain a degree word. Whatever the optimal account of the details may be, here too the facts cut across syntactic category. The feature [+gradable] is very likely necessary for an adequate account of degree modifiers. Generalizing to the entire class of degree words, *so, how, too, very*, note that such specifiers occur freely not only with APs but also with (most) metaphorical PPs, as illustrated in (18).[10]

(18) a.   They seemed $\begin{Bmatrix} \text{so} \\ \text{too} \\ \text{very} \end{Bmatrix}$ foolish.

   b.   They seemed $\begin{Bmatrix} \text{so} \\ \text{too} \\ \text{?very} \end{Bmatrix}$ $\begin{matrix} \text{in love} \\ \text{at home.} \\ \text{out of shape.} \end{matrix}$

   c.   How good of you!

   d.   How out of shape Lee looked!

   e.   How at home the hosts made us feel!

   f.   How out of character Pat seemed in that role!

   g.   Just how out of his mind do you think he is?

Observe that although metaphorical PPs take such adjective specifiers, locative and directional PPs do not, as illustrated by the ungrammaticality of the examples in (19).

(19) a. *How at the railroad crossing they live!

    b. *How to town they went!

This is presumably due to the fact that most locatives are not gradable. It cannot be a restriction against their taking any kind of modifier, however, since certain specifiers such as *right* are good:

(20) a. They live right at the railroad crossing.

    b. They went right to town.

On the other hand, unlike adjectives, metaphorical PPs also allow *much*, as shown in (21).[11]

(21) a. How much out of shape.

    b. So much at home.

    c. Too much in love.

    d. Very much down in the dumps.

This is exactly what one would expect of PPs in Jackendoff's framework. The generalization seems to be that metaphorical PPs can take either the specifiers suited to their syntactic category, or the specifiers suited to their grmmatical function as predicate complements.[12]

1.4. *Enough-shift*

Another difference between the specifiers of A and P lies in the position of *enough*, "the most syntactically exceptional word in the specifier system" (Jackendoff (1977, p. 150)). Bresnan (1973) pointed out that *enough* obligatorily follows adjectives, adverbs and quantifiers, and optionally follows nouns; she proposed a local transformation, *Enough*-shift, to move *enough* around the head. But suppose the head is a preposition.[13] The examples below illustrate the behavior of *enough* when it modifies a gradable, metaphorical PP.

(22) a. Robin seems $\left\{ \begin{array}{l} \text{* enough sensible.} \\ \text{sensible enough.} \end{array} \right\}$

b. Robin seems enough $\left\{ \begin{array}{l} \text{in love.} \\ \text{at home.} \\ \text{over the hill.} \\ \text{out of shape.} \end{array} \right\}$

c. * Robin seems $\left\{ \begin{array}{l} \text{in enough love.} \\ \text{at enough home.} \\ \text{over enough the hill.} \\ \text{out enough of shape/out of enough shape.} \end{array} \right\}$

d. ?? Robin seems $\left\{ \begin{array}{l} \text{in love enough.} \\ \text{at home enough.} \\ \text{over the hill enough.} \\ \text{out of shape enough.}^{14} \end{array} \right\}$

Clearly the rule of *Enough*-shift blocks if the head is a preposition. Here at last we have a criterion that seems to be purely syntactic; in English, *enough* follows adjectives, but precedes prepositions.

This curious fact about *enough*, namely, that it follows adjectives but precedes prepositions, may reflect a more general prohibition in English, as sketched below in (23).

(23)

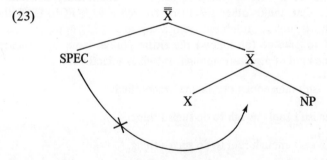

It is a well-known fact about English that adverbs can occur between a verb and a PP-complement, but not between a verb and its object.

(24) a. * Kim spoke quickly the words.

b. Kim spoke quickly to the children.

Perhaps the behavior of *enough* reflects not the category of the head, but rather the nature of the complement. That is, it can be positioned between an adjective and a PP-complement, but not between an adjective and a NP-complement. This fact cannot be attributed to an adjacency constraint on case assignment, since adjectives are assumed not to be case-assigners.

As the German data discussed by van Riemsdijk (1983) illustrates, in languages where complements precede the head, the specifier may intervene between an NP-complement and the head. But in languages in which the head of the phrase precedes its complements, (23) may well reflect a universal prohibition. German provides no relevant evidence, since NP-complements can never follow an adjectival head. But facts like the English ones obtain in both Russian (M. Halle, personal communication) and Norwegian.[15] The Norwegian adjective **redd** 'afraid' behaves just like English *near* with respect to the placement of **nok** 'enough'.[16]

(25) a. Han er redd (for) ulver.

     He is afraid (of) wolves.

  b. Han er redd nok $\left\{ \begin{array}{c} * \emptyset \\ \text{for} \end{array} \right\}$ ulver.

     He is afraid enough of wolves.

Thus it seems that the idiosyncratic behavior of *enough* is not really category-specific, as it first appeared to be. The exceptionality of *enough* lies in the fact that unlike other specifiers, *enough* always FOLLOWS the head of the phrase, unless prohibited from doing so by (23), in which case it will be forced to precede (or follow) the entire phrase. Note that *enough* must follow one kind of predicate nominal as well as adjectives:[17]

(26) a. He isn't man enough to assume responsibility.

  b. Lee isn't fool enough to do such a thing.

  c. * Lee isn't enough fool to do such a thing.

If this is the correction generalization, then a clear prediction is made: *enough* should be able to follow even prepositions in two cases: if the preposition takes a PP-complement, as in (27) and if the preposition is used intransitively, i.e. with no complement, as in (28) (see Jackendoff (1973)). This prediction seems to be largely borne out.[18]

(27) a.   Lee isn't down enough in the dumps yet to seek professional help.

   b. ? Lee isn't enough down in the dumps yet to seek help.

   c.   The cat wouldn't go up enough into the tree.

   d. ? This theory is still up enough in the air.[19]

(28) a.   The cat wouldn't go $\begin{Bmatrix} * \text{ enough up.} \\ \text{up enough.} \end{Bmatrix}$

   b.   Lee isn't down enough to seek professional help.

   c.   It doesn't stick up enough for me to reach it.

The conclusion is that *enough* follows the head of the phrase it modifies unless prohibited from doing so by (23). The original statement that *enough* precedes prepositions is clearly wrong, since, as we have just seen, it can follow a preposition which does not take a NP-complement. However we can still use the *enough*-test to distinguish between adjectives and prepositions. Although *enough* may precede or follow prepositions, depending on the nature of its complement, it may never precede an adjective.

(29) a.   Nothing is $\begin{Bmatrix} * \text{ enough good.} \\ \text{good enough.} \end{Bmatrix}$

   b.   Nothing is $\begin{Bmatrix} * \text{ enough close} \\ \text{close enough} \end{Bmatrix}$ to the beach.

   c.   Nothing is $\begin{Bmatrix} * \text{ enough near (the beach).} \\ \text{near enough (to) (the beach).} \end{Bmatrix}$

This turns out to be an extremely useful test.

1.5. *Other Syntactic Tests*

The results of the preceding sections clearly leave us with an impoverished set of criteria for identifying categories. Subcategorization, coordination and degree modifier tests were all shown to cut across syntactic categories. Only the position of *enough* relative to the head of a phrase turned out to be usable in distinguishing adjective from preposition. Other strictly categorial facts seem to be various morphological tests, such as the ability to take a synthetic comparative and superlative, the ability to take an *un*-prefix, which attaches to adjectives only (D. Siegel (1973)), and the ability to occur in prenominal position.[20, 21]

(30) a. Lee is even $\begin{cases} \text{more out of shape} \\ \text{* outer of shape} \\ \text{* inner shape} \end{cases}$ than I thought.

b.* Americans tend to be un-in-shape.

c.* Pat felt un-at-home.

d.* The two in-love senior citizens walked hand-in-hand down memory lane.

Note that the synthetic comparatives in (30a) are impossible despite the fact that these lexical forms exist independently as adjectives, as in *the outer wall, the inner sanctum* (cf. Note 6).

2. SYNCHRONIC STATUS OF *LIKE, WORTH, NEAR*

In this section we will show that *like* and *worth* are best analyzed as prepositions, whereas *near* passes all the tests for adjectivehood, making it perhaps the only surviving relic of the class of transitive adjectives.[22] (Of course, the NP-complement of *near* also alternates with a PP-complement, as in *near to* NP, just as one would expect of an adjectival head.) In the next section, I will discuss each of these words in more detail.

2.1. *Like*

It is generally agreed that *like* is a preposition in Modern English. Note the position of *enough* relative to *like* and related words, namely, *likely* and *alike*.

(31) a. That's a(n) $\begin{cases} \text{* enough likely} \\ \text{likely enough} \end{cases}$ story.

b. Chris looks $\begin{cases} \text{enough like you} \\ \text{* like enough you} \\ \text{? like you enough}^{[23]} \end{cases}$ to be your twin.

c. They look $\left\{ \begin{array}{l} \text{enough alike} \\ \text{alike enough} \end{array} \right\}$ to be twins.

d. How much are they $\left\{ \begin{array}{l} \text{*old?} \\ \text{alike?} \end{array} \right\}$

Enough must follow the clearly adjectival *likely*, just as we would expect. On the other hand, it must precede *like*, again as expected if *like* is a preposition rather than an adjective. As illustrated in (31c), *enough* can either precede or follow the adjective *alike*, which is exceptional in taking degree phrases, as noted by Jackendoff (1977, p. 155), and illustrated by the contrast in (31d).

There do exist a few marginal adjectival uses of *like* in prenominal position, as illustrated in (32).

(32) a. The like-subject constraint was proposed by Perlmutter.

b. You'll need boots, raincoats, and the like.

It seems to me that the phrase *and the like* is best analyzed as a NP with null head, and that *like* is in the position of an adjective. But such prenominal uses of *like* are clearly not productive.[24] Thus it is impossible to say:

(33) * Lee bought a new car and I bought $\left\{ \begin{array}{l} \text{a} \\ \text{the} \end{array} \right\}$ like.

Since prenominal use of *like* is nonproductive, the existence of the phrase *and the like* would be very weak justification for a synchronic assignment to the category A.

Nor is there any support for adjectivehood from the morphology. Neither *like* nor *unlike* have synthetic comparatives. Despite the fact that the negative prefix *un-* attaches only to adjectives, and that *unlike* clearly means 'not like', this would also be very weak justification. The relationship between the two words is not that of a synchronically productive word formation rule. See Section 3 below.

As we have argued above in Section 1.1., the fact that *like* can be used as predicate complement to verbs like *seem* does not mean that it is being used as an adjective in such cases. Observe that even when *like* is being used as a predicate complement, as in (34), it behaves like a P syntactically, the same applies to *unlike*.

(34)   Toby seems $\left\{\begin{array}{l} \text{very much} \\ \text{enough} \end{array}\right\}$ like his grandfather.

In other words, it is unnecessary to assign dual categorization to *like*, one as P and one as A. Rather, we can give a single assignment as P.

2.2. *Worth*

As counterintuitive as it may at first appear, *worth* is best analysed as a preposition.[25] It certainly passes the diagnostic tests for preposition as well as *like* does, even better in fact, since there is no *unworth* with a presumably adjectival base. This probably reflects the fact that *unworth*, when it did exist, was always restricted to clearly adjectival uses, namely attributive and intransitive, which have been replaced by *unworthy*. I conclude that analyzing *worth* as a P is more a problem for the linguist's conscious mind than for his unconscious.

The *enough*-test gives somewhat odd results for *worth*, which seems to be only marginally gradable, but the relative judgments are clear, as indicated in (35).

(35) a.   Sailing is great fun, but owning your own boat isn't

$\left\{\begin{array}{l} \text{enough worth the trouble} \\ *\text{worth enough the trouble} \\ ?? \text{worth the trouble enough} \end{array}\right\}$ for me to want to buy one.

   b.   Owning your own boat isn't sufficiently worth the trouble.

We find exactly the same pattern of judgments in (35) as we found for metaphorical PPs in (22) above. If *worth* were analyzed as an adjective, and if *enough*-shift is obligatory, then it would be difficult to explain why the phrase [*enough worth* NP] is acceptable. Except for *alike*, no other adjective phrase allows this possibility. The existence of [*worth enough*] is not counter-evidence: it is clear that in this phrase, *enough* is not a degree word modifying *worth*, but is instead the object complement of *worth*. Consider the contrasts in (36).

(36) a. $\left\{\begin{array}{l} \text{old} \\ \text{worth} \end{array}\right\}$ enough.

b. How much are they $\left\{ \begin{array}{l} \text{* old?} \\ \text{worth?} \end{array} \right\}$

c. What are they $\left\{ \begin{array}{l} \text{* old?} \\ \text{worth?} \end{array} \right\}$

The ungrammaticality of (36b) with *old* is due to a violation of the Left-Branch Condition; the grammatical examples with *worth* in (36b, c) are simply instances of preposition-stranding, after *wh*-movement of the object.[26] Thus despite the superficial similarity, the phrases in (36a) are quite different syntactically.

If *worth* was an adjective, then the only remotely plausible analysis would be to claim that the NP-complement were an inverted measure phrase; i.e. that the NP is base-generated in preadjectival position, parallel to *six feet tall* and *one year old*, but that *worth* was idiosyncratic in requiring inversion. Such an analysis would run into several problems. First, unlike other adjectives taking measure phrases, *worth* would require an obligatory measure phrase, as shown by the ungrammaticality of (37a). Second, lots of non-measure phrases occur, including definite NPs, as illustrated in (37b).

(37) a. * Lee is worth.

b. It's worth $\left\{ \begin{array}{l} \text{the time and trouble.} \\ \text{a second look.} \\ \text{it.} \\ \text{half a dozen of those other ones.} \\ \text{all the rest of them put together.} \\ \text{every penny.} \end{array} \right\}$

c. It's very much worth it.

d. It seems five times more worth it now than it did last year.

Third, the degree phrase and the NP-complement can cooccur, as illustrated in (37c, d).

Thus it seems reasonable to conclude that *worth* is a perfectly well-behaved preposition in modern English.[27]

2.3. *Near*

If *worth* is usually misanalyzed as an adjective, *near* on the other hand is usually misclassified as a preposition. The reason is obviously because it takes an NP-complement, and because it can be used with verbs such as *put* that strictly subcategorize for locatives, or verbs such as motional *go* which subcategorize for directionals.[28]

(38) a. Kim put the lamp near the bed.

b. Don't go near the water!

Closer examination, however, shows that *near* is best analyzed as an adjective. Contrast the behavior of *near* with that of *like* discussed above in Section 2.1., indicating that *near* is not a preposition, despite the fact that it takes a NP-complement. Note further that the mediating preposition *to*, normally optional, becomes obligatory when the phrase is modified by *enough*. Even when *near* is used locatively, it behaves syntactically like an adjective.[29] It takes a synthetic comparative and superlative, and *enough* follows the head rather than preceding it, as it would if *near* were a preposition.

(39) a. Kim put the lamp nearer (to) the bed.

b. Don't go any $\left\{ \begin{array}{l} \text{nearer} \\ \text{* more near} \end{array} \right\}$ (to) the water!

(40) a. Kim put the lamp $\left\{ \begin{array}{l} \text{near enough to the bed to read.} \\ \text{* enough near (to) the bed.} \end{array} \right\}$

b. Chris didn't go $\left\{ \begin{array}{l} \text{* enough near} \\ \text{near enough} \end{array} \right\}$ (to) the water to get wet.

Moreover, there exist attributive prenominal uses of *near*:

(41) a. the near shore.

b. a near miss.

c. Take the nearest one to you.

d. They remained near strangers after (nearly) twenty years of marriage.

If one wanted to claim that all locative phrases are syntactically PPs in English, one could assign the structure in (42), which would automatically solve the problems just noted by analyzing *near* as an adjective specifier.

(42)

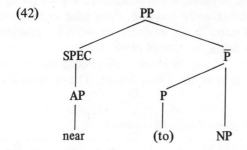

While this structure is even plausible for some verbs, where *near* is only optionally present, as in (43a), this isn't usually the case, as shown in (43b).

(43) a. Lee pulled the child $\left\{ \begin{array}{l} \text{near (to) her.} \\ \text{to her.} \end{array} \right\}$

b. Lee put the toy box $\left\{ \begin{array}{l} \text{near the door.} \\ \text{* to the door.} \end{array} \right\}$

The crucial difference in (43b) is clearly whether the PP is locative or directional. That contribution to meaning is associated only with HEADS of phrases, not with modifiers. Therefore *near* must be the head in (43b), and instead of the phrase structure in (42), we must be dealing with a locative AP.

This conclusion should not be at all surprising. *Close to* and *far from* are exactly parallel to *near to*, and *close* and *far* are clearly adjectives.

(44) a. Lee pulled the child $\left\{ \begin{array}{l} \text{close to her.} \\ \text{closer to her.} \end{array} \right\}$

b. Lee put the toy box $\left\{ \begin{array}{l} \text{far from the door.} \\ \text{far enough from the door.} \\ \text{* from the door.} \end{array} \right\}$

The fact that these phrases are locatives accounts for their use with verbs like *put*, while the fact that they are syntactically APs accounts for the existence of the synthetic comparatives and the position of *enough* with respect to the head.

2.4. *Summary*

The following table summarizes the results of this section and the criteria that
I have been using to distinguish between A and P. Entries are given for the
'typical' A or P, since for almost every criterion, there exist exceptional
lexical items whose categorial status is not in doubt. In order to facilitate
comparison, criteria have been defined so that all entries for A are '+', and all
entries for P are '−'. Remember that only locatives or directionals behave like
'typical' Ps with respect to those tests that I have argued to be semantically
or functionally based.

(45)   Diagnostic Criteria for A versus P

	A	P	*like*	*worth*	*near*
(a) semantic or functional					
occurs as pred. comp. to *seem*, etc.	+	−	+	+	+
degree modification by *very*	+	−	?	−	+
degree modification by *how, so, too*	+	−	+	?	+
(b) morphological					
has synthetic comparative	+	−	−	−	+
can be base for negative *un*-prefix	+	−	(+)	−	(−)
can inflect and agree (NA for modern Eng.)	+	−			
(c) strictly categorial					
prenominal position in NP	+	−	−	−	+
occurs 'intransitively'[30]	+	−	−	−	+
occurs with postmodifier *enough*	+	−	−	−	+
degree modifiers without *much*	+	−	−	−	+
can be 'stranded' (NA for mod. English)	+	(−)			

Criteria can be divided into two distinct types: morphological and distributional. Morphological evidence can come from either inflectional or derivational morphology. Distributional evidence, as I have argued here, can also be
divided into two types: that which has a semantic or functional basis, and
that which appears to be more strictly syntactic. We will now procede to a
more general consideration of the various diagnostic criteria.

Evidence from derivational morphology is notoriously unreliable as evidence for category assignment. Often the processes are not fully productive,
and speakers do not make synchronic connections between diachronically
related forms. Thus the non-existence of **unnear* does not show that *near*

is not an adjective, and the existence of *unlike* shows only that *like* was not yet a preposition at the time the word was created, and says nothing about its synchronic status. Evidence from comparatives is unfortunately also unidirectional, since not all adjectives are gradable. If a word does have a synthetic comparative, then it seems reasonable to conclude that it is an adjective rather than, say, a preposition; but lack of a synthetic comparative shows nothing. If two words bear a productive synchronic relation, then morphological evidence counts; if they have a synchronically nonproductive relation, then the morphological evidence shows nothing. Obviously it can be hard to tell in a particular instance whether the relation is synchronic, since there is always the possibility of a relic. But relics characteristically lack the full range of uses of a productively related form. A typical example is that of *elder*, historically the comparative of *old*; but *elder* cannot be used everyplace that *older* can, and in fact is most typically a noun, as in *the elders of the church*. By comparison the relation between *near* and *nearer* is clearly productive.

Inflectional morphology clearly can serve to identify syntactic categories unambiguously, but it is obviously not applicable as a diagnostic for adjectives in modern English. In languages where adjectives inflect for case, number and/or gender, prepositions are characteristically invariant. Thus inflectional evidence is sufficient to distinguish between the two categories. This is true even in languages like Spanish and Norwegian, which although they lack case, still have productive number and gender agreement on adjectives. However, since modern English has completely lost all adjectival inflection, adjectives and prepositions alike are morphologically invariant. Hence the language learner (and the linguist) must rely on more syntactic evidence. It is this fact that made the categorial reanalysis from A to P possible.

As noted above, nonmorphological criteria can be divided into two types: the essentially semantic or functional distributional criteria, and the more strictly syntactic criteria. One of the major points of Jackendoff (1972) is that many apparently syntactic constraints follow from semantic constraints, so that once a language learner has learned the meaning of the word or construction, the observed syntactic distribution will follow automatically. Where supposedly syntactic criteria turn out to have a semantic basis, we should not be surprised to find exceptions to a generalization which is expressed in terms of syntactic categories. This is precisely what we have seen for the strict subcategorization and specifier systems of predicate complements in English. The kind of modifiers that a phrase takes may have a semantic explanation, but the position that these modifiers take relative to the head of the phrase is a strictly syntactic, language-specific fact. For example, the fact that *enough* can be a modifier tells us nothing about the syntactic category of the phrase it modifies, but its position relative to the head of the phrase does.

Let me emphasize that I do not wish to claim that all syntactic generalizations can or should be reduced to semantics; to do so would unnecessarily complicate the grammar. Syntactic categories and phrase structure rules are still needed to capture generalizations about the internal structure of phrases. A good example comes from numerals.[30] Numerals are sometimes considered to be just a special subclass of adjectives, since some of the ways in which they behave differently from typical adjectives seem to have plausible semantic explanations, e.g., the fact that they do not take degree modifiers, and the fact that there can be at most one of them per NP. But not all restrictions on numerals have semantic accounts. For example, the fact that they must be the first of any sequence of adjectives in English cannot be made to follow from the semantics in any obvious way. This suggests that we need to have a special phrase-structure position for numerals, as distinct from adjectives. Therefore it should come as no surprise that in some languages, e.g. French, numerals precede the head noun whereas normal attributive adjectives follow.

An even better example is the category Determiner, which could, in fact, be defined as the 'first position' in the NP. Consider the so-called possessive adjectives in Romance languages.[31] Possessives are Determiners in French, just as they are in English, but not in Italian.

(46) a. son livre/ *le   son livre   (French)
         *his book/ *the his book*

     b. il   sou libro   (Italian)
         the his book

It is hard to imagine what a semantic explanation of this fact would be.

To sum up, we expect semantically-based facts to be universal, and strictly syntactic facts such as relative position to be language-specific.[32] Phrase structure rules seem to be the appropriate place to state such syntactic facts.

3. DIACHRONIC CHANGES

In the previous section, I have argued for a distinction between those category tests with a semantic or functional basis and those which reflect strictly syntactic generalizations. Further support for the distinction as drawn in the table of diagnostic criteria in (45) comes from the historical data. If we look at the syntactic changes that *like* and *worth* have and have not undergone as a result of the categorial reanalysis from adjective to preposition, it seems clear that the phrase-structure rules, or the generalizations they express, play an important role in the identification of syntactic categories.[33] In (47)– (49), examples of *like* at various stages in the history of English are given, at points when it still behaved syntactically like an adjective with respect to (productive) prenominal use, synthetic comparison, etc. Typically adjectival uses of *like* in Old English, (Chaucerian) Middle English and (Shakespearean) Early New English are given; the fact that these sentences would be ungrammatical in modern English shows that the category change has had some syntactic consequences. For each time period, the (a)-examples contain synthetic comparatives, the (b)-examples illustrate an intransitive predicative use, and the (c)-examples illustrate the prenominal attributive use. Any further examples provide other syntactic evidence relevant to category identification.

(47) **Old English** [34]

    a. Se lichoma waes   slæpendum men *gelicra*   *ð*onne
        the body   was [to] sleeping   men   more-like than [to]
        deadum.
        dead [men]

        The body was more like a sleeping man than a dead man.

    b. Næs   se   wæstm *gelic*
        Not-was the fruit   alike

        The fruit was not alike.

    c. Ealle men hæfdon [*gelicne* fruman].

        All men had a like beginning.

As illustrated in (47a), OE **gelic** takes dative complements which typically precede the head.

In ME, we find complements to *like* expressed either as a NP, or as a PP introduced by *to*. For the most part, the complement can precede the preposition only if it is a pronoun. Note the existence of [*like thereto*] illustrated in (48d); however we never find *[*therelike*], which we would expect to find if *like* were a preposition, since virtually all monosyllabic prepositions could invert with a pronominal object *there*. An example of stranding as the result of *wh*-movement is given in (48e). Since preposition-stranding was not generally possible in Chaucerian ME (Grimshaw (1975), Allen (1977)), this provides yet further evidence that *like* was categorized as an adjective.

(48) **Middle English (Chaucer)**[35]

    a. if it be *liker* love or hate.

    b. an house ... uncovered ... and a chidynge wyf been *lyke*.

    c. A *lyk* dreme dreymt þai both.

    d. Then have I not, ne no thing [*lyk* thereto].
        ... ne feynen it, ne be evene [*lik* to it].
        ... that in this world ne was ther noon [it *lyche*] /*therelike.

    e. 'And what soun is it *lyk*?' quod he.

By Shakespeare's day, PP-complements to *like* were less frequent than for Chaucer, although still possible.[36] Prenominal uses seem to be quite productive still. Intransitive uses are common in the meaning of 'likely'; note the position of *enough*. The example in (49e) shows that *like* can be stranded; but by this point in time, *wh*-movement can strand prepositions as well. All in all, the evidence suggests that *like* is still an adjective.

(49) **Early New English (Shakespeare)**[37]

    a. ... the boy *liker* in feature to his father Geoffrey.
        ... and earthly power doth then show *likest* God's.
        You would shew yourselves much *liker* to God who is love
        and *unliker* to Satan the accuser. (1670, Baxter)
        Swift ... the *likest* author we have to Rabelais. (1859, Masson)

    b. T'is *like* to be loud weather.
        And [*like* enough] the duke hath taken notice.

    c. And here I take the *like* unfeigned oath.
        Should a *like* language use to all degrees.

    d. His child is *like* to her, fair as you are.

    e. What was he *like*?

It is obvious that a categorial reanalysis has since taken place. I have not yet had time to try to pinpoint just when this took place, or to determine whether the changes in use took place rather quickly, or only gradually over the intervening centuries. What is clear, however, is that just the right conditions existed in English for the reanalysis of the head from A to P. The necessary conditions are given in (50).

(50) (i) loss of all adjectival inflection which could identify a lexical item as A;

    (ii) parallelism between AP and PP in the position of the complement relative to the head.

The categorial reanalysis reflects the fact that prepositions characteristically take NP-complements, while adjectives do not. At a point in time when virtually all adjectival complements are PPs and not NPs, the following two phrase structure rules are motivated.

(51) a. $PP \rightarrow P\ NP$

   b. $AP \rightarrow A\ (PP)$

There will, however, be no rule (51c) introducing transitive adjectives.[38]

(51) c. $*AP \rightarrow A\ (NP)$

In the postverbal position of predicate complements, either a PP or an AP is allowed. But given the sequence in (52), the phrase structure rules in (51) provide a unique answer to the questions of what syntactic category X belongs to: anything that is obviously not a verb can only be a preposition![39]

(52) $V\ [X\ NP]_{XP}$

A similar reanalysis occurred in some dialects of Dutch.[40] In both German ⸀ and Dutch, adjectival complements typically occur to the left of the head, as illustrated in (53a). An exception in Dutch, however, is **lijk** 'like'.

(53) a. [NP *waard*]

    worth NP

   b. [*lijk* NP]

    like NP

Since there is no adjectival inflection in predicative position in Dutch, the
exceptional order in (53b) establishes the necessary parallelism with PP,
and makes the categorial reanalysis possible. Since preposition-stranding is
impossible in Dutch, the following contrast is found.

(54) a. *Wat is hij lijk? (P)

     What is he like?

   b. Wat is hij waard? (A)

     What is he worth?

Once *like* and *worth* were identified as prepositions rather than adjectives
in English, then all their clearly adjectival uses, as defined by the phrase-
structure rules in (55), were forced out and replaced by related forms.[41]

(55) a. AP → A (PP) intransitive

   b. NP → (Det) (AP) N prenominal

Like was replaced by *likely* and *alike* in its two intransitive uses, and *worth*
was replaced by *worthy* both intransitively and prenominally.

On the other hand, neither the meaning of *like* nor its uses in predicate
complements and adverbials have changed in the least. The examples in
(56) below illustrate the various predicative and adverbial uses of *like* in
Shakespeare's work.[42] Similar examples could have been given from Old
English and Middle English. These examples show that the adjective *like* had
the same predicate complement and adverbial uses as the preposition *like* has
today.[43]

(56) a. **Predicate complement**

     Yet he looks like a king!
     How like a fawning publican he looks!
     How like Eve's apple doth thy beauty grow!

   b. **Manner adverbial**

     Common people swarm like summer flies.
     Few in millions can speak like us.
     Though thou canst swim like a duck . . .

c. **Disjunct**

Therefore, like her, I sometime hold my tongue.
That we (like savages) may worship it.
Virginity breeds mites, much like a cheese.

The fact that the category change has not affected *like*'s use in predicate complements supports the claim that subcategorization for such complements should not be stated in terms of syntactic category.

4. CONCLUSION

In this paper I have argued for the categorial reanalysis of two transitive adjectives in the history of English; in so doing, I have had to examine the various criteria used to identify syntactic categories. Both synchronic and diachronic evidence shows that certain criteria are actually not category-specific; in particular, it was shown in Section 1 that subcategorization, coordination and cooccurrence with certain degree modifiers cut across syntactic categories, thus undermining the traditional arguments that these phenomena are based on phrase structure categories. This result is important for our understanding of the nature of these fundamental grammatical phenomena, and their representation in grammatical theory. The distinction between functionally or semantically based criteria and truly categorial or structural criteria not only helps to explain the grammatical consequences of the categorial reanalysis but also helps to clarify the overall structure of the grammar.

A number of linguists (e.g. Heny (1979), Chomsky (1981)) have recently suggested that the base component of the grammar, i.e. the phrase structure rules, can be virtually eliminated since the information they provide about subcategorization is already implicitly given in the lexicon. Commenting on the possible interpretation of the otherwise unnecessary phrase-structure rules as redundancy rules relating subcategorization frames of lexical items, Chomsky notes that "apart from order, the rule of the categorial component serves no function as a redundancy rule" (1981, p. 32). As he observes, the existence of a phrase-structure rule stating optional expansions of some syntactic category does not eliminate the need to provide subcategorization information for each lexical item belonging to that category. It does not, however, follow, as Chomsky suggests, that the categorial component does no work. The role of the phrase-structure rules *qua* 'redundancy rules' is nonetheless a significant one in the assignment of lexical items to syntactic categories, as shown by the categorial reanalysis reported here. However redundant the phrase-structure rules seem to be, we need them to account for the cases of categorial reanalysis discussed in Section 3.

But we can draw an even stronger conclusion. The redundancy between phrase structure rules and strict subcategorization frames can be eliminated in two different ways: we could eliminate the phrase structure rules altogether, as Chomsky and Heny suggest, or alternatively, we could eliminate from the strict subcategorization frames (i.e., the lexical entries) precisely that information that the phrase structure rules express. That is, we could eliminate the redundancy not by getting rid of the base component of the grammar, but rather by changing the nature of the lexical entries. One solution is to eliminate linear order and categorial information from subcategorization frames, and instead subcategorize only for functional and semantic categories. In fact, this is the view of subcategorization in Lexical-Functional Grammar (Bresnan (1981), (in press)) and implicitly in Relational Grammar (Perlmutter (ed.) (to appear)). In LFG, it is assumed that lexical items subcategorize for grammatical functions, not constituent structure categories.[44] Grammatical functions are then mapped onto the particular phrase-structure rules and inflectional morphology of each language. This mapping can change independently of lexical subcategorization frames, which can be relatively invariant across languages and through time.

Within such a theory of grammar, the syntactic effects of the categorial reanalysis of *like* (Section 3) are exactly as expected. Phrase-structure rules are needed to explain the categorial reanalysis that took place in the history of English: what made this particular reanalysis possible is that the phrase-structure expansion of PP closely resembled the structures in which these adjectives appeared. When the English case-inflections were lost, the object function had to be encoded in phrase structure configuration rather than in case. But these adjectives now appeared in the phrase structure configuration [X NP], with an object complement, violating the unmarked universal that adjectives and nouns do not take direct objects. Thus, the phrase structure rules play an explanatory role in the historical changes discussed in Section 3. Strict subcategorization frames expressed in terms of syntactic category do not; in fact, the arguments of Section 1 undermine the evidence traditionally used for subcategorization by category.

Thus the categorial reanalysis of certain adjectives supports a theory of subcategorization based on grammatical functions rather than phrase structure categories, and also demonstrates the importance of the base component. If the role of phrase structure rules is to account for language-particular structural facts, as argued at the end of Section 2, then they can plausibly be thought of as independent of lexical structure. The structural aspects of traditional subcategorization frames can be factored out of the lexical entry, and represented explicitly in the grammar in the form of phrase structure rules.

Brandeis University

NOTES

* Preparation of this paper was supported in part by National Science Foundation Grant No. BNS-78 16522 to Brandeis University. Valuable feedback on the ideas in this paper and on an earlier version was provided by a number of people, including Joan Bresnan, Jane Grimshaw, Frank Heny, Ray Jackendoff, Ewan Klein, Peter Peterson and Henk van Riemsdijk.
[1] See, however, Bowers (1975), Hendricks (1977), Nanni (1980), Berman (1974), E. Siegel (1976).
[2] Hendricks (1978) takes the even stronger position that the phrase-structure rules generate no post-head complements to adjectives. Apparent exceptions are generated by a local rule adjoining an S-bar or PP within V-bar as right sister to A. It is unclear to me whether this analysis is compatible with the categorial reanalysis discussed here. However, it seems to me that there are independent reasons for the fact that complex APs cannot occur prenominally in English, a fact which is a major motivation for his position (cf. Note (21) below).
[3] Platzack's (1980) study of Swedish adjectives shows that the diachronic picture is more complicated in ways that I have not had time to investigate. Of particular relevance is the extent of influence from German.
[4] For example, see Wasow's classic paper (1977) concerning the distinction between verbal and adjectival passives. Although his diagnostics do distinguish adjectives from verbs, this paper shows that only some of them are actually suffiicient criteria for adjectivehood, in the sense of distinguishing adjectives from prepositions. The main purpose of this section is to sort out those diagnostics which are not category-specific. See also Wasow, Note 9.
[5] See, e.g., Nanni (1980), who argues that one source of strings like *easy to please* is as base-generated (lexically derived) complex adjectives.
[6] As pointed out to me by J. Grimshaw (personal communication), who also provided several of the relevant examples, the phenomenon of category conversion raises nontrivial questions about the internal structure and morphology of lexically reanalyzed phrases which I will ignore here. Note however, that although converted words normally inflect like the category they become (Quirk *et al.*, Appendix I), (e.g. *They are 'has-beens'*), converted adjectives do not take synthetic comparatives or superlatives, even when they are monosyllabic.

(i) That's the 'in' thing to do.

(ii) * That's the 'innest' thing to do.

[7] In fact, of the examples in (9), (d, e) are decidedly better than (a–c).

[8] The obvious problem is to determine where the boundary between syntax and semantics lies. In this paper I am assuming that a syntactic category is one defined by the phrase-structure rules. At issue then is whether the phrase-structure rules should be allowed to include features such as [± gradable] or [± predicate].

[9] See Grimshaw (1981b, in prep) for further discussion. Dick Carter points out (personal communication) that some verbs which take predicate complements seem to impose categorial restrictions as well. For example, the verb *become* takes NP and AP complements but does not appear to allow any of the metaphorical PPs, as illustrated in the near minimal pair below.

 (i)   Lee became mad.

 (ii)   * Lee became out of his mind.

Since these seem to be semantically equivalent predicates, the categorial difference must account for the difference in acceptability. Further reflection shows that the difference must be semantic in nature, rather than categorial, since as Joan Bresnan points out (personal communication), (iii) is impossible even though *lunatic* is an adjective that seems roughly synonymous with *mad*.

 (iii)   * Lee became lunatic.

Moreover, if the conclusions drawn in Section 2 about the synchronic status of *like, worth* and *near* are correct, then there are certain PPs that occur with *become*, as well as certain APs that do not:

 (iv)   Robin became more and more $\left\{ \begin{array}{l} \text{like her brother.} \\ \text{unlike his former self.} \end{array} \right\}$

 (v)   With his real estate holdings, Robin has become worth a fortune.

 (vi)   * Robin has become near the edge of bankruptcy.

Thus, it seems that *become* takes gradable nonlocative XCOMPs of any category, although the necessary degree of gradability is obviously more restricted than for specifiers (see Section 1.3.), or for complements to most other linking verbs.

Note that these contrast between (i) and (ii) provides further evidence against the lexical conversion analysis of predicative PPs: if they are lexicalized complex adjectives, it would be impossible to distinguish between examples like (i) and (ii). The only PPs which can be used as complements to *become* are those which can also occur prenominally (cf. (5a)):

 (iii)   Over the years, Lee/the sweater became out of shape.

[10] I have no explanation for why *very* seems less felicitous than the other degree words with many such PPs. Such examples are often heard, and certain of them, especially those which have been converted to adjectives, sound perfect to me, e.g. *very out of shape*. Also curious is the fact that the exclamation *How in love they are*! seems decidedly better than the question *How in love are they*?.

[11] So do predicate nominals:

(i)   He's very much a fool.

(ii)   He's very much the perfect gentleman.

[12] The only systematic exception is that if the PP contains an adjective, e.g. *in good spirits* or *in good shape* as opposed to just *in shape*, then no specifier seems to be possible:

(i)   * How (much) in good spirits did you find the patient?

(ii)   * How (much) in good shape should you be to run a marathon?

[13] Neither Bresnan (1973) nor Jackendoff (1977) included prepositions in their accounts of the syntax of *enough*.

[14] The judgments indicated here are mine; for at least some speakers, the examples in (22d) are acceptable. This might follow from their being converted adjectives, with *enough* following the entire complex word.

[15] Because of the word order constraint requiring that the finite verb be in second position (cf. Maling and Zaenen (1981)), in Norwegian it is possible for adverbs to occur between the finite verb and its NP-complement, but they cannot occur between a nonfinite verb and a NP-complement. One can easily imagine a raising-type analysis of the 'Verb-Second' word order constraint which would account for this fact about adverb placement in Norwegian, in conjunction with the prohibition sketched in (23). Nonfinite verbs form a single constituent with their complements. If finite verbs, on the other hand, are 'raised' into a separate Aux node, they would not form a single constituent with their complements, and hence (23) would not be relevant.

[16] Lars Hellan informs me that there are four adjectives in Norwegian which can take direct NP-complements: redd 'afraid', lik 'like', naer 'near', and verd 'worth'. They inflect like adjectives unless they have a following NP-complement, in which case they are invariant, and do not exhibit agreement with the subject. It is interesting that of these four, only redd and naer have synthetic comparatives.

[17] Examples like these are discussed in Bresnan (1973), where it is proposed that *enough*-shift requires a null specifier. Frank Heny (personal communication) points out examples like (i) below, which have interesting implications for an *of*-insertion analysis of complements to (deverbal) nouns.

(i)   There was destruction enough of small towns during the war.

[18] Obviously relevant is the question of whether the first P in such phrases is the head, or just a specifier; see Section 2.3. below, and also Waksberg (1977) for discussion. It isn't clear how to tell for metaphorical PPs.

[19] Note however that *out of* does not behave as predicted:

(i)   * He isn't yet out enough of shape.

(ii)   ? The cat wouldn't come out enough of the bag.

(iii)   The cat wouldn't come out enough from the bag.

One might wish to argue that *out of shape* has been lexicalized as an adjective, and hence cannot be split up, especially since (ii) seems at least marginally better. But the same pattern holds of *out of* in phrases which cannot appear prenominally:

(iv)   * He doesn't seem out enough of it to be institutionalized.
         He doesn't seem enough out of it to be institutionalized.

(vii)   * He seems out enough of his mind to be deemed crazy.
         He seems enough out of his mind to be deemed crazy.

Perhaps *out of* has simply been lexicalized as a complex preposition taking a NP-complement.

Other complex PPs with *of* behave similarly.

(iv)   ? He was living just off enough of the main street for it to be quiet.

(v)   He was living just enough off (of) the main street for it to be quiet.

In this case, the optional *of* seems to be ignored for the purposes of the constraint in (23).

20 Although only adjectives may occur in prenominal position, they may themselves be lexicalized complex adjectives with internal structure, e.g. that of PP. Thus I consider the examples of prenominal PPs given earlier to be adjectives nonetheless, and hence prenominal position is a good criteria for distinguishing categories.

21 R. Oehrle (personal communication) suggested to me that the restriction against PPs in prenominal position may have nothing to do with syntactic category, but may be accounted for by whatever rules out (i).

(i)   * a [yellow with age] manuscript.

Williams (1982) has argued that English has a 'Head-Final Constraint', which requires that prenominal phrasal modifiers of N must be head-final. Maling (1970) proposed essentially the same constraint, albeit in a bidirectional form, requiring that the head of the phrasal modifier be adjacent to the head N. Note, however, that even if such an adjacency constraint accounts for the failure of PPs to occur prenominally, it does not account for the differences between *near* and *like*, nor does it explain why in Modern English, the heads do not inflect like typical adjectives:

(ii)   * I've never seen a man liker him.

(iii)   I've never seen a man more like him.

22 R. Oehrle (personal communication) suggests that *due* may be another surviving transitive adjective; note that it occurs prenominally in such phrases as *in due course* and that its NP-complement also alternates with a PP-complement, as in *due to*. Not all speakers accept *due* NP, however. A clearer example is *opposite*, mentioned by Ross (1972). I have not had time to consider these and other possible exceptions, if any, to the generalization that adjectives in English do not take NP-complements, but do not consider them serious counterexamples. See Note (39) below.

²³ This last example is possibly a VP modifier, as in *to laugh enough* or *to look around enough*. Contrast the pattern in (31b) with complex adjecive phrases such as *yellow (enough) with age*.

²⁴ Unlike many other languages, English usually requires pronominal rather than null heads in examples like (33) below. In general, null heads are allowed only with generic interpretation, as in (i), or with superlatives, as in (ii) (See Quirk *et al.* (1972)).

(i)   Only the very rich live in Manhattan.

(ii)   We use only the very best/strongest.

Note the degree modifier *very* and the synthetic comparative; in inflectional languages, the adjective would be marked for gender, number and case. Since generics are semantically (and grammatically) plural, the generic reading is unavailable for examples like (33); the null-head analysis of the phrase is impossible, and the sentence is out. Only the fixed expression *and the like* survives.

Since on a nongeneric reading of such phrases a word cannot be an adjective, the only available analysis is that it is a noun; this seems to have occurred in examples like (iii), as shown by the plural endings.

(iii)   Did you ever see the likes of him?
         Did you see the others?
         Do come in, my dears/my dearests.

The earliest citation of the plural *likes* in the OED is 1787. Note that there must be a category distinction between the converted nouns in (iii) and the adjectives in null-head NPs as in (i)−(ii), which never take plural endings. There is no semantic explanation for this fact. Even superlatives, which might be argued to have a unique reference and hence fail to pluralize, allow plural pronominal heads:

(iv)   We chose the biggest ones.

²⁵ The fact that our first intuitions about *worth* and *near* turn out to be wrong shows how misguided the attempt to provide notional definitions of categories is.

²⁶ I don't know what to make of the fact that *worth* does not pied-pipe (nor does *like*). As Emmon Bach pointed out to me, *worth* is also unusual in being a *tough*-predicate that takes gerundive rather than infinitival complements:

(i)   This matter is well worth looking into.

(ii)   This problem is worth your having Lee look into.

This peculiarity seems to be independent of the categorial assignment of the head. Visser (1963, vol. II, Section 1058) cites both *worth* and *past* as adjectives taking *ing*-complements with non-subject gaps, although he notes that the categorial status of the head is in certain cases unclear.

²⁷ There is also a noun *worth*, as illustrated below:

(i)   At least you got your money's worth.

(ii)   Don't underestimate the worth of descriptive syntax.

[28] As opposed to *go* in *go wild, go bananas, go mad*, etc., which does take adjectives.

[29] The only indication that *near* is a less than perfect adjective is the oddness of using the locative specifier *right*, as pointed out to me by H. van Riemsdijk. Note the contrast between *near* and *close*:

(i)   Put it right near the door!

(ii)   ? Put it right close to the door!

(iii)   ? Put it right near to the door!

[30] This is clearly an oversimplification, since I would like to allow for the analysis of verbal particles and certain adverbs as intransitive prepositions (see Jackendoff (1973) and references therein).

[31] Pointed out to me by F. Heny (personal communication).

[32] I owe this example to J. Grimshaw (personal communication).

[33] As J. Lyons puts it, "What may be universal in human language are the combinatorial properties of the major categories relative to one another". (1968, p. 333)

[34] I will not document here any changes in the use of *near* which may have occurred, since they would not be the result of a category change.

[35] Examples were taken from Bosworth-Toller (1898).

[36] Examples were taken from Tatlock & Kennedy (1963).

[37] I have no idea why this possibility for PP-complements was lost.

[38] These examples and those in (53) below were culled from Spevack (1973) and from the OED; unless indicated otherwise, the examples are from Shakespeare.

[39] Thus I agree completely with Wasow (1977, fn. 10) that "a single lexical item (or even two or three) appearing in a given environment seems like very weak justification for adding a phrase structure rule to the grammar". Hence I am claiming that the existence of *near* and *opposite* does not justify postulating (48c). Nor does the idiom *by and large* justify a phrase-structure rule allowing the conjunction of P and A!

[40] In the absence of inflection, even verbs and prepositions may temporarily be confused. My favorite example is the line from Handel's *Messiah*, where . . . *we like sheep* is repeated for quite some time before the concluding VP *have gone astray* forces the correct analysis.

[41] I owe this observation to A. Zaenen and Guido Thys (personal communication).

[42] Another possible example of the influence of the phrase-structure rules is the development of *like* as a subordinating conjunction in spoken English; this development can be seen as a natural consequence of the rule PP $\longrightarrow$ P S as a way of introducing subordinate clauses in English, as suggested by Emonds. Despite being condemned by prescriptive grammarians, this usage is the only real possibility in spoken American English, since for many speakers, *as* is restricted to the written language.

[43] See Quirk *et al.* (1972, Ch. 8) for a discussion of the grammatical distinction between adverbial adjuncts and disjuncts.

[44] Note that contrary to the claim that adverbs do not strictly subcategorize anything (Jackendoff (1977, p. 78), adverbs can and do take X-bar complements in some languages. In Icelandic, for example, líkur 'like' has the same three uses illustrated in (53). The predicate complement use exhibits adjectival agreement; both adverbial uses, however, have the invariant neuter singular nominative inflection characteristic of

adverbs. As either an adjective or an adverb, it can take a NP-complement. The exact nature of the relation between adjective and adverb is an interesting problem for future research, but I know of no independent motivation for claiming that their complements are attached at different levels.

45 See especially Grimshaw (1981b, in prep.), who argues for this position based on the grammatical relations of subject and direct object.

BIBLIOGRAPHY

Allen, C.: 1977, *Topics in Diachronic Syntax*, unpublished Ph.D. dissertation, U. Massachusetts, Amherst.

Baker, C. L. and J. McCarthy (eds.): 1981, *The Logical Problem of Language Acquisition*, MIT Press, Cambridge, Mass.

Baltin, M.: 1978, *Toward a Theory of Movement Rules*, unpublished Ph.D. dissertation M.I.T.

Berman, A.: 1974, 'Adjectives and Adjective Complement Constructions in English', Report No. NSF-29, Department of Linguistics, Harvard University.

Bosworth-Toller: 1898, *An Anglo-Saxon Dictionary*, Oxford University Press.

Bowers, J.: 1975, 'Adjectives and Adverbs in English', *Foundations of Language* 13, 529–562.

Bresnan, J.: 1973, 'Syntax of the Comparative Clause Construction in English', *Linguistic Inquiry* 4, 275–344.

Bresnan, J.: 1978, 'A Realistic Transformational Grammar', in M. Halle, J. Bresnan, and G. Miller (eds.), *Linguistic Theory and Psychological Reality*, MIT Press, Cambridge, Mass.

Bresnan, J.: 1980, 'The Passive in Lexical Theory', Occasional Papers No. 7, MIT Center for Cognitive Science; to appear in Bresnan (in press).

Bresnan, J.: 1981, 'Control and Complementation', to appear in Bresnan (in press).

Bresnan, J. (ed.): in press, *The Mental Representation of Grammatical Relations*, MIT Press (to appear 1982).

Chomsky, N.: 1981, *Lectures on Government and Binding*, Foris, Dordrecht.

Crystal, D.: 1967, 'Word Classes in English', *Lingua* 17, 24–56.

Dik, S.: 1968, *Coordination: Its Implications for the Theory of General Linguistics*, North-Holland, Amsterdam.

Emonds, J.: 1976, *A Transformational Approach to English Syntax*, Academic Press, New York.

Grimshaw, J.: 1975, 'Evidence for Relativization by Deletion in Chaucerian Middle English', *NELS* V, pp. 216–224.

Grimshaw, J.: 1981a, 'Form, Function and the Language Acquisition Device', in C. L. Baker and J. McCarthy (1981), pp. 165–182.

Grimshaw, J.: 1981b, 'Subcategorization and Grammatical Relations', paper presented at the Harvard Mini-Conference on the Representation of Grammatical Relations, December 12, 1981.

Grimshaw, J.: in prep., 'Theories of Subcategorization', Linguistics Program, Brandeis University.

Hendricks, R.: 1978, 'The Phrase Structure of Adjectives and Comparatives', *Linguistic Analysis* 4, 255–299.

Heny, F.: 1979, Review article, Chomsky, N., *The Logical Structure of Linguistic Theory, Synthese* 40, 317–352.

Jackendoff, R. S.: 1972, *Semantic Interpretation in Generative Grammar*, MIT Press, Cambridge, Mass.

Jackendoff, R. S.: 1973, 'The Base Rules for Prepositional Phrases', in S. Anderson and P. Kiparsky (eds.), *A Festschrift for Morris Halle*, Holt, Rinehart and Winston, New York, pp. 345–856.

Jackendoff, R. S.: 1977, *X-bar Syntax: A Study of Phrase Structure*, Linguistic Inquiry Monograph Two, MIT Press, Cambridge, Mass.

Kaplan, R. and J. Bresnan: 1980, 'A Formal System for Grammatical Representation', Occasional Papers No. 13, MIT Center for Cognitive Science; to appear in Bresnan (ed.).

Lightfoot, D.: 1980, 'The History of NP Movement', in T. Hoekstra, H. van der Hulst, and M. Moortgat (eds.), *Lexical Grammar*, Foris, Dordrecht, pp. 255–284; also in C. L. Baker and J. McCarthy (1981), pp. 86–119.

Lyons, J.: 1968, *An Introduction to Theoretical Linguistics*, Cambridge University Press.

Maling, J.: 1979, 'Adjective Phrases and the Order of Constituents', unpublished generals paper, MIT.

Maling, J. and A. Zaenen: 1981, 'Germanic Word Order and the Format of Surface Filters', in F. Heny (ed.), *Binding and Filtering*, Croom-Held, London and MIT Press, Cambridge Mass., pp. 255–278.

Oxford English Dictionary, A New English Dictionary on Historical Principles, Clarendon Press, Oxford.

Nanni, D.: 1980, 'On the Surface Syntax of Constructions with *Easy*-type Adjectives', *Language* 56, 568–581.

Perlmutter, D. (ed.): to appear, *Studies in Relational Grammar*, Chicago University Press.

Peterson, P.: 1981a, 'Problems with Constraints on Coordination', *Linguistic Analysis* 8, 449–460.

Peterson, P.: 1981b, *The Progressive Construction in English*, unpublished Ph.D. dissertation, University of Newcastle, N.S.W., Australia.

Pinker, S.: 1980, 'A Theory of the Acquisition of Lexical-interpretive Grammars', Occasional Papers No. 6, MIT Center for Cognitive Science; to appear in Bresnan (ed.).

Platzack, C.: 1980, 'Adjectives with Noun Phrase Complements in Swedish – A Phenomenon with Implications for the Theory of Abstract Cases', unpublished ms., Institute for Nordic Languages, University of Lund, Sweden; revised version to appear in *The Linguistic Review*.

Quirk, R., S. Greenbaum, G. Leech, and J. Svartvik: 1972, *A Grammar of Contemporary English*, Seminar Press, New York; Longman Group Ltd., London.

Riemsdijk, Henk van: 1983, 'The Case of German Adjectives', this volume. An earlier version appeared in J. Pustanowsky and V. Burke (eds.), *Markedness and Learnability*, U. Mass. Occasional Papers in Linguistics 6, pp. 148–173.

Ross, J. R.: 1972, 'The Category Squish: Endstation Hauptwort', *CLS* 8.

Schachter, P.: 1977, 'Constraints on Coordination', *Language* 53, 86–103.

Siegel, D.: 1977, 'Nonsources of Unpassives', in J. Kimball (ed.), *Syntax and Semantics* 2, Seminar Press, New York, pp. 301–317.

Siegel, E.: 1976, *Capturing the Adjective*, unpublished Ph.D. dissertation, University of Massachusetts, Amherst.

Spevack, M.: 1973, *The Harvard Concordance to Shakespeare*, the Belknap Press of the Harvard University Press, Cambridge, Mass.

Tatlock, J. S. P. and A. G. Kennedy: 1963, *A Concordance to the Complete Works of Geoffrey Chaucer*, Peter Smith.

Visser, F.: 1963, *A Historical Syntax of the English Language*, Vol. I–IIIb, E. J. Brill, Leiden.

Waksberg, J.: 1977, 'The Structure of Prepositional Phrases in the X-bar Theory', unpublished ms., Brandeis University.

Wasow, T.: 1977, 'Transformations and the Lexicon', in P. Culicover, T. Wasow, and A. Akmajian (eds.), *Formal Syntax*, Academic Press, New York, pp. 327–360.

Wasow, T.: 1980, 'Major and Minor Rules in Lexical Grammar', in T. Hoekstra, H. van der Hulst and M. Moortgat (eds.), *Lexical Grammar*, Foris, Dordrecht, pp. 285–312.

Williams, E.: 1980, 'Predication', *Linguistic Inquiry* 11, 203–238.

Williams, E.: 1982, 'Another Argument that Passive is Transformational', *Linguistic Inquiry* 13, 160–163.

Q2